The Baldrige Assessor's Workbook

How to Perform the Examiner's Role for Internal and External Assessments

Kicab Castañeda-Méndez

QUALITY RESOURCES®
A Division of The Kraus Organization Limited
New York, New York

Most Quality Resources books are available at quantity discounts when purchased in bulk. For more information contact:

Special Sales Department
Quality Resources
A Division of The Kraus Organization Limited
902 Broadway
New York, NY 10010
212-979-8600
800-247-8519

Printed in the United States of America

01 00 99 98 97   10 9 8 7 6 5 4 3 2 1

The paper used in this publication meets the minimum requirements of American National Standard for Information Sciences—Permanence of Paper for Printed Library Materials, ANSI Z39.48-1984.

ISBN 0-527-76325-X

Library of Congress Cataloging-in-Publication Data
Castañeda-Méndez, Kicab.
        The Baldrige assessor's workbook : how to perform the examiner's role for internal and external assessments / Kicab Castañeda-Méndez.
                p. cm.
        ISBN 0-527-76325-X (pbk. : alk. paper)
        1. Malcolm Baldrige National Quality Award. 2. Total quality management—United States—Evaluation—Handbooks, manuals, etc.
I. Title.
HD62. 15.C373   1997
658.5'62'07973—dc21   97-26526
                                                                                          CIP

Acknowledgments

Many people contributed to this book as colleagues in award processes, co-examiners on teams, contributors to award processes, co-teachers on training, reviewers of suggestions or training proposals or manuscripts, or clients who provided me feedback.

In particular, I thank Harry Hertz, Mary Bostwick, and Dick Eppig for my Baldrige training.

I thank those people involved with the launching and sustaining of the Connecticut Award for Excellence (CAFE) who influenced and believed in me: Bill Mason, Ernest Nagler, Brenda Samuels Woods, Chuck Micelli, Bonnie Delaney, John DeGrandis, Mike Herrington, Steve Baum, and Sandra Biloon.

I thank those examiners who contributed to my understanding of the Criteria: CAFE examiners Bob Thulin, Hilary Estey, Walt Cederholm (also Baldridge), Maureen Boyle-Henninger, Elyse Dent, Al Gaige, Claire Nolin, Dennis Dell'Accio, Steve Korwin (also Baldrige); Baldrige examiners Scott Nadel and Mark Blazey.

Special clients who helped in the development of my training materials include: Life Laboratories (especially Ken Geromini); Lawrence Hospital (especially Steve Schoener, Rita Dipippo, Nancy Graham, and Roger Dvorak); and Hartford Hospital (especially John Fagan).

I am always grateful to Cindy Tokumitsu from Quality Resources.

Dedication

In memory of my sweet brother, Omar, whose total dedication to writing continuously inspires me.

Contents

PART I
AN OVERVIEW

PART II
THE MALCOLM BALDRIGE AWARD

PART III
THE EXAMINER'S TASKS

PART IV
THE ORGANIZATION'S TASK

PART V
INFORMATION FOR AWARD COMMITTEES
AND SELF-ASSESSING ORGANIZATIONS

PART VI
APPENDICES

List of Figures and Tables

Foreword

It is always foolish—perhaps even dangerous—to use any complex tool without proper guidance. And if ever there was a complex tool of management, it is the Malcolm Baldrige National Quality Award criteria and process. Since its inception a decade ago, the Baldrige process has served for many organizations as a powerful, integrating framework for organizational excellence. But for others, unfortunately, it has become a "black hole," consuming much energy and effort but emitting little useful outcome. As often happens, the blame has generally been placed on the tool, when the fault lies more with the craftspeople who have been unable to use the tool effectively.

To provide an evolutionary approach to utilizing the Baldrige process fully, many states, including Connecticut, through the Connecticut Award for Excellence (CAFE) have developed a "step" or "three-level award" process. This provides organizations with a means to embrace the national Baldrige process in increasingly sophisticated incremental steps, leading to the full scope of the Baldrige process. A valuable role played by these state award processes is to provide, consistently and credibly, key ingredients to a complete Baldrige-based improvement process—examiner competence, scoring consistency, and feedback usefulness—that most organizations cannot provide for themselves.

The Baldrige Assessor's Workbook is a convergence of several years of learning and experience at both the state and national level. Perhaps more important, it has been designed in full recognition that the success of a self-assessment or application process is dependent on the skill of the craftspeople. The workbook's scope, structure, tools, and examples are intended to instruct and to aid facilitation of the process. Its uniqueness, and power, come from the focus on the entire Baldrige *process*. While others have devoted many pages to understanding the Criteria, *The Baldrige Assessor's Workbook* provides excellent insights into

- the work and process of examining an application,
- developing consistent application scores as a foundation for measuring future improvements, and
- preparing a Feedback Report that can be used by executives and leaders without requiring them to become Baldrige examiners.

Those organizations that choose to build internal self-assessment capabilities will find this workbook an invaluable assistant. For those just beginning a self-assessment process, the details of the approach to the three-level award provides a logical and tested process for starting a limited but sound process and evolving into the fully mature Baldrige scope.

For many of us who have been associated with the Baldrige process, the relationship has gone beyond a mere "association." Like any activity with a compelling vision and purpose, it has become a passion. Just one exposure to an organization that lives the Baldrige principles changes forever one's definition of ''excellence.'' Things once considered just theoretical suddenly are recognized as achievable. This passion has infected Kicab Castañeda-Méndez. This workbook is his way of serving his passion for Baldrige excellence, as well as his natural needs as a teacher. I am confident you will find it effective in achieving its purpose—transmitting the power of the Baldrige process.

G. Michael Herrington
Vice President, Quality and Operations, World Color
Examiner, Malcolm Baldrige National Quality Award, 1990–1991
Judge, Connecticut Award for Excellence, 1994–1997

Preface

The Baldrige Criteria define a total quality management organization. They do so in a way that is useful for any organization in any industry. Because of this, organizations have used the Criteria as part of the way they operate: to provide feedback in a continuous improvement cycle.

The Baldrige process consists of an organization describing itself relative to the Criteria; trained examiners review the description to provide a useful evaluation. For example, all 1996 Baldrige winners won their state quality award the year before (and used that feedback to make further improvements) and received feedback for at least three consecutive years prior to winning.

The national Baldrige Award is limited in the number of winners it can recognize each year and has limited resources. The effect is that not all applicants receive the same level of detail in their feedback. Baldrige-based state quality awards contribute to the Baldrige process in three ways. They have adopted the same criteria, created other award levels, and recognize many more applicants. The result is that organizations can receive comprehensive feedback regardless of where they are in their quality journey.

In addition, many organizations use this process internally for self-assessment, to provide feedback on their own schedule and on the criteria they feel are more relevant to their particular stage of development.

Still, these uses of the Baldrige Criteria would be more valuable if additional people understood the Criteria as examiners do. Unfortunately, not everyone can be an examiner. So, one purpose of this workbook is to bring the training to all.

To do this, other issues must be resolved. Based on my experience as a 1997 Baldrige examiner, a senior examiner from 1994 to 1997 for the Connecticut Award for Excellence (CAFE), a provider of self-assessment workshops to organizations, and a trainer of CAFE examiners, I have identified several areas in which this process can be improved. By *this process*, I mean the process of providing value-added feedback to organizations for improvement, whether it comes from the national, state, or internal award processes or from internal or external assessments.

Several issues arose during my Baldrige training. These focused primarily on understanding the explanations in the Criteria and the information for Baldrige examiner trainees on writing comments and scoring to remove some apparent inconsistencies:

- The definitions in the Scoring System (page 33, *1997 Criteria**) use words such as appropriateness, effectiveness, consistently, innovation, significant, adaptations, rate, and breadth; the Scoring Guidelines (page 34, *1997 Criteria*) do not use these words, but others: systematic approaches,

---

**1997 Criteria for Performance Excellence*, available from National Institute of Standards and Technology, Route 270 and Quincy Orchard Road, Administration Building, Room A537, Gaithersburg, MD 20899-0001; Tel: 301-975-2036; Fax: 301-948-3716; E-mail: oqp@nist.gov; Web Address: http://www.quality.nist.gov/.

addressing Item requirements, deployment to areas or work units, continuous improvement, key areas, current performance levels, trends, and comparisons.

- The Scoring System includes information on assignment of scores that uses the phrases "*basic* objectives of the Items" and "*principal* activities covered in the Item"; the Scoring Guidelines do not use these phrases, but others, such as "*primary* purposes of the Item," "*overall* purposes of the Item," and "*all* the requirements of the Item" (italics added).
- The definition of Deployment (page 33, *1997 Criteria*) says it "refers to the extent to which the applicant's approach is applied to *all requirements of the Item*" (italics added), but says "use of the approach by all appropriate work units" is a factor used to evaluate deployment; the Response Guidelines (page 37, *1997 Criteria*) say "deployment can be shown compactly by using tables that summarize what is done in different parts of the company."
- The Response Guidelines (page 37, *1997 Criteria*) recommend showing activities are systematic, which means "they 'build in' evaluation and learning, and thereby gain in maturity"; the Scoring Guidelines separate evaluation, learning, and maturity from being systematic.
- Trainees are given examples of strong and weak comments and informed that using the terms *good*, *excellent*, and *poor* make the comment judgmental and therefore weak, yet the Scoring Guidelines (p. 34) use these exact words to differentiate between different scores, such as "excellent analysis," "early good performance levels," "no . . . poor performance levels," and "good to very good relative performance levels."

At both the state and national levels, we had concerns during examiner training and the consensus process about the scorebooks:

- First-time trainees spend 20–40 hours preparing their training scorebook, often doing it incorrectly and poorly, resulting in frustration, a sense of wasted time, and, sometimes, loss of examiners.
- Scoring after training may not be noticeably less variable than before training.
- Some examiners focus on defending their scores (which is *not* the product) during consensus rather than refining and agreeing on a set of comments (which *is* the product) first.
- Consensus varies in duration, preparation, and quality of feedback reports within teams and across teams.
- Site visits vary in focus, accomplishment, and preparation for the final feedback report.
- Final feedback reports have less information than the scorebooks, information that applicants would find valuable.

Multilevel awards need to address several other issues:

- How can each award level be evaluated so there is consistency across award levels?
- How can the feedback report be consistent across the award levels?
- How can the instructions and Criteria for the award levels be consistent and easily understood by applicants?

- How can we define the "lower" award levels so that "winners" are defensible models?
- How can training prepare examiners for any award-level applicant?
- How can training for all award levels be manageable and rigorous but not harsh on trainees?

Organizations applying for quality awards or using the Criteria for self-assessment have other concerns:

- How can they understand what the Criteria ask without becoming examiners?
- How can they do a self-assessment without having employees be examiners?
- How can they use the Criteria to identify more clearly where they are in their journey?
- How can they better understand feedback from themselves and others without becoming examiners?
- How can they better use the feedback?

This workbook offers a solution to these issues.

WORKBOOK DESIGN

Each chapter of this workbook begins with an overview and a list of learning objectives. This is followed by presentation of the material, examples, and exercises. The answers to the exercises are in Appendix B. Readers unfamiliar with the Baldrige Criteria will maximize their benefits by doing all exercises. Experienced assessors can be more selective in the exercises they choose to do.

There are six parts to the workbook. Part I has two introductory chapters. Chapter 1 answers the question, Why an assessor's workbook? In this chapter, I present an overview of an examiner's roles and explain a typical award process (e.g., the Baldrige Award and a state award), focusing on the feedback subprocess. Because for most awards the purpose (and product) is feedback for continuous improvement, I describe how the feedback process is a measurement tool. This leads naturally to identifying sources of variation in this measurement. One purpose of this workbook is to show how to reduce this variation, thereby increasing the value of the feedback.

In Chapter 2, I identify five audiences with interests addressed in this workbook. This chapter includes how each audience can use the workbook, the benefits to these people (whether award examiners or internal assessors) who have an interest in the Criteria without an interest in becoming an assessor, and the benefits to organizations (e.g., organizations doing a self-assessment) that have an interest in the Criteria without an interest in applying for an award.

Part II contains an introduction to the Baldrige Award. Chapters 3 and 4, respectively, explain two aspects of the award: the Criteria and the Scoring Guidelines. The information on the Criteria includes not only the criteria and how to understand them, but also their purposes and roles, their core values, and their critical characteristics. The Scoring Guidelines are analyzed and explained so that they are more useful and meaningful to all assessors for providing value-added, clear, and actionable feedback.

In Part III, Chapters 5 to 10, respectively, address the six critical tasks of examiners in the feedback process: Interpreting the Application, Writing Comments, Scoring Comments, Reaching Consensus, Visiting Sites, and Writing the Feedback Report. Readers unfamiliar with the Criteria can plan to spend 50, 60, or more hours doing all the exercises in the Part III chapters. This workbook is equivalent to a full semester's course. More experienced examiners can spend less time by being more selective, but have this workbook as a permanent reference.

Chapter 11 of Part IV is useful for organizations writing an award application or preparing documentation for a self-assessment.

Part V contains information for quality award organizing committees and organizations applying for external awards or doing self-assessments. Chapter 12 describes a method for defining three award levels that allow improved feedback to all organizations, regardless of where they are on the quality journey. Chapter 13 provides a detailed framework using the material in this workbook for training examiners. Thus, it is useful information not only for organizing committees, but also for organizations wishing to develop their own internal award.

There are four appendices in Part VI. These include a glossary of key terms, answers to the exercises, a case study, and the 1997 Malcolm Baldrige National Quality Award Criteria.

The chapters should be done sequentially by first-time readers unfamiliar with the Baldrige Criteria. The chapters are designed so that you have mastery of the material to make the next theme more comprehensible. Others may find value immediately by reading the specific chapter that interests them.

I welcome all comments and ideas for further improving this workbook.

Kicab Castañeda-Méndez
84 Old South Salem Road
Ridgefield, Connecticut
E-mail: kicab@aejes.com

I

AN OVERVIEW

1

Why an Assessor's Workbook?

THE ROLE OF AN EXAMINER

Several excellent books exist on the Malcolm Baldrige National Quality Award Criteria. So, why another? This book does not just explain the Criteria. It leads you through exercises to understand the Criteria as an examiner would, not just as a casual observer or interested applicant. The word *assessor* is used because you may use what you learn from this workbook whether you are an actual award examiner or an internal or external evaluator of your own or someone else's organization.

The purpose of this book is to make you an organization's assessor who uses the Baldrige Criteria for assessment to improve. The basis for this assessment is the Feedback Process (see Figure 1.1). The Feedback Process described in Figure 1.1 is generic to accommodate its different uses, such as for the national award, state quality awards, other types of awards, and self-assessment. Your Feedback Process may differ from this generic model. This workbook, however, will prepare you for most assessment processes. Or, conversely, you will be prepared to help develop variations on this assessment process.

The primary purpose of the Feedback Process is to provide information to applicants so they can improve their organizations. The information comprises comments on the organization's strengths and areas for improvement. These comments, with a summary, are the feedback report. The more specific and detailed that information is, the more useful and actionable the feedback will be. Obviously, a specific and detailed feedback report requires the examiner to thoroughly understand and know how to apply the Criteria. It also requires the examiner to set aside personal beliefs and biases and focus on what the Criteria require.

As an examiner, you must be an expert on the Criteria and the Feedback Process—not on the organization, its industry, or relevant comparisons of its processes. As an examiner, you must use your experience and knowledge to judge whether what an organization is doing is *consistent* with the Criteria—not whether what it is doing is *correct*. As an examiner, you must let the evidence and data speak for themselves.

THE FEEDBACK PROCESS

Figure 1.1 shows the key steps of the Feedback Process. Depending on the particular process for providing feedback (e.g., for the national or state award and number of levels), applicants may receive feedback after the individual scorebooks are produced, after consensus, or after a site visit. The solid arrows denote the path that maximizes the value of the feedback to the applicant because it is based not only on a documented description of the organization but on personal observations from a well-defined data collection process.

The organization's task is to understand its quality management systems

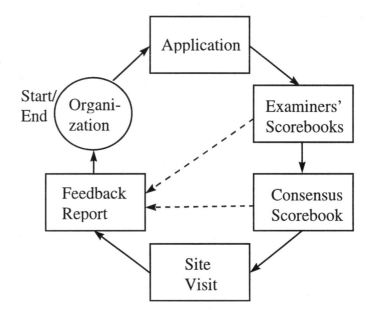

Figure 1.1 The Feedback Process.

and processes, the knowledge and skills of its people, and the capabilities of its resources and to present this information to the examiner through an application. The application consists of descriptions of the organization's systems and processes, identification of the organizational parts using these systems and processes, and a summary of results on measures of these systems and processes.

The Criteria determine how these descriptions, identifications, and results are presented. Three or more examiners (this varies by award, e.g., state or national, and by award level; see Chapter 12) develop individual scorebooks. Each scorebook contains the examiner's comments (see Chapter 6) and scores (see Chapter 7). We can view these scorebooks as prototypes of the feedback report.

These individual scorebooks are the basis for the consensus process by which the same examiners form a team and collaborate to produce a consensus set of comments and scores and prepare for a site visit. The purpose of the site visit is to secure additional information to clarify and confirm the consensus scorebook comments and to discover any relevant information not in the application. After the consensus process and site visit, the team leader heads the development of the feedback report, which is sent to the applicant on approval of, say, the judges. For examinations that are not based on an award, the procedure may vary. It may not include judges, consensus, site visits, or any combination of these.

EXAMINATION AS A MEASUREMENT TOOL

The Feedback Process is a measurement tool. This measurement tool begins with the organization developing the written application and ends with the organization receiving a feedback report. A measurement tool is a system of several components (Table 1.1): an object to be measured, a procedure for measuring, a scale for distinguishing measures, a measurement, and a criterion or decision-rule for evaluating or making a decision based on the measurement. Each component is essential for producing a valid and reliable measurement.

Some things can be measured directly, such as a person's weight. Other things must be measured indirectly, such as a person's intelligence or comprehension. This measurement tool, the Feedback Process, does not directly measure the object it is intended to measure: the organization's quality systems. It measures them indirectly by measuring their description in the application. Thus, questions of validity are appropriate.

Unfortunately, the examiner, regardless of training, competence, and expertise, cannot adequately ensure validity. The examiner cannot ensure that the description is complete and accurate. However, for applicants using this workbook, we can expect to improve the validity of the measurement by improving the correctness of the description in the application. We expect this when you use the knowledge and skills gained from this workbook to help your organization develop its application (see Chapter 2, ''Audience and Benefits'').

This measurement tool has two scales. One scale is quantitative, ranging from 0 to 1000. For external award assessments, judges may use this scale to determine whether further refinement of the measurement is needed through a site visit (see Chapter 9) and whether to give recognition to applicants. The second scale is qualitative, with two possible values: strength (denoted with a +) and Area for Improvement (denoted by a −). Examiners apply this scale to their comments.

The feedback report is the result of the measurement. It contains both a numerical score and a set of Strength and Area for Improvement comments. While the score might seem to be the only actual measurement, the qualitative measurement from the comments provides the greatest value for measuring progress. For example, all 1996 Baldrige Award winners previously won a state quality award; they used the comments from the feedback reports, not the scores, to continue their quality journey.

The value of this measurement comes not only from the examiners' perceived value in scoring and consensus and from the judges' perceived value in rendering a decision for site visits or recognition, but also from the appli-

Table 1.1 The Baldrige Examination as a Measurement Tool

MEASUREMENT COMPONENT	*Baldrige Examination*
Object to be measured	Organizational quality management systems and processes; extent of their relevant use; their absolute and relative performance
Procedure	The Feedback Process
Scale	Quantitative: 0-1000; Qualitative (two values): Strength, Area For Improvement
Measurement (result)	Feedback report: qualitative comments and quantitative scores
Criterion or decision-rule	Customer-perceived value; recognition

cant's perceived value of the information for improving their organization's quality efforts.

In the national and state processes, examiners' scorebook comments have references to the specific criteria (see Chapters 3 and 6), which they remove in their feedback report (see, for example, any Baldrige case study feedback report). This is done because these feedback reports are comments to the applicant on the most important strengths and areas for improvement as judged by the examiners from the application. To accomplish this requires skill in interpreting the application and a well-written application, but also subjectivity on the part of examiners.

Since this workbook cannot substitute for actual training, in which there is constant feedback from the trainer and facilitators, we take a different perspective. The approach in this workbook prepares you for becoming a Baldrige assessor and also prepares you for being an expert source to your organization and others.

The feedback report from this workbook's Feedback Process aims to increase the value and comprehensiveness and decrease the subjectivity inherent in feedback reports. The three ways it differs from the national, some state, and other award feedback and internal assessments are as follows:

1. The feedback report that you will learn how to produce includes the specific criterion and scoring dimension to which each comment refers. For applicants who do not have complete understanding of the Criteria (that is, most applicants), these references are invaluable. Not all awards provide this information in their feedback reports.
2. You will not be asked to judge whether something is "most important" to an applicant. This requires you to be subjective, especially regarding an application that is weak in stating what is important. The next section shows how reducing variation and making clearer the specific purposes of each step of the process can reduce this subjectivity.
3. Rather than select the "most important areas" for comments, you will comment on all Criteria (see Chapters 3 and 6). The rationale for this is that if it is important enough to include in the Criteria, it is important enough for the applicant to receive comments.

With these three changes, examiners better inform applicants of at least two things when the application is incomplete, inadequate, or did not receive a perfect score: (1) areas of failure to understand the Criteria and (2) areas in which they need to focus their efforts.

REDUCING MEASUREMENT VARIATION

As with all measurement tools, sources of variation detract from the usefulness and reliability of the measurement (see Figure 1.2). The application may be inaccurate because the developers of the application had varying, incomplete, and/or mistaken understanding of the Criteria and scoring guidelines; their knowledge of the organization was incomplete or incorrect; or their writing skills were weak.

The individual examiner's comments and scores may differ significantly

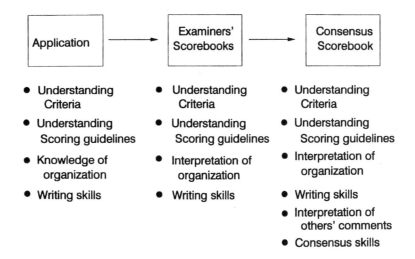

Figure 1.2 Sources of variation in the Feedback Process.

because the examiners have different understandings of the Criteria, have different understandings of the scoring guidelines, interpreted the application differently, or have different writing skills. The consensus scorebook may be inaccurate because the consensus team members had different skills in working as a team or had different skills for performing the consensus.

One objective of this workbook is to show how to reduce the effect of several sources of variation. In particular, by showing many people how to be examiners, I expect to reduce variation in eight areas:

1. understanding the Criteria,
2. understanding the Scoring Guidelines,
3. interpretation of the application,
4. skills in writing comments,
5. skills in scoring comments,
6. ability to work as a team when consensus is required,
7. collecting information from the site visit when applicable, and
8. ability to summarize a complete set of comments.

In Figure 1.3, you can see that the consensus part of the award process has different sets of comments and scores as inputs and a single set of

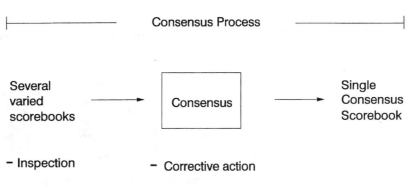

Figure 1.3 Consensus process as part of the award process.

comments and scores as the output. If the objective of the Feedback Processes is to produce this single set of comments and scores, then in my mind consensus is a failure cost (i.e., it was not done right the first time). It consists of inspecting the individual comments and scores and when these are viewed as varying "too much" or no individual scorebook is comprehensive, then the corrective action is to have the examiners rectify the differences and inadequacies of their scorebooks through consensus.

What if there never was (significant) variation or incompleteness among the examiners' scorebooks? There would be no need do consensus. Some would, and have, argue that we can never eliminate variation or inadequacies. Others have argued that variation among the individual scorebooks is good. One reason given for wanting scorebook variation is that individual examiners may miss something in the application. So, with more examiners, there might be a greater chance of finding whatever is missing.

This reminds me even more of inspection: one inspector cannot find all the defects, so increase either the number of inspectors or the number of inspections. For those who recall Deming's exercise of inspecting a paragraph to count the number of times the letter *e* occurred, you will remember that the moral of his exercise is that going to, or increasing the frequency to 100% inspection does not improve the accuracy.

If the examiners are not more learned or do not have a better "inspection" process, adding more inspections of an application will neither increase the quality of the final product nor remove the causes of the poor quality.

Another purpose of this book is to reduce (my vision is to eliminate) variation at the first step of the measurement process, the scorebooks, and the first step of the feedback report process, the application. This workbook shows you how to design quality into the scorebooks and applications.

We can view examiners as part of a product development process by which they take raw material, the application, and use it to produce a product, the feedback report. The scorebooks are prototypes of the feedback

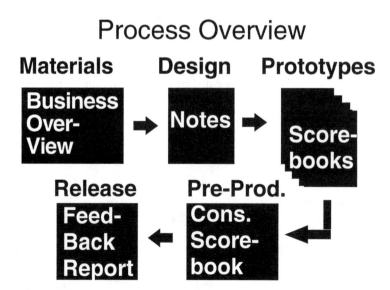

Figure 1.4 Production process view of examination process: Raw materials (application) to final product (feedback report).

report (Figure 1.4). Increasing the quality of the raw material and the proto-types makes the final product better. If the prototypes have flaws, so will the final product. If the prototypes are not tested, the final product will likely fail in the hands of the user, the applicant. The remaining chapters show you how to "qualify" the raw material and how to design the proto-types so that the final product has customer-perceived value.

2

Audience and Benefits

Of the 50 states, 40 have some kind of quality award, and several have more than one. Numerous organizations have instituted internal awards. Most of these awards are Baldrige-based.

This workbook is for organizations and individuals who use or plan to use the Baldrige Criteria as the basis for assessment for continuous improvement. For this purpose, the material presented is general enough to apply to these various uses but specific enough to understand the Criteria and the role of the examiner in the Feedback Process.

Figure 2.1 shows how the chapters of this workbook relate to the Feedback Process. In addition, the figure indicates why the organizations and individuals for whom this workbook was written can benefit from it.

AUDIENCE

This book is for five audiences: individuals, organizations doing a self-assessment, organizations applying for a quality award, organizations developing an internal Baldrige-based award, and organizations that provide or have internal Baldrige-based quality awards. After reading the description of each audience, refer to Figure 2.1 to identify which chapters would benefit you.

Individuals

This workbook is for those individuals interested in

- becoming an examiner for their state Baldrige-based quality award or the Malcolm Baldrige National Quality Award,
- becoming an examiner for their employer's, association's, or other organization's Baldrige-based quality award,
- developing an application for their organization for a Baldrige-based quality award, or
- developing a quality management system in their unit, department, function, area, or section.

Regardless of your interest, if you are unfamiliar with the Baldrige Criteria, read Parts I–III of this workbook in the order presented, do all exercises, and compare your work to the answers in Appendix B to increase your knowledge and improve your skills. Using this workbook will make the examiner training for the state and national awards much easier. Your understanding of how an examiner views the Criteria and your understanding of the linkages among the Baldrige systems will make you invaluable to your organization when it applies for an award and to your work unit's quality management system development.

If you are already familiar with the Criteria (e.g., an examiner or contributor to the writing of an application), select chapters to refresh your memory or to refine your skills. Part V may be of additional value to you.

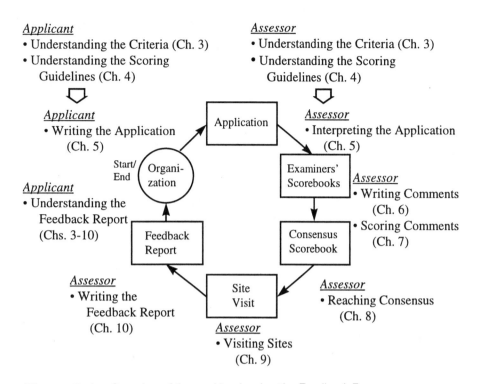

Figure 2.1 Overview of the workbook using the Feedback Process.

Organizations Doing a Self-Assessment

This workbook is helpful to organizations doing a self-assessment

- so they know what to assess about their organization,
- so they know what information to collect and prepare,
- so they know how to prepare the self-assessment, and
- so they know how to improve using the results of the self-assessment.

By having key people use the book as a minicourse, you develop in-house expertise on developing an application and scoring it without the cost of outside consultants or without being restricted to the time schedule of your state, national, or other award. Chapter 11 helps you develop your documentation (''application''), and Chapters 3–10 gives you insight on how to get the most from your self-assessment report.

Organizations Applying for a Baldrige-Based Award

This workbook is helpful for organizations applying for a national, state, or other Baldrige-based quality award

- so they can better know what examiners look for,
- so they can better prepare their application,
- so they can better decide the award level (see Chapter 12) at which to apply,

- so they can better plan their efforts to develop an application,
- so they can better understand the feedback report from the examiner's perspective, and
- so they can increase the value from the application, examination, and feedback processes.

Read Chapter 11 for tips on applying and Chapters 12 and 13 next to get an overview of a three-level award. Identify a few key individuals in the organization who are interested in being experts on the Criteria. Assign them this workbook and have them proceed as for individuals, above. With senior management, decide the award level for which you will apply and prepare an application at that level using these key people as in-house experts on the Criteria and how an application should be written.

Organizations Developing an Internal Baldrige-Based Award

This workbook is for organizations developing an internal Baldrige-based award

- so they can have internal examiners who understand the Criteria,
- so they can have clearly defined levels that recognize logical progression,
- so they can recognize successful efforts in different areas, and
- so they can progress more deliberately in their own quality journey.

This workbook can supplement the information you should get from other companies with Baldrige-based awards, the state quality awards, and NIST (National Institute for Standards and Technology) for the national award. Chapter 12 specifically defines a three-level award that you may wish to use, and Chapter 13 shows how education and training of examiners and applicants can be done consistently and effectively. The remaining chapters help you develop modules with objectives and procedures for training examiners.

Organizations Providing or Internally Using Baldrige-Based Quality Awards

Organizations with Baldrige-based quality awards in place can use this workbook

- so they can improve the training of their examiners,
- so they can improve the quality of their applications, and
- so they can improve (or develop) consistent three-level award programs.

If the purpose of your Baldrige-based state quality award is to bring organizations along the quality journey, then going to a multilevel award is critical. Several states already have done so. Chapter 12 describes how you can either enhance your multilevel award or modify your single-level award to be a multilevel one. This workbook can also serve as a supplement to your training program for your examiners (Chapter 13). It reinforces ideas you already teach and provides an easy reference for your examiners before, during, and after training.

BENEFITS TO READERS, THEIR ORGANIZATIONS, AND ASSOCIATIONS

This is a *workbook*. Every year, a very small number from all interested people are selected to be examiners for state and national quality awards. The training is rigorous and exhausting—and valuable. The value is threefold:

1. Individual examiners become experts on the Baldrige Criteria.
2. These individuals can assess their own and other organizations using a proven total quality framework.
3. These individuals can help their own and other organizations develop their quality management systems more effectively and efficiently.

The closer this nation and the individual states come to having all individuals competent to understand and use the Criteria, the greater the effect on all organizations and state and national economies.

This book would make this goal more realistic and make the training more uniform because reducing variation is, after all, a quality goal. There are three other goals. First, with many more individuals trained as examiners within an organization, the quality of applications should increase, making the task of preparing and writing an application less expensive but more productive and valuable for applying organizations. Second, some states have multiple award levels to recognize different stages of development. This workbook develops examiners with an understanding of three stages of organizational maturity. This will help organizations better prepare for each level and have a better understanding of what is required for each. This will help reduce the overwhelming effect the Baldrige Criteria's notes, descriptions, and comments have on first-time readers. Third, both applicants and examiners will have a higher quality product—the feedback report from the examiners to the applicant.

While most awards provide an inexpensive way to get feedback relative to the national award, an organization may wish feedback faster, that is more specific, or at a different time than scheduled by external awards. So, many organizations do self-assessments and develop their own internal awards. They also benefit from this workbook by using it to develop their self-assessment.

II

THE MALCOLM BALDRIGE AWARD

3

Getting to Know the Criteria

OVERVIEW The first step for examiners and applicants is to understand the Criteria (see Figure 3.1). Failure to do so adequately causes three problems: (1) collecting irrelevant or incorrect information with respect to the Criteria, (2) writing ambiguous or incorrect responses to the Criteria, and (3) examining the responses inappropriately relative to the Criteria. In this chapter, we address these problems by showing you what information is asked for in the Criteria. In Chapters 6 and 7, we show you how and where to write responses to that information and how to examine your responses. If readers include information collectors, application writers, and application examiners, this chapter will help reduce variation in understanding the Criteria through improved applications.

OBJECTIVES By completing the exercises in this chapter, the reader will be able to

- identify the 1997 Criteria's 7 Categories, 20 Items, and 50 Areas to Address,
- identify to which of two classes an Item belongs,
- explain what is examined in each Category,
- explain what needs to be described or summarized in each Item
- explain what information must be supplied in each Area to Address,
- use the glossary and notes to explain what technical information is asked for in the Criteria, and
- use the glossary, notes, and core values to explain linkages among the Criteria.

Note that all references to and quotations from the Criteria in this workbook pertain to the 1997 Malcolm Baldrige National Quality Award Criteria.

INTRODUCTION Variation in scorebooks sometimes occurs because examiners have different understandings of the Criteria. The Baldrige Award Criteria should be understood in the context of their roles:

1. They form a basis for making awards.
2. They form a basis for giving feedback to applicants.
3. They help improve performance practices and capabilities.
4. They facilitate communication and sharing of best practices information among U.S. organizations of all types.
5. They serve as a working tool for understanding and managing performance, planning, training, and assessment.

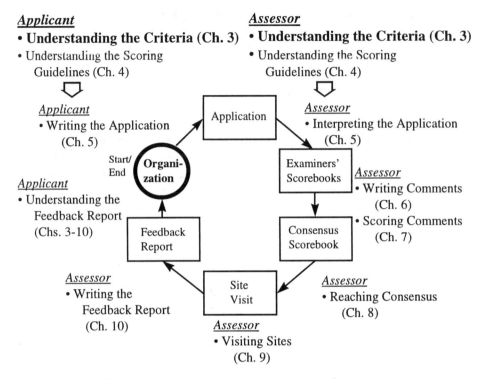

Figure 3.1 The Feedback Process: Understanding the Criteria.

To fulfill these roles, the Criteria are designed to help companies enhance their competitiveness through focus on dual, results-oriented goals: delivery of ever-improving value to customers, resulting in marketplace success; and improvement of overall company performance and capabilities. The accomplishment of these goals is enhanced by four specific characteristics:

1. The Criteria focus on business results, balancing customer satisfaction/retention, financial and marketplace performance, product and service performance, productivity and operational effectiveness and responsiveness, human resource performance/development, supplier performance/development, and public responsibility/good citizenship.
2. The Criteria are nonprescriptive and adaptable in that they do not prescribe specific tools, techniques, systems, and measures; how the organization should be organized; and what functions or departments it should have.
3. The Criteria support a systems approach to companywide goal alignment through linkages among the Criteria and feedback between processes and results via learning cycles that include planning, execution, assessment, and revision.
4. The Criteria permit goal-based diagnosis through the use of 20 results-oriented requirements and a set of scoring guidelines.

Figure 3.2 shows the underlying concept of the Criteria and how the scoring guidelines and learning cycles form the basis for the results-oriented requirements. Typically, an organization develops an approach to an organizational issue by designing and developing a system, process, procedure, or method. Once developed, the approach is used (deployment) where appli-

Underlying Concept

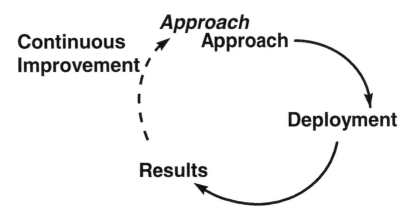

Figure 3.2 Underlying concept of the Criteria.

cable, perhaps starting in one appropriate area before fully deploying the approach. Results are often collected. The Criteria require that the results form the basis for changing the approach to get better results. The results are the basis for fact-based, continuous improvement. This closed loop forms a learning cycle that is not typically found in organizations to the extent required by the Criteria.

The Criteria have three levels of detail: Categories, Items, and Areas to Address (or, briefly, Areas). The Baldrige Award has always had seven Categories, although Category names have changed slightly from time to time and in 1997 the Category order changed. The number of Items in the Baldrige Award has changed over the years, with 1997 having 20 Items. Items focus on one aspect of what is examined in the Category. The most dramatic changes have occurred in the Areas, both in content and in number. The greatest changes occurred from 1994 to 1995, when the number of Areas was reduced from 91 to 54, and from 1996 to 1997, when it was reduced from 52 to 30 and the Criteria's format was made more consistent across Items and Areas.

CATEGORIES

The seven 1997 Categories are

1. Leadership,
2. Strategic Planning,
3. Customer Focus and Satisfaction,
4. Information and Analysis,
5. Human Resource (HR) Development and Management,
6. Process Management, and
7. Business Results.

The 1997 Criteria describe the relationship among the Categories (see Figure 3.3).

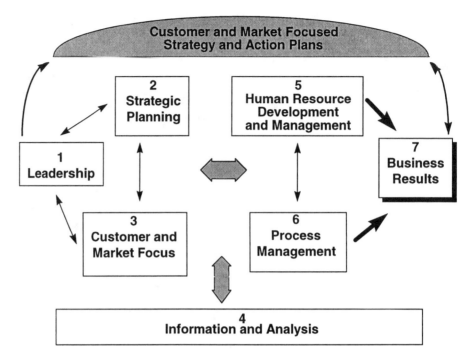

Figure 3.3 The Baldrige Framework.

EXAMPLE **1 Leadership (110 points)**
The Leadership Category examines senior leaders' personal leadership and involvement in creating and sustaining values, company directions, performance expectations, customer focus, and a leadership system that promotes performance excellence. Also examined is how the values and expectations are integrated into the company's leadership system, including how the company continuously learns and improves and addresses its societal responsibilities and community involvement.

The description of each Category is general and uses the key verb *examines*. Thus, Category 1 Leadership examines the following:

- senior leaders' personal leadership and involvement in creating
  values
  company directions
  performance expectations
  customer focus
  a leadership system
- senior leaders' personal leadership and involvement in sustaining
  values
  company directions
  performance expectations
  customer focus
  a leadership system
- how the values are integrated into the company's leadership system
- how the expectations are integrated into the company's leadership system
- how the company continuously learns and improves

- how the company addresses its societal responsibilities
- how the company addresses its community involvement

Exercise 3.1   1. What do Categories 2–7 examine?

ITEMS   Item numbers come after the Category number, such as 4.3 refers to the third item of Category 4. The two classes of Items, based on the type of information requested, are Approach-Deployment and Results. Every Item has a symbol that identifies to which class it belongs. The symbol is an oval with either "Approach-Deployment" or "Results" written in the oval.

Approach-Deployment Items always ask for descriptions of how and where things are done, using the verb *describe*. At the Item level, it becomes clearer what the applicant has to do and what the examiner must evaluate. The sentence or two of each Approach-Deployment Item identifies the primary purposes or basic objectives of the Item.

EXAMPLE   **1.1   Leadership System (80 pts.)**
Describe how senior leaders guide the company in setting directions and in developing and sustaining an effective leadership system.

For this Item, the examiner is looking for descriptions of senior leaders' activities in

- setting directions,
- developing a leadership system,
- sustaining the leadership system, and
- ensuring the leadership system is effective.

Exercise 3.2   The Items in 1997 Categories 1–6 are Approach-Deployment Items.

1. What must be described in Item 1.2?
2. What must be described in Items 2.1–2.2?
3. What must be described in Items 3.1–3.2?
4. What must be described in Items 4.1–4.3?
5. What must be described in Items 5.1–5.3?
6. What must be described in Items 6.1–6.3?

Results Items always ask for data on achieving the purposes of the Item. This includes data on measures and/or indicators and comparison data. The applicant must "summarize" these data as results. In the 1997 Criteria, all results are reported in the five Items of Category 7.

EXAMPLE   **7.1   Customer Satisfaction Results (130 pts.)**
Summarize the company's customer satisfaction and dissatisfaction results.

Exercise 3.3   1. What must be summarized in Item 7.2?
2. What must be summarized in Item 7.3?
3. What must be summarized in Item 7.4?
4. What must be summarized in Item 7.5?

AREAS AND SUBAREAS

Areas define what specifically must be addressed in each Item. Areas are denoted by letters after the Item number, such as 3.2a denotes the first Area (the letter *a*) of the second Item (the number *2*) in Category 3. Areas can have subAreas, which are denoted by numbers in parentheses after the Area letter, such as 5.2a(4) refers to the fourth subArea in Area a of Item 2 in Category 5.

Areas for Approach-Deployment Items use the word *how* to indicate that a description of a process or a procedure is required. The *1997 Criteria* provide help in understanding the meaning of the word *how*: "Applicant responses should outline key process information such as methods, measures, deployment, and evaluation/improvement factors."

Areas for Result Items state in the summary the performance area for which data are required. In all Results Areas, "current levels and trends" of, and "appropriate comparative data" for, the particular measures and/or indicators are required.

EXAMPLE: AREA FOR AN APPROACH-DEPLOYMENT ITEM

In your response (to Item 3.1), address the following Area:

a. Customer and Market Knowledge

Provide a brief outline of how the company learns from its current and potential customers and market to support the company's overall business needs and opportunities. Include

(1) how customer groups and/or segments are determined or selected, including the consideration of customers of competitors and other potential customers and markets. Describe how the approaches to listening and learning vary for different customer groups; . . .

EXAMPLE: AREA FOR A RESULTS ITEM

In your response (to Item 7.2), address the following Area:

a. Financial and Market Results

Provide results of

(1) financial performance, including aggregate measures of financial return and/or economic value, as appropriate; and

(2) marketplace performance, including market share, business growth, and new markets entered, as appropriate. Provide all quantitative measures and/or indicators of performance, current levels, and trends. Include appropriate comparative data.

Exercise 3.4

1. How many Areas do the following items have?
   1.2 ____   2.1 ____   4.1 ____   5.2 ____   6.3 ____   7.1 ____
2. How many subAreas do the following Areas have?
   1.2a ____   3.1b ____   4.3b ____   5.3c ____   6.2a ____   7.5a ____
3. What must be described in Area 2.1b? 3.2b(3)? 4.3a(2)? 5.2a(5)? 6.3a(2)?
4. What must be summarized in Area 7.1a? 7.2a(2)? 7.3a? 7.4a? 7.5a?

GLOSSARY AND NOTES

Because some words and phrases have technical meanings in the Criteria, they are explained in notes to the Items or in the glossary.

EXAMPLE   SubArea 1.1a(4) asks "how senior leaders review the company's overall performance," while Area 4.3b asks "how company performance and capabilities are reviewed."

Question: What is the difference between these two Areas?

Answer: The Note to Item 1.1 explains. "Company performance reviews are addressed in Item 4.3. Responses to 1.1a(4) should therefore focus on the senior leaders' roles in the review of overall company performance, not on the details of the review."

Exercise 3.5   Use the glossary and notes in the Criteria to answer the following questions.

1. To what does "alignment" refer? See glossary and Areas 2.1b and 2.2a.
2. To what does "measures and/or indicators" refer? See glossary and Areas 2.2c, 3.2b(2) and note N1, 4.3a, 5.3c(1) and note N3, 6.1b(2) and note N5, 6.2a(4) and note N3, and 6.3a(2) and Note.
3. What does "performance" mean? See glossary and Areas 7.1a (notes N1 and N3), 7.2a (Note), 7.3a (note N1), 7.4a (Note), and 7.5a (notes N1–N3).
4. To what does "strategy development process" refer? See note N1, Item 2.1.
5. To what does "leadership system" refer? See glossary and Area 1.1a(2).
6. To what does "cycle time" refer? See glossary and Areas 2.2b(1), 4.1a(3), 6.2a(5), and 7.5a.
7. To what does "work and job design" refer? See note N1 to Item 5.1.
8. What might be appropriate indicators for employee well-being, satisfaction, and motivation? See note N3, Item 5.3 and note N2, Item 7.3.
9. To what does "process" refer? See glossary, Category 6 and its three Items, and note N1, Item 6.2.
10. To what does "action plans" refer? See glossary and Area 2.2a.

CORE VALUES

The Award Criteria are based on 11 core values and concepts, which are fully explained in *1997 Criteria* on pages 39–41. These values and concepts are the foundation for integrating key business requirements within a results-oriented framework. These core values and concepts include the belief that customers judge quality; senior leaders must be role models; success is achieved through continuous improvement and learning and increasingly depends on the knowledge, skills, and motivation of its work force; time performance is a critical process measure; prevention by designing quality into products, services, and processes provides a competitive edge; market leadership requires a strong future orientation; appropriate measures and results on those measures are critical to effective decision-making; overall company goals are better achieved through partnerships; and companies have responsibilities to their communities.

Exercise 3.6   For each core value listed below, check how it is an integral part of the Criteria by reading the referenced Criteria.

1. Customer-driven quality: Category 3 and Areas 2.1a(1), 1.1a(2) and (3), 4.3a(1), 5.1a(2), 6.1a(1), 6.1b(2), and 6.2a(1).
2. Leadership: Category 1 (see Note, Item 1.1) and Item 4.3.
3. Continuous improvement and learning: Areas 1.1a(3), 1.1a(4), 1.2a(2), 1.2b, 2.1b, 2.2b(1), 3.1a(3), 3.2a(1), 4.1a(4), 4.2a(4), 4.3b, 5.1b, 5.2a(5), 5.3c, 6.1b(3), 6.2a(5), and 6.3a(3).

4. Employee participation and development: Category 5 and Areas 2.1b, 2.2a, and 2.2b(1). See also the definition of performance in the glossary.
5. Fast response: Areas 2.2b(1), 3.2a(2), 3.2b(1), 4.1a(3), 5.1a(2), 6.1a(3), 6.2a(5), and 7.5a.
6. Design quality and prevention: Areas 6.1a(2) and 6.1a(3), 6.2b(2), 6.2a(2), and 6.2a(4); 6.3a(1) and 6.3a(2); 5.1a(1), 5.1a(2); 5.2a(1), 5.2a(2); 4.1a(2), 4.1a(3); 3.2a(1); 2.1b and 2.2a.
7. Long-range view of the future: 2.2a and 2.2c.
8. Management by fact: see referenced Criteria for continuous improvement and learning.
9. Partnership development: Item 6.3 and Area 2.1a(5).
10. Company responsibility and citizenship: Item 1.2 and 7.5.
11. Results focus: Category 7, Item 1.2, and Item 4.3.

4

Getting to Know the Scoring Guidelines

OVERVIEW

Once applicants and examiners understand the Criteria, they can enhance that understanding by understanding the scoring guidelines (see Figure 4.1). Key issues underlying the scoring guidelines include the scale of 0 to 1000, which is anchored at 500 and not at 1000 or 0; the scoring system explanation does not readily match the scoring guidelines; and there are six dimensions to scoring but no unequivocal way to blend these scoring dimensions to yield a single score. In this chapter, I show how to reduce the effect of these factors so that readers of this workbook will have reduced variation in understanding the Scoring Guidelines.

OBJECTIVES

By completing the exercises in this chapter, the reader will be able to

- explain the difference between Approach, Deployment, and Results,
- explain the difference between Approach-Deployment Items and Results Items,
- explain the content of the scoring guidelines,
- explain why there are seven scoring dimensions,
- explain each scoring dimension, and
- identify the scoring dimensions for each class of Item.

INTRODUCTION

You cannot understand the Scoring Guidelines without understanding the difference between Approach, Deployment, and Results. Page 33 of the *1997 Criteria*, in the section, ''Scoring System: Approach, Deployment, Results,'' explains these three terms.

Approach
''Approach'' refers to how the applicant addresses the Item requirements—the method(s) used. The factors used to evaluate approaches include:

- ■ appropriateness of the methods to the requirements,
- ■ effectiveness of use of the methods, and the degree to which the approach:

    — is systematic, integrated, and consistently applied
    — embodies evaluation/improvement/learning cycles
    — is based upon data and information

- ■ evidence of innovation and/or significant and effective adaptations of approaches used in other types of applications or businesses.

Deployment
''Deployment'' refers to the extent to which the applicant's approach is applied to all requirements of the Item. The factors used to evaluate deployment include:

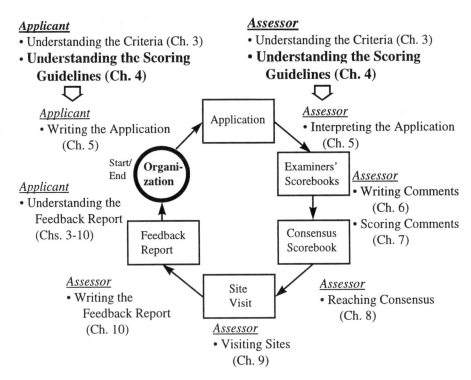

Applicant
• Understanding the Criteria (Ch. 3)
• **Understanding the Scoring Guidelines (Ch. 4)**

Applicant
• Writing the Application (Ch. 5)

Applicant
• Understanding the Feedback Report (Chs. 3-10)

Assessor
• Writing the Feedback Report (Ch. 10)

Assessor
• Understanding the Criteria (Ch. 3)
• **Understanding the Scoring Guidelines (Ch. 4)**

Assessor
• Interpreting the Application (Ch. 5)

Assessor
• Writing Comments (Ch. 6)
• Scoring Comments (Ch. 7)

Assessor
• Reaching Consensus (Ch. 8)

Assessor
• Visiting Sites (Ch. 9)

Application

Start/End Organization

Examiners' Scorebooks

Feedback Report

Consensus Scorebook

Site Visit

Figure 4.1 The Feedback Process: Understanding the Scoring Guidelines.

■ use of the approach in addressing business and Item requirements
■ use of the approach by all appropriate work units.

Results
"Results" refers to outcomes in achieving the purposes given in the Item. The factors used to evaluate results include:

■ current performance
■ performance levels relative to appropriate comparisons and/or benchmarks
■ rate, breadth and importance of performance improvements
■ demonstration of sustained improvement and/or sustained high-level performance.

SCORING GUIDELINES

The Scoring Guidelines are shown in Table 4.1. There is one set of guidelines for Approach-Deployment Items and another for Results Items. Both sets have five scoring rows, excluding the header row. Each scoring row identifies a different scoring range:

• Row 1 identifies a score of 0%.
• Row 2 identifies scores from 10% to 30%.
• Row 3 identifies scores from 40% to 60%.
• Row 4 identifies scores from 70% to 90%.
• Row 5 identifies a score of 100%.

Table 4.1 Scoring Guidelines

SCORE	APPROACH/DEPLOYMENT
0%	• no systematic approach evident; anecdotal information
10% to 30%	• beginning of a systematic approach to the primary purposes of the Item • early stages of a transition from reacting to problems to a general improvement orientation • major gaps exist in deployment that would inhibit progress in achieving the primary purposes of the Item
40% to 60%	• a sound, systematic approach, responsive to the primary purposes of the Item • a fact-based improvement process in place in key areas; more emphasis is placed on improvement than on reaction to problems • no major gaps in deployment, though some areas or work units may be in very early stages of deployment
70% to 90%	• a sound, systematic approach responsive to the overall purposes of the Item • a fact-based improvement process is a key management tool; clear evidence of refinement and improved integration as a result of improvement cycles and analysis • approach is well deployed, with no major gaps; deployment may vary in some areas or work units
100%	• a sound, systematic approach, fully responsive to all the requirements of the Item • a very strong, fact-based improvement process is a key management tool; strong refinement and integration — backed by excellent analysis • approach is fully deployed without any significant weaknesses or gaps in any areas or work units

SCORE	RESULTS
0%	• no results or poor results in areas reported
10% to 30%	• early stages of developing trends; some improvements *and/or* early good performance levels in a few areas • results not reported for many to most areas of importance to the applicant's key business requirements
40% to 60%	• improvement trends *and/or* good performance levels reported for many to most key areas of importance to the applicant's key business requirements • no patterns of adverse trends *and/or* poor performance levels in areas of importance to the applicant's key business requirements • some trends *and/or* current performance levels — evaluated against relevant comparisons and/or benchmarks — show areas of strength *and/or* good to very good relative performance levels
70% to 90%	• current performance is good to excellent in most areas of importance to the applicant's key business requirements • most improvement trends *and/or* performance levels are sustained • many to most trends *and/or* current performance levels — evaluated against relevant comparisons and/or benchmarks — show areas of leadership and very good relative performance levels
100%	• current performance is excellent in most areas of importance to the applicant's key business requirements • excellent improvement trends *and/or* sustained excellent performance levels in most areas • strong evidence of industry and benchmark leadership demonstrated in many areas

In this chapter, the assigned scores of each row are ignored. The assigned scores are discussed again in Chapter 7, "Scoring Comments." Here, we are interested only in the definition of each row for the two types of Items. These definitions identify what are called the *scoring dimensions*.

For the purposes of this chapter, the Scoring Guidelines are better presented as in Table 4.2. Notice that, except for Row 1 in Table 4.1 for Approach-Deployment Items, there are three bulleted phrases that define the scoring row. These phrases identify three scoring dimensions of Approach-Deployment Items:

1. the extent the Approach is systematic and addresses all that is asked for in the Item (e.g., Row 2 says, "Beginning of a systematic approach to the primary purposes of the Item"),

Table 4.2 Scoring Dimensions for the Scoring Guidelines

APPROACH-DEPLOYMENT ITEMS

Score	Systematic	Deployment	Continuous Improvement
0%	No system evident	No evidence of deployment	No evidence of continuous improvement
10% to 30%	Beginning of systematic approach to primary purposes of the Item	Major gaps in deployment that would inhibit achieving primary purpose of Item	Transition from reacting to problems to a general improvement orientation
40% to 60%	Sound system responsive to primary purposes of Item	No major gaps in deployment; some areas or work units in early stages	Fact-based improvement process; more emphasis placed on improvement than reaction to problems
70% to 90%	Sound system responsive to overall purposes of Item	Well deployed; may vary in some areas or work units	Clear evidence of refinement and improved integration from cycles and analyses
100%	Sound system fully responsive to all Item requirements	Fully deployed without significant gaps or weaknesses	Key management tool: strong integration and excellent analyses

RESULTS ITEMS

Score	Key Areas	Levels and/or Trends	Comparisons
0%	None to few reported	[No favorable levels or trends]	[No comparisons]
10% to 30%	Few key areas reported	Some early good performance levels and/or early stages of setting trends [some favorable levels and/or trends]	[Few fair comparisons]
40% to 60%	Many key areas reported	Many improvement trends and/or good performance levels; no adverse trends and/or no poor performance levels [no unfavorable levels and/or trends]	Some performance levels and/or trends show good to very good comparisons
70% to 90%	Most key areas reported	Good to excellent performance levels and/or sustained trends [most levels and/or trends good to excellent and sustained]	Many to most levels and/or trends show very good and leadership comparisons
100%	Most key areas reported	Sustained excellent performance levels and/or excellent improvement trends [most levels and/or trends excellent and sustained]	Industry and benchmark leader in many areas

2. the extent the Approach is used by all appropriate areas or units of the organization (e.g., Row 4 says, "Approach is well deployed, with no major gaps; deployment may vary in some areas or work units"),
3. the extent the Approach is continuously improved through data and evaluation (e.g., Row 4 says, "a fact-based improvement process is a key management tool; clear evidence of refinement and improved integration as a result of improvement cycles and analyses").

These three features or scoring dimensions are called the Systematic, Deployment, and Continuous Improvement dimensions, respectively, in Table 4.2.

These scoring dimensions can be illustrated using Figure 4.2 to show the relationship between Approach-Deployment and Results. In Figure 4.2, the top half of the figure includes Approach (Systematic), Deployment, and

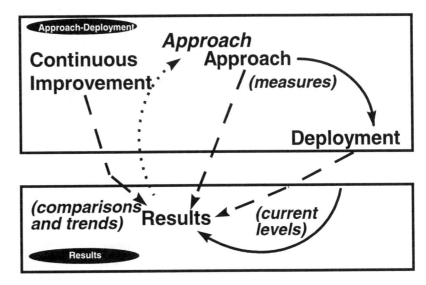

Figure 4.2 Integration of the scoring dimensions and the underlying concept of the Criteria.

Continuous Improvement. These are the three Approach-Deployment scoring dimensions.

At first glance, it appears that there is a discrepancy between the description of Approach and Deployment in "Scoring System: Approach, Deployment, Results" (see pages 25–26 in the workbook), and the Scoring Guidelines for Approach-Deployment. This description mentions the factors' appropriateness, effectiveness, integration, innovation, and business requirements, while not one of these factors is mentioned in the Scoring Guidelines; the description has five factors (marked ■) while the Scoring Guidelines have three.

To help you understanding this apparent discrepancy, you need to understand how the factors mentioned in the description of the Scoring System are folded into the Scoring Guidelines. The scoring dimensions defined in this workbook group the description factors as follows:

- *Systematic* means "systematic, integrated . . . appropriateness of the methods to the requirements [and] use of the approach in addressing business and Item requirements."
- *Deployment* means "consistently applied . . . use of the approach by all appropriate work units."
- *Continuous Improvement* means "embodies evaluation/improvement/learning cycles" that are "based upon data and information" with "evidence of innovation and/or significant and effective adaptations of approaches used in other types of applications or businesses."

While the word *Deployment* is used both as an Item identifier and a scoring dimension, the context will make it clear which is meant if "scoring dimension" is not included.

Since an examiner cannot judge whether the applicant's approaches are "significant adaptations" or whether these are "effective" from the description alone, we infer these notions of innovation in several ways. One way is by evidence that the approaches have been improved, which is exemplified through the second bullet of each row for Approach-Deployment in Table 4.1. Another way is through Results. The applicant's measures and/or indicators of its Approaches should show evidence that the approaches are good relative to other businesses (e.g., competitors and benchmarks). This aspect of Approach-Deployment connects the methods to Results, which we discuss below.

The key distinction between Approach and Deployment can be seen by the two Approach-Deployment scoring dimensions, Systematic and Deployment. The former refers to the purposes of the method defined by the Areas' requirements, while the latter refers to parts of the organization that use the approach. This distinction is clarified through the "Guidelines for Responding to Approach/Deployment Items" on page 37 of the *1997 Criteria*.

1. **Understand the meaning of ''how.''**
   Items requesting information on approach include Areas that begin with the word ''how.'' *Applicant responses should outline key process information such as methods, measures, deployment, and evaluation/improvement factors.* Responses lacking such information, or merely providing an example, are referred to in the Scoring Guidelines as *anecdotal information.*

2. **Write and review response(s) with the following guidelines, questions, and comments in mind:**
   ■ Show *what* and *how.*
      — Does the response show what is done, and does it give a clear sense of how?
   ■ Show deployment
      — Does the response give clear and sufficient information on deployment of the approach addressed in the response? Deployment can be shown compactly by using tables that summarize what is done in different parts of the company.

For example, Item 5.3 asks for a description of ''how the company maintains a work environment and work climate that supports the well-being, satisfaction, and motivation of employees.'' Area requirements include ''factors such as health, safety, and ergonomics.'' Later in the Item it states that the applicant should ''note significant differences, if any, based upon different health and safety factors in the work environment of employee groups or work units.'' Showing how the company maintains a work environment refers to the Systematic dimension, while showing what is done in different work environments and for different employee groups refers to the Deployment dimension. If some work environments or employee groups do not use the approach, then there are gaps in the Deployment of the approach.

Another apparent discrepancy is between the definition and use of the word *systematic.* Applicants are likely to be influenced by the Response Guidelines on pages 36 and 37 in the *1997 Criteria*: ''Approaches that are systematic use data and information for improvement and learning. In other words, approaches are systematic if they ''build in'' evaluation and learning, and thereby gain in maturity (p. 37).

Examiners, however, are influenced by the Scoring Guidelines, which separate systematic (as in ''a sound systematic approach, responsive to the overall purposes of the Items") from evaluation, learning, and maturity (as in "a fact-based improvement process is a key management tool; clear evidence of refinement and improved integration as a result of improvement cycles and analysis"). While the intention of the Criteria is to integrate methods with improvement, assessors can and should recognize these as distinct components to enhance the value of feedback. This becomes more evident in Part III, where commenting and scoring are addressed, and in Part IV, where different award levels are addressed.

APPROACH-DEPLOYMENT ITEMS

Systematic

The Scoring Guidelines identify four degrees of responsiveness to Item requirements that indicate how much of the Item purposes are addressed by the method: none, primary, overall, and full. The primary purposes of an Item are defined by the description following the Item title (Figure 4.3). This would be reflected by a score in the range of 40% to 60% on this scoring dimension. Full purposes of an Item include all Areas and subAreas to Address. This would be reflected by a score of 100% on this scoring dimension. Overall purposes of an Item are more than the primary purposes but less than the full purposes. This would be reflected by a score in the 70% to 90% range on this scoring dimension. A score of 0% on this scoring dimension means that there is no systematic approach, or, if there is one, it does not address any Item requirements.

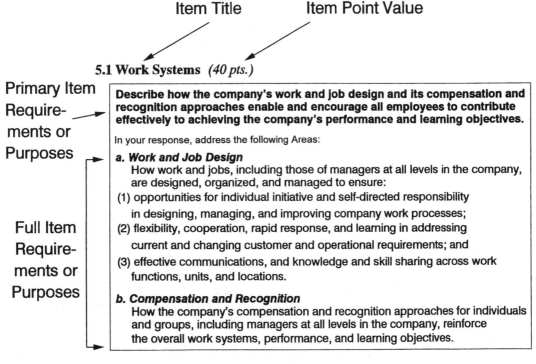

Figure 4.3 Item format and contents.

Further distinctions are made using the phrases "beginning of a systematic approach" and "sound, systematic approach." We already learned that the word *systematic* is troublesome, but we can clarify its meaning through the scoring dimensions Systematic and Continuous Improvement.

In addition, the Response Guidelines in the *1997 Criteria* also help us. They include a section on understanding the meaning of "how." This includes "methods, measures, deployment, and evaluation/improvement factors." The last two terms—deployment and evaluation/improvement—refer exactly to the scoring dimensions Deployment and Continuous Improvement. So, the first two are included in Systematic: methods and measures. This matches the illustration in Figure 4.2. So, a "beginning of a systematic approach" would not have both methods and measures. A score of 10–30% on the Systematic scoring dimension means that the applicant describes some details of the methods addressing the primary purposes or full details of the method but does not include measures.

Exercise 4.1

1. What are the primary purposes of Item 2.2? Item 4.3?
2. What are the full requirements of Area 2.2b? Area 5.1b?

Deployment

The scoring dimension Deployment refers to the extent the Approach is being used in all areas of the organization in which it should be. This decision is not left to the judgment of the examiner. The Applicant should identify, either in the response itself to the Criteria or in the Business Overview, the areas for which the Approach is applicable. There are many ways to divide an organization into "areas" or "work units" for deployment purposes. These divisions are answers to such questions as the following:

- Who are the senior leaders?
- Who are the major competitors or competitor groups?
- Who are the primary customers or customer groups?
- What are the principal products or services?
- What are the key support functions?
- What are the major company locations or sites?
- What are employee classifications or groups?
- Who are the major suppliers or supplier groups?

Table 4.3 identifies the areas or work units for each Approach-Deployment Item in the Criteria. For example, full deployment for Item 1.1 means that every member of the leadership system must be involved according to the Areas in this Item. If they are not all involved, then there is not full "use of the approach by all appropriate work units."

Exercise 4.2

For this exercise, refer to the case study in Appendix C.

1. Look at the organization chart Figure 0-1 in the Business Overview of the case study. Who are the work units for Item 1.1, Leadership (i.e., who are all the senior leaders)?
2. Look at the Business Overview, Section 1 ("Basic Description of Company") of the case study. What are the work units for Category 5, Human Resource Development and Management (i.e., what are the employee categories)?

Table 4.3 Definition of "Areas or Work Units" for Approach-Deployment Items

ITEM	APPROACH	DEPLOYMENT AREAS OR WORK UNITS
1.1	Leadership System	Values, directions, expectations, customer focus, and commitment to entire organization and key stakeholders.
1.2	Company Responsibility and Citizenship	Key communities. See Notes N1 and N2.
2.1, 2.2	Strategic Plan: Development and Company Strategy	Plans to all levels: company/executive level, process level, and work unit/individual job level. See page 21 of *1997 Criteria*, description of Strategic Planning and also definition of *performance* in glossary, especially paragraph 3.
3.1, 3.2, 3.3	Customer/Market Knowledge, Relationship, Satisfaction	Key customer groups and markets segments.
4.1, 4.3	Information, Data; Analyses	To all work units and partners; key customers and suppliers/partners or customer and supplier/partner groups. See note N1, Item 4.1.
4.2	Comparisons	Key measures, as appropriate, compared to key competitors. See Note to item 4.2.
5.1, 5.2, 5.3	Work Systems; Education, Training, Development; Well-being, Satisfaction	All employee categories.
6.1	Product/Service Processes	Core products/services; key production/delivery processes.
6.2	Support Processes	Key support functions. See Note N1.
6.3	Supplier and Partnering Processes	Major suppliers/partners or supplier/partner groups.

3. Look at the Business Overview, Section 3 ("Supplier and Partnering Relationships" of the case study. What are the work units for Item 6.3, Management of Supplier and Partnering Process (i.e., who are the major suppliers and how are suppliers categorized)?

4. Look at the Business Overview, Section 4 ("Competitive Factors") of the case study. What are the work units for Item 4.2, Selection and Use of Comparative Information and Data (i.e., who are the major competitors)?

Continuous Improvement

An Area to Address has a continuous improvement element to it when it specifically asks for (1) how something is evaluated and (2) how the results from the evaluation are used to improve and/or reinforce the specific behavior or performance for which it was designed. Review Exercise 3.6, number 3, which refers to the core value "continuous improvement and learning." The list of Areas related to this core value are 1.1a(3), 1.1a(4), 1.2a(2), 1.2b, 2.1b, 2.2b(1), 3.1a(3), 3.2a(1), 4.1a(4), 4.2a(4), 4.3b, 5.1b, 5.2a(5), 5.3c, 6.1b(3), 6.2a(5), and 6.3a(3). When you did this exercise, you should have noticed that each Area used words like review, evaluate, and track, followed by improve and reinforce. For example, Item 1.1 has one Area (1.1a) and four subAreas: 1.1a(1) through 1.1a(4). Area 1.1a(4) asks: "*how senior leaders* review *the company's overall performance, and use the review process to* reinforce *company directions and* improve *the leadership system*" (emphasis added). SubArea 1.1a(4) is referred to in this workbook as the continuous improvement element of Item 1.1.

For each year from 1994 to 1997, approximately 60% to 80% of Approach-Deployment Items have a continuous improvement element, that is, an Area or subArea that asks how the company "evaluates and improves" the Approach(es) to be described in that Item. Other Items do not use this exact phrase, but ask for continuous improvement because they ask how information on performance is collected and then ask how that information is used to reinforce or improve. Continuous improvement refers to the extent the application describes how it collects performance information, uses this information to improve, and how often it has improved.

Exercise 4.3　Confirm that each (sub)Area listed in Exercise 3.6, number 3, is a Continuous Improvement Area.

RESULTS ITEMS

For Results Items, Table 4.1 identifies four features that the applicant must show

1. key measures and/or indicators for the Approach (e.g., Row 3 says, "improvement trends and/or good performance levels reported *for many to most key areas of importance to the applicant's key business requirements*"),
2. current performance levels for the Approach's measures and/or indicators (e.g., Row 3 says, "improvement trends and/or *good performance levels* reported for many to most key areas of importance to the applicant's key business requirements"),
3. trends for the Approach's measure and/or indicators (e.g., Row 3 says, "*improvement trends* and/or good performance levels reported for many to most key areas of importance to the applicant's key business requirements" and "no patterns of adverse *trends*"), and
4. comparisons for the Approach's measures and/or indicators (e.g., Row 3 says, "some trends and/or current performance levels—*evaluated against relevant comparisons and/or benchmarks*—show areas of strength and/or good to very good *relative* performance levels").

These four features are called Key Areas, Levels, Trends, and Comparisons in Table 4.2.

The bottom half of Figure 4.2 illustrates these four features in the Approach-Deployment-Results-Continuous Improvement learning cycle. This half of the figure includes only Results, but the long-dashed arrows show how to derive measures, Levels, Trends, and Comparisons from Approach-Deployment. Applicants identify measures in the Business Overview and Approach-Deployment Items when they are asked for key requirements, stakeholder needs, strategic goals, and the like. So, measures emanate from approaches. Levels are current performances on deployed approaches. Results also include Trends and Comparisons. Trends are Levels for previous periods and Comparisons are Levels for other organizations. Trends and Comparisons show relative comparisons to internal and external targets, respectively, and therefore are evidence of continuous improvement.

The first, second, and fourth bullets in Table 4.1 correspond to the three Results scoring dimensions Levels, Comparisons, and Trends, respectively.

"Rate" of performance improvement is implicitly included in the Scoring Guidelines by how fast the improvement has occurred. "Breadth" is implicitly included by the extent most areas of importance have measures so breadth is tied to Deployment.

Key Areas   The fourth scoring dimension, Key Areas, derives from the word *importance*. Notice that, starting with the second row of the Results section in Table 4.1, the phrase "areas of importance to the applicant's key business requirements" appears. These Scoring Guidelines recognize that all organizations have measures, data, and results. Typically, better organizations have more measures, data, and results for what is important to them. Thus, the Scoring Guidelines make "areas of importance to key business requirements" a part of the Scoring Guidelines through the scoring dimension called Key Areas.

Key Areas are typically identified in the Business Overview (in which it is required, but applicants do not always comply with this requirement); in the statements of vision, mission, and values; and in the strategic plan. The examiner should not make subjective decisions about whether something is or is not (should or should not be) important to the applicant. If the applicant has failed to identify this in the Business Overview, the examiner has no choice but to note that key business requirements—what is important to the business—have not been stated. Sometimes, the examiner can infer these requirements from other statements.

The *1997 Criteria* make it easy for applicants to list their Key Areas and for examiners to identify them. (See also the definition of performance in the glossary and each Item in Category 7.)

EXAMPLE   Read "Preparing the Business Overview," Section 2 ("Customer requirements") of the Criteria (page 35) or refer to the corresponding pages of Chapter 3 in this book. This section asks for customer requirements. It lists on-time delivery, low defect levels, price demands, and after-sales services as examples of key customer requirements for products and services.

Read Colony Fasteners, Incorporated's (CFI's) response to this request in the case study in Appendix C, "Business Overview." In the "Customer Requirements" section, there are five key requirements itemized: delivery, quality, price, responsiveness, and ease of doing business. In addition, the case study states that CFI's credo is: *To All Customers, We Promise Service, Satisfaction, and Value.* Therefore, an examiner can infer that CFI includes service, satisfaction, and value as key areas of importance to the applicant's key business requirements.

Exercise 4.4   For this exercise, refer to the Criteria.

1. What Key Areas are identified in Item 1.2? Where are the results reported?
2. What Key Areas are identified in Item 2.2? Where are the results reported?
3. What Key Areas are identified in Item 3.2? Where are the results reported?
4. What Key Areas are identified in Item 4.3? Where are the results reported?
5. What Key Areas are identified in Item 5.1? Where are the results reported?
6. What Key Areas are identified in Item 5.2? Where are the results reported?
7. What Key Areas are identified in Item 5.3? Where are the results reported?
8. What Key Areas are identified in Item 6.1? Where are the results reported?

9. What Key Areas are identified in Item 6.2? Where are the results reported?
10. What Key Areas are identified in Item 6.3? Where are the results reported?

Exercise 4.5   For this exercise, refer to the case study in Appendix C.

1. Read the response to Area to Address 6.3a(1), ''Process Design,'' in the case study. What key supplier requirements are identified?
2. Read the response to Area to Address 6.1b(1), ''Key Processes and Requirements,'' in the case study. What key process requirements are identified?

Levels

Levels refers to the current value of the measure and/or indicator. If the measure is taken annually (quarterly, etc.), then the applicant must report the value of the measure and/or indicator for the year (quarter, etc.) of the application. CFI reports on an annual basis. Therefore, all results should be reported annually.

EXAMPLE   In the last example, we discovered that CFI identified five key customer requirements. Figure 7.1-4 in the case study shows CPS' customer satisfaction for these requirements. Satisfaction is measured on a five-grade scale: A, B, C, D and F. The current Levels are delivery, between D and C; price, between B and A; quality, between B and A; responsiveness, between B and A; and ease of doing business, between D and C.

Exercise 4.6   For this exercise, refer to the case study in Appendix C.

1. One key supplier requirement is illustrated in Figure 7.4-2. What is it and what is its current Level?
2. Figure 7.5-2 has results for one key process requirement. What is it and what is its current Level?

Trends

Trends refers to patterns of the current and previous Levels. If the applicant is measuring annually (quarterly, etc.), then Trends are defined as the current year (quarter, etc.) and one or more previous years (quarters, etc.). The more previous Levels there are, the more evidence exists to show if a Trend is sustained, the rate of improvement is fast, or the Trend is adverse.

EXAMPLE   In Figure 7.1-4 of the case study, there are no Trends for customer satisfaction as only 1996 results are shown.

Exercise 4.7   For this exercise, refer to the case study in Appendix C.

1. For the key supplier requirement illustrated in Figure 7.4-2, state whether there are adverse, sustained, or improving Trends and for how long a period?
2. For the key process requirement illustrated in Figure 7.5-2, state whether there are adverse, sustained, or improving Trends and for how long a period?

Comparisons

Baldrige defines two types of Comparisons. The first type is an industry comparison. The applicant compares the current or trend levels against competitors, industry averages, peer groups, and best in class. The second type is called benchmarking. The applicant compares the current or trend levels against the best performance for that measure and/or indicator of the process that is benchmarked regardless of where and in what industry it occurs.

EXAMPLE

Figure 7.1-4 of the case study shows CPS customer satisfaction ratings of five key customer requirements. The results include comparisons to a competitor and to a benchmark. CPS is worse than the best competitor for delivery and ease of doing business, equal to the best competitor for quality, and better than the best competitor for price and responsiveness. CPS is worse than the benchmark on all requirements except price, for which it is slightly worse.

Exercise 4.8

For this exercise, refer to the case study in Appendix C.

1. One key supplier requirement is illustrated in Figure 7.4-2. To what are the results compared and how do they compare?
2. Figure 7.5-2 has results for one key process requirement. To what are the results compared and how do they compare?

Exercise 4.9

This exercise is designed to check your understanding of all seven scoring dimensions. They are hypothetical situations and do not refer to the case study; the references are Items or Areas to Address. For each situation below, indicate the type of issue by putting the appropriate abbreviation after the sentence: SY = Systematic, DE = Deployment, CI = Continuous Improvement, KA = Key Area, LE = current Level, TR = Trend, and CO = Comparison.
What is the scoring dimension issue, if the applicant's response to

1. 1.2a(1) did not address ethical conduct? _____
2. 7.3a did not include data for previous years? _____
3. 4.2a(4) did not describe how effective use of data are evaluated and improved? _____
4. 7.1a did not include how their competitors did? _____
5. 7.5a did not include data on support services and Area 6.2a(1) did not list any requirements? _____
6. 1.1a did not include two of the six senior executives? _____
7. 6.3 listed four criteria for qualifying suppliers; no data were reported on them in 7.4a? _____

III

THE EXAMINER'S TASKS

5

Interpreting the Application

OVERVIEW

Interpreting the application is easier for the examiner and should be more accurate when both the examiner and the applicant have full understanding of the Criteria and Scoring Guidelines (see Figure 5.1). An applicant who understands how an examiner interprets the application can prepare a better application: the people who provide the descriptions of the organization will have complete and correct information and the people who write the application will write clear and correct descriptions. In this chapter, you learn what basic but critical information the Criteria ask for and how to search for that information in the application. If readers include information collectors, application writers, and application examiners, this chapter helps reduce variation in understanding an organization through improved applications.

OBJECTIVES

By completing the exercises in this chapter, the reader will be able to

- explain the purpose of the Business Overview,
- cite the two types of information the Business Overview provides to examiners,
- prepare Criteria-related notes on an application for writing comments, and
- interpret the application relative to the Criteria.

**INTRODUCTION:
THE BUSINESS
OVERVIEW**

By doing Exercises 4.5–4.7 of Chapter 4, you should already have an appreciation for the information the Business Overview conveys. We now explore in more detail its significance and what information it should contain.

Every application must contain a Business Overview. The Criteria's explanation of the Business Overview improved significantly in 1996 from 1995. Table 5.1 shows the instructions for preparing the Business Overview. The first two paragraphs tell us how important the Business Overview is and what role it plays for applicants, examiners, judges, and organizations preparing for self-assessment.

Without the Business Overview, examiners would have to guess subjectively what is relevant and important to the applicant's business. With a Business Overview, examiners do not have to guess.

The Business Overview contains the information needed to ''design'' our prototypes of the Feedback Report: the Scorebook. There are two pieces of information that you must extract from the Business Overview: (1) what is

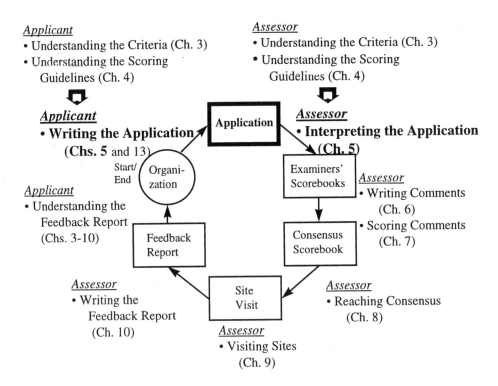

Applicant
- Understanding the Criteria (Ch. 3)
- Understanding the Scoring Guidelines (Ch. 4)

Assessor
- Understanding the Criteria (Ch. 3)
- Understanding the Scoring Guidelines (Ch. 4)

Applicant
- **Writing the Application** (**Chs. 5** and **13**)

Application

Assessor
- **Interpreting the Application** (**Ch. 5**)

Start/End Organization

Applicant
- Understanding the Feedback Report (Chs. 3-10)

Examiners' Scorebooks

Assessor
- Writing Comments (Ch. 6)
- Scoring Comments (Ch. 7)

Feedback Report

Consensus Scorebook

Assessor
- Writing the Feedback Report (Ch. 10)

Site Visit

Assessor
- Reaching Consensus (Ch. 8)

Assessor
- Visiting Sites (Ch. 9)

Figure 5.1   The Feedback Process: Interpreting the application.

important enough to the organization to include in its total quality efforts and (2) what is important enough to the organization to measure.

The first piece of information recognizes that not every system, process, work unit, or area of the organization can be addressed by its quality efforts because of limited time and resources. Therefore, the organization must define what has highest priority. The organization's quality efforts must extend to these areas.

The second piece of information is also critical. As examiners, we see a snapshot of the organization. We cannot know—and we should not impose our subjective ideas—on what needs to be measured specifically. The Criteria identify general areas (e.g., products and services) and themes (e.g., waste and cycle time), but the specific measures and/or indicators are the organization's choice. The organization must tell us, the reviewers of the application, its choices in the Business Overview.

Note: The entire case study is prepared to read and sound like a real award application, with its strong points and its flaws. This will provide more valuable training than would a perfectly polished piece, because this is what internal and external examiners work with from organizations.

Exercise 5.1

Prepare a separate sheet with the Business Overview sections and subsections. Title the sheet "Key Business Factors Worksheet."

Read the section "Business Overview" in Appendix C, Case Study. As you read it, take notes by writing phrases for each description. For example, in Section 1, "Basic Description of the Company," the first entry is "Nature of Business." Your notes to this part could be: *world leader in the design and manufacture of fasteners: pins, bolts, rivets, screws, and specialty fasteners.*

Table 5.1   Instructions for Preparing the Business Overview

PREPARING THE BUSINESS OVERVIEW

The Business Overview is an outline of the applicant's business, addressing what is most important to the business, the key factors that influence how the business operates, and where the business is headed. In simplest terms, *the Business Overview is intended to help Examiners understand what is relevant and important to the applicant's business.*

The Business Overview is of critical importance to the applicant because:
■ it is the most appropriate starting point for writing and self-assessing the application, helping to ensure focus on key business issues and to achieve consistency in responses, especially in reporting business results; and
■ it is used by the Examiners and Judges in all stages of application review, including the site visit.

Guidelines for Preparing the Business Overview
The Business Overview consists of five sections as follows:

1. Basic description of the company.
This section should provide basic information on:
■ the nature of the applicant's business: products and services;
■ company size, location(s), and whether it is publicly or privately owned;
■ the applicant's major markets (local, regional, national, or international) and principal customers (consumers, other businesses, government, etc.). (Note any special relationships, such as partnerships, with customers or customer groups.);
■ a profile of the applicant's employee base, including: number, types, educational level, bargaining units, and special requirements; and
■ major equipment, facilities and technologies used

If the applicant is a subunit of a larger entity, a brief description of the organizational relationships to the parent company and percent of employees it represents should be given. Briefly describe also relationships of the applicant's product and services to those of the parent company and/or other subunits of the parent company. If the parent company provides key support services, these should be briefly described.

2. Customer requirements
This section should provide information on:
■ key customer requirements (for example, on-time delivery or low defect levels, price demands, and after-sales services) for products and services. Briefly describe all important requirements, note any significant differences, if any, in requirements among customer groups.

3. Supplier relationships
This section should provide information on:
■ types and numbers of suppliers of goods and services;
■ the most important types of suppliers, dealers, and other businesses; and
■ any limitations or special relationships that may exist in dealing with some or all suppliers.

4. Competitive factors
This section should provide information on:
■ the applicant's position (relative size, growth) in the industry;
■ numbers and types of competitors;
■ principal factors that determine competitive success such as productivity growth, cost reduction, and product innovation; and
■ changes taking place in the industry that affect competition.

5. Other factors important to the applicant
This section should provide information, as appropriate, on:
■ major new thrusts for the company such as entry into new markets or segments;
■ new business alliances;
■ introduction of new technologies;
■ the regulatory environment affecting the applicant, such as occupational health and safety, environmental, financial, and product;
■ *changes in strategy; and*
■ unique factors.

Page Limit
The Business Overview is limited to four pages. These four pages are not counted in the overall application page limit. Typing instructions for the Business Overview are the same as for the application. These instructions are given in the *1997 Application Forms and Instructions* booklet.

> It is strongly recommended that the Business Overview be prepared first and that it be used to guide the applicant in writing and reviewing the application.

READING THE ENTIRE APPLICATION

For readers who have read and assessed an application before and are familiar with the Criteria, the *1997 Criteria* can significantly reduce the amount of note taking. Item format is highly consistent, with fewer Areas that need a response. Taking notes can be done more simply and directly, as shown below.

If this is your first time reading and/or assessing an application, taking notes is essential to accurate interpretation of the application and to reduce time in assessment, resulting in more useful feedback for the applicant. With the improvements in the *1997 Criteria*, you can take notes in two phases. In the first phase, restrict yourself to each Item. In the second phase, refine your notes by using the explicit linkages (discussed later) among Items.

The following procedure will help you organize your thoughts, notes, and time for the first phase in taking notes to interpret the application. After you finish each category, take a break.

1. Take an hour or so to skim the case study. This will give you an overview of the organization and understand its jargon, organizational relationships, and internal operations and measures.
2. Take notes on one Item at a time. Prepare your work area by having within reach only the page from the Criteria with the Item for which you will be taking notes, the case study, a pen or pencil, a highlighter, and perhaps a separate sheet for notes identified with the Item number.
3. Read the Item description to understand the primary purposes of the Item. Read each Area and/or subArea. Finally, read the relevant section of the case study. This is usually indicated by the Item number and Area. If the applicant has done an excellent job in writing the application, sections will be further identified by subArea.
4. Take notes:
   a. In the application, highlight the section(s) that you feel responds to each (sub)Area.
   b. Mark the section(s) with the appropriate notation, such as ''1.1a(2).''
   c. Write key phrases on the sheets on which you are taking notes (the Criteria page itself and/or a separate sheet).
   d. Reference the highlighted area by including in your notes the column, page, and, as appropriate, figure and/or table number. (If you do not include this reference now, when you are reviewing your notes or discussing with others, you will spend extra time searching, and sometimes even fail, to find your reference.)
   e. For Category 7, it may be useful to use a table (e.g., Table 5.2) to keep track of the measures that should have results reported. Those key measures should be listed in Categories 1–6, addressing Item 7.1 customer satisfaction, Item 7.2 financial and market, Item 7.3 human resource, Item 7.4 supplier/partner, and Item 7.5 company-specific performance. They should include current level; levels for previous periods (months, quarters, years, as appropriate) to form trends; levels for competitor(s), industry average/best, and/or benchmarks for comparisons.

Phase 1 is finished when you have done Steps 1–4 for every Item in every Category. In Phase 2, use Figure 5.2 and Tables 5.3 and 5.4 to refine your

Table 5.2   Format for Summarizing Notes on Results for Category 7

Instructions: In the KEY AREA column, enter one of the five performance areas (see Category 7) per block of rows. In the MEASURE column, list the specific *key* measures (as shown by the example in italics using the case study) for that KEY AREA. In the LEVEL column, state what the current level is for each measure and state how it compares to its goal or maximum performance (e.g., "Favorable" or "Unfavorable") or some subjective assessment of performance (e.g., "Poor," "Good," or "Excellent"). In the column TREND, state whether the trend over the past 3 or more periods is favorable or unfavorable and whether sustained or not. In the column COMPARISON, state whether the comparison of LEVEL or TREND to an external target (e.g., industry average, best-in-class, best competitor, benchmark) is worse, equal, or better. Also note to whom the comparison is made. Do not use internal goals for this column.

KEY AREA	MEASURE	LEVEL	TREND	COMPARISON (versus whom?)
Customer Satisfaction	*A-D, F rating on delivery*	*1996: C/D-CPS (poor); C/B - CAS, DAS, NSS good (subjective)*	*No trend data*	*Worse than goal, best competitor, and benchmark*
Financial and Market				
Human Resource				
Supplier/Partner				
Company-specific (product/service, support processes, other)				

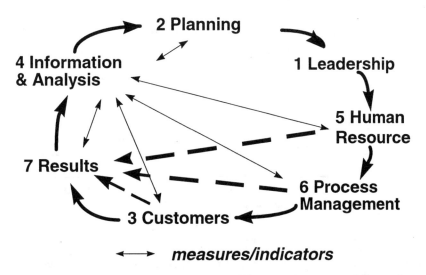

Figure 5.2   Relationships among Categories, measures and/or indicators, and Results.

Table 5.3 Relating Information from the Business Overview to the Criteria

The following list shows where the information from the Business Overview goes in your notes. When recording, indicate with "(BOV)" where you got the information:

1. Basic description of the company
- products and services: *Item 6.1 Management of Product and Service Processes*
- applicant's major markets and principal customers: *Category 3 Customer and Market Focus*
- profile of employee base: *Category 5 Human Resource Development and Management*

2. Customer requirements
- key customer requirements: *Category 3 Customer and Market Focus*

3. Supplier and partnering relationships
- types, numbers of suppliers; most important types of suppliers: *Item 6.3 Management of Supplier and Partnering Processes*

4. Competitive factors
- number and types of competitors: *Category 4 Information and Analysis; Category 7 Business Results*
- principal factors that determine competitive success: *Category 2 Strategic Planning*

5. Other factors
- major new thrusts; business alliances: *Category 2 Strategic Planning; Category 3 Customer and Market Focus*
- regulatory environment: *Item 1.1 Leadership*
- changes in strategy: *Category 2 Strategic Planning*

Table 5.4 Linkages between Approach-Deployment (A-D) Items and Results Items

CATEGORY	A-D AREA TO ADDRESS: topic	RESULTS ITEM
1 Leadership	1.2a(1): regulatory, legal, and ethical requirements	7.5 Company-Specific (see note N1, Item 1.2)
3 Customer and Market Focus	3.2a: accessibility and complaint management	7.5 Company-Specific (see note N3, Item 3.2)
	3.2b: customer satisfaction determination	7.1 Customer Satisfaction
4 Information and Analysis (see note N2, Item 4.3)	4.3a(1) customer-related performance	7.1 Customer satisfaction
	4.3a(2) operational performance, including product and service	7.3 Human Resource 7.5 Company-Specific
	4.3a(3) competitive performance	7.1-7.5
	4.3a(4) financial and market-related performance	7.2 Financial and Market
5 Human Resource	5.3c: employee well-being and satisfaction	7.3 Human Resource
6 Process Management: product/service processes	6.1b(1) and (3): product/service requirements and improvement	7.5 Company-Specific
6 Process Management: support processes	6.2a(3) and (5): support requirements and improvement	7.5 Company-Specific
6 Process Management: supplier/partner processes	6.3a: supplier/partner requirements and improvements	7.4 Supplier and Partner

notes. Figure 5.3 shows a different perspective on the relationship among the Categories. It also shows how Results are linked to Approach-Deployment by Category and how the Categories are linked by measures/indicators. Table 5.3 shows you how to use information from the Business Overview to augment your notes. Table 5.4 lists the linkages among the Items. As you become more proficient with the Criteria, use the linkages alluded to in Chapter 3, Exercise 3.5, and Table 5.3. (Note: Sometimes it is better for an applicant to include some information in a related section than where asked. Because the applicant has a limited number of pages to describe the organization, do not penalize the applicant for trying to respond to the Criteria with this constraint. While you may not be obligated to search everywhere for information, you are obligated to use information you find in other sections to prepare your feedback. Understanding the linkages makes it easier for you to accomplish this.) More sophisticated linkages can be found in Mark Blazey's book, *Insights to Excellence 1997: An Inside Look at the 1997 Baldrige Award Criteria* (Milwaukee: Quality Press, 1997).

Exercise 5.2   Read the entire application for Colony Fasteners, Incorporated; write, amend, and enhance your notes and confirm the sources of your notes with appropriate highlighting and notation in the case study. You should plan to spend 60–90 minutes per Category reading and writing. For this reason, take a break after each Category.

These notes help the examiner understand the organization and prepare the stage for writing comments. This understanding alleviates the subjectivity that can enter the examination process. If answers (or information) cannot be found, the examiner must state that the application does not include this information. This does not mean there is no answer. It means only that the examiner has no data (yet) with which to evaluate the applicant on the criteria.

6

Writing Comments

OVERVIEW

The product of the Feedback Process is the feedback report. Examiners must learn how to maximize the value of the feedback report to the applicant (the customer) through the comments they write (see Figure 6.1). In this chapter, the type of comments best suited for the feedback report are called value-added, nonprescriptive comments. Applicants can benefit from this chapter by better understanding what examiners look for and how they should write comments. Because the applicant must read and understand these comments, applicants will find them more valuable when they understand how and why examiners write what they do in feedback reports. As a result of this chapter, I expect scorebooks, consensus comments, and feedback reports to be much better written and expect there will be much less variability in how they are written.

OBJECTIVES

By completing the exercises in this chapter, the reader will be able to (1) explain the two types of comments examiners write for scorebooks and feedback and (2) write comments to an application that are value adding and nonprescriptive.

UNDERSTAND-ING THE INTEGRATION OF THE CRITERIA, THE SCORING GUIDELINES, AND THE APPLICATION

Comments are based on three sources of information:

1. The Criteria, which state what information the application must contain
2. The application, which contains the information requested
3. The scoring guidelines, which quantify the extent the information in the application complies with the Criteria

Comments represent the examiner's identification of the applicant's Strengths and Areas for Improvement. Different examiners have different experiences. To the extent diverse experiences help to understand the Criteria and help to write nonprescriptive comments, they are helpful. To the extent diverse experiences cause examiners to propose solutions, reject other's solutions, or implicitly evaluate based on factors other than those in the Criteria, they are not helpful. So, one purpose of training on writing comments is to overcome the potentially adverse use of diverse experiences.

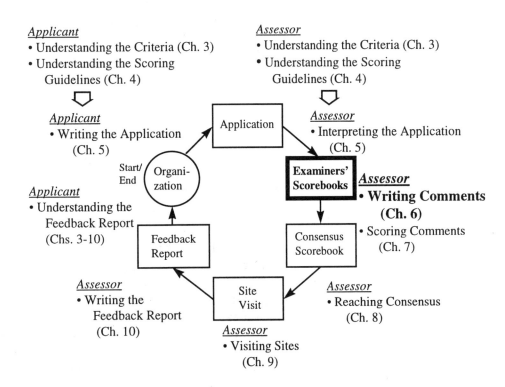

Applicant
• Understanding the Criteria (Ch. 3)
• Understanding the Scoring
  Guidelines (Ch. 4)

Applicant
• Writing the Application
  (Ch. 5)

Applicant
• Understanding the
  Feedback Report
  (Chs. 3-10)

Assessor
• Writing the
  Feedback Report
  (Ch. 10)

Assessor
• Understanding the Criteria (Ch. 3)
• Understanding the Scoring
  Guidelines (Ch. 4)

Assessor
• Interpreting the Application
  (Ch. 5)

Assessor
• **Writing Comments
  (Ch. 6)**
• Scoring Comments
  (Ch. 7)

Assessor
• Reaching Consensus
  (Ch. 8)

Assessor
• Visiting Sites
  (Ch. 9)

Application

Start/
End | Organi-
zation

Examiners'
Scorebooks

Consensus
Scorebook

Feedback
Report

Site
Visit

Figure 6.1   The Feedback Process: Writing comments.

In theory, if two well-trained examiners use the *same application and Criteria*, there should be no variation in their comments on the application. This happens when examiners

• understand what the Criteria ask for,
• understand the purpose of comments,
• understand the scoring guidelines,
• heed the instructions for commenting, and
• have good writing skills.

Commenting requires that the examiner understand what is asked in each Area to Address because the Criteria are specific in these sections. Commenting requires that the examiner understand the purpose of commenting, which is to provide useful feedback to the applicant without being prescriptive. Commenting requires that the examiner understand the scoring guidelines because the scoring guidelines identify the extent to which the application responds to the Areas to Address. Commenting requires that the examiner follow the guidelines for commenting so that the highest quality feedback is attained. Commenting requires writing well and consistently.

**WRITING
VALUE-ADDED
AND NON-
PRESCRIPTIVE
COMMENTS**

Comments are the result of the examiner applying the Criteria and the scoring guidelines to the application. There are two types of comments: (1)

comments that identify Strengths and (2) comments that identify Areas for Improvement.

Value-added comments take into account the Business Overview and the scoring dimensions by

- identifying by Area, and if applicable by subArea, the aspects to which the application has responded when the comment is a Strength,
- identifying by Area, and if applicable by subArea, the aspects to which the application has not responded when the comment is an Area for Improvement, and
- identifying scoring rows for the applicable scoring dimensions.

Nonprescriptive comments do not implicitly or explicitly recommend or reject specific procedures, tools, techniques, systems, and the like. Comments that are value added and nonprescriptive in the senses above make the task of scoring easier and, most importantly, tell the applicant exactly which areas need further work (Areas for Improvement) and the areas in which they must maintain their level of performance (Strengths), but not how.

So, comments are value added and nonprescriptive when

1. They are legible.
2. They are in complete sentences.
3. They identify the specific (sub)Area to Address.
4. They identify the scoring dimension(s) to which they apply.
5. For Strength comments, they use the applicant's words to describe and summarize and the Criteria's words to identify to what the comment applies.

   a. For Approach-Deployment Items, write comments that describe the approach (Systematic), list the work units using the approach (Deployment), and/or indicate the extent of improvement cycles (Continuous Improvement).
   b. For Results Items, write comments that identify whether results are for areas of importance (Key Areas), whether current performance (Levels) is good, whether historical performance patterns (Trends) are favorable or not, and/or identify to what the comparisons are made and how they compare (Comparisons).

6. For Area for Improvement comments, they use the Criteria's words to specify what is unclear or missing and explicitly identify the scoring dimension and rank.

   a. For Approach-Deployment Items, write comments that describe which Areas to Address are missing (Systematic), which work units are not using the approach (Deployment), and cite the extent of lack of improvement (Continuous Improvement).
   b. For Results Items, write comments that identify the key measures (Key Areas) that do not have results or have poor results (Levels), describe adverse patterns (Trends), or identify missing or poor comparisons (Comparisons).

7. The Strength and Area for Improvement comments for an Item address the Item in its entirety and nothing else.

This list may seem intimidating to those unfamiliar with how to write comments. However, a simple exercise should reveal not only why this list is needed, but how you might derive it yourself. Consider the following comment on Colony Fasteners, Incorporated (CFI), the case study organization:

> ''Internal customers are neither included nor consulted.''

Now, try to identify to what this refers. If you have difficulty or find it impossible, then you can begin to appreciate the need to refer to the specific (sub)Area to Address. Since this is an Area for Improvement comment, you can perhaps also begin to appreciate the need to include some specific words in the Criteria to clarify the comment further.

This exercise suggests that one way to check your comments is by seeing to what extent they would stand alone.

TIPS FOR WRITING COMMENTS

It is not essential that you start with Category 1 when writing comments. Different examiners start with different Categories. Some prefer to start with Category 3, Customer Focus and Satisfaction, to see how customer oriented the organization is. Others start with Category 2, Strategic Planning, because this gives an overview of the organization, its action plans, and key measures.

The key to writing comments that add value is in identifying Areas for Improvement. Appropriate Area for Improvement comments will also prepare you for the subsequent tasks of an examiner, such as scoring and preparing for site visits. The following tips and examples of sentence structures for writing Area for Improvement comments will help achieve these objectives. The headings relate to the scoring dimensions used in this workbook.

Systematic: Response missing part or all of an Area to address

- It is unclear that (*quote from the Criteria*).
- Apparently (organization name) does not (*quote from Criteria*).
- There is no description of (*quote from Criteria*).

Deployment: Major gaps or not fully deployed

- It appears that Criteria are not deployed to (*deployment units*).
- It is not clear that (*deployment units*) use the approach to (*quote from Criteria*).

Continuous Improvement: Not fact based, no cycles of refinement

- There is no evidence of refinement of (*approach*) through cycles and analyses.
- It is unclear how many cycles of refinement (*approach*) have been performed.

Areas, Levels, Trends, Comparisons: Missing key measures, results, or comparisons

- There are no data/measures for (*Key Area*).
- Levels are (*unfavorable; poor*) relative to (*maximum/minimum on scale; goals*).
- There are no data for previous (*periods*).
- Trends for the past (*number*) (*periods*) are unfavorable.
- There are no comparisons.
- Comparisons against (*name*) are (*unfavorable; poor*).

Exercise 6.1   For each comment below, state what makes it value added or not and whether it is prescriptive. The numbers in brackets identify the Area to Address to which the comment refers.

1. [5.3a] The organization has a good system to ensure a safe and healthful work environment.
2. [5.3c] The response does not state how it addresses employees' views of management and leadership.
3. [5.1b] The company needs to include cash bonuses as union worker compensation.
4. [5.2a] The company's Training and Education Support System is used to identify potential career paths and aids employees in selecting appropriate training.
5. [5.2a(5)] It is unclear how the organization's evaluation and improvement of education and training take into account company performance.

Table 6.1 shows a form for writing comments.[1] This form is useful for all comments and all Items. The table has three sections. The top section is an identifier that includes a place to state the primary purposes of the Item (since comments are grouped by Item for scoring) and either organizational deployment units (Work Units) or Key Areas of measures (Key Areas). When writing comments to an Approach-Deployment Item, cross out Key Areas and when writing comments to a Results Item cross out Work Units. In the space between ''Work units/Key Areas'' and the top of the table, write the Item number (e.g., 5.3), the Item title (e.g., Employee Well-Being and Satisfaction), and the points for the Item in parentheses after the title, such as (30 pts.).

The next two sections are for comments. The middle section is for Strength comments and the third section is for Area for Improvement comments.[2] The scoring dimension(s) (Score Dim.) to which the comment applies goes in the left-most column, the Area and/or subArea to Address goes in the middle column (Area to Address), and the comments are placed in the right-hand column. In the ''Scoring Dim.'' column use the following abbreviations: SY for Systematic, DE for Deployment, CI for Continuous Improvement, KA for Key Area, LE for Levels, TR for Trends, and CO for Comparisons.

Figure 6.2 shows a decision tree for determining the types of comments examiners make. The examiner determines the type (Approach-Deployment or Results) of Item

---

[1]This form is different from what is used by Baldrige and some state examiners. It is enhanced by including the identifier section. It is also streamlined by excluding redundant information (see Footnote 2).

[2]Typically, an examiner places +'s or double +'s and −'s or double −'s to indicate the examiner's judgment of how strong or weak the application is because the examiner does not provide comments to all Areas and subAreas. In addition, the +'s and −'s are not included in the Baldrige and some other award feedback reports. Clearly, these notations are for examiners only for scoring individually and in consensus and for identifying site visit issues. Since here we do provide comments to all Areas and subAreas, these distinctions are not necessary because these judgments are made through the scoring system.

Table 6.1   Comment and Scoring Worksheet

<u>Purposes</u>
<u>Work Units/Key Areas</u>

Score Dim.	Area to Address	STRENGTHS

Score Dim.	Area to Address	AREAS FOR IMPROVEMENT

Comment and Scoring Work Sheet   Percent Score ____

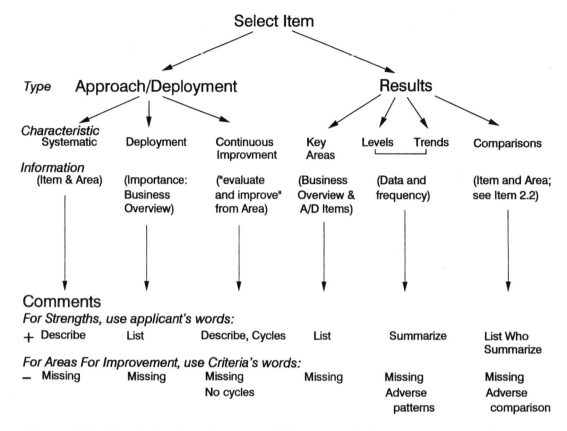

Figure 6.2 Decision tree for writing value-added, nonprescriptive comments.

on which the examiner is commenting. Each Item type has different scoring dimensions. Figure 6.2 shows where the information for the Item dimension is found. Not only should comments be at the subArea levels when they exist, but they should also address the scoring dimension of the Item.

SIX-STEP PROCEDURE

An examiner takes six steps to produce comments for an Item:

1. Identify the type of Item—Approach-Deployment or Result.
2. Identify the primary purposes of the Item.
3. If it is an Approach-Deployment Item, identify what constitutes full deployment and cross out *Key Areas*. If it is a Result Item, identify the Key Areas and/or measures and cross out *Work Units*.
4. For each (sub)Area to Address, write value-added, nonprescriptive Strength and Area for Improvement comments in the right column.
5. For each comment, denote the scoring dimension(s) to which it applies in the left column and the specific (sub)Area to which it applies in the middle column.
6. Check that the set of comments for the Item addresses the Item in its entirety and nothing else.

EXAMPLE

Let us see how to apply this six-step procedure using Item 5.3 and the response to Item 5.3 in the case study (Appendix C).

Criteria

5.3 Employee Well-Being and Satisfaction (30 pts.)

Describe how the company maintains a work environment and a work climate that support the well-being, satisfaction, and motivation of employees.

In your response, address the following Areas:

a. Work Environment

How the company maintains a safe and healthful work environment. Include how employee well-being factors such as health, safety, and ergonomics are included in improvement activities. Briefly describe key measures and targets for each important factor. Note significant differences, if any, based on different health and safety factors in the work environments of employee groups or work units.

b. Employee Support Services

How the company supports the well-being, satisfaction, and motivation of employees via services, facilities, activities, and opportunities.

c. Employee Satisfaction

How the company determines employee well-being, satisfaction, and motivation. Include (1) a brief description of formal and informal methods used. Outline how the company determines the key factors that affect employee well-being, satisfaction, and motivation and assesses its work climate. Note important differences in methods, factors, or measures for different categories or types of employees, as appropriate; and (2) how the company relates employee well-being, satisfaction, and motivation results to key business results and/or objectives to identify improvement activities.

Step 1: Identify the type of Item.
Answer: This is an Approach-Deployment Item.

Step 2: List the primary purposes of the Item.
Answer: Item 5.3's primary purposes are description of how the company maintains a work environment and work climate that supports employees' (1) well-being, (2) satisfaction, and (3) motivation.

Step 3: Since this is an Approach-Deployment Item, identify what constitutes full deployment and cross out *Key Areas*.
Answer: All employees, noting "any significant differences among employees or employee groups" or "different categories or types of employees."

So, for the case study, full deployment means all categories of employees: hourly (HRL), salary exempt (SE), salary nonexempt (SNE); U.S. workers and non-U.S. workers (see page iii of the Business Overview); all major locations—Philadelphia, Los Angeles, Dearborn, Santa Ana, Milwaukee, Jacksonville, Macon, and foreign locations (see page ii of Business Overview).

Step 4: Write value-added and nonprescriptive Strength and Area for Improvement comments.
Answer: Read the applicant's response to Area to Address 5.3a. If the Approach "maintains a safe and healthful work environment," it must address

two aspects: (1) how employee well-being factors "such as health, safety, and ergonomics are included in improvement activities;" and (2) state the key "Measures and targets for each important factor." One Strength comment for 5.3a could be: *To prevent accidents or incidents proactively, Safety Awareness Teams regularly audit each plant and improvement teams are assigned to find root causes.* One Area for Improvement comment for 5.3a could be: *It is not clear that the environment, health, and safety (EHS) efforts are applied to all locations since data in Figure 7.3-1 (Lost Work Day Cases) refer only to U.S. locations. The responses do not address potential differences among employee groups (e.g., locations, jobs).*

Critique   The Strength comment repeats the response using the words in the application. The two clauses come from the third and second paragraphs, respectively, in the applicant's response to this Area to Address. Confirm this by finding them in the case study and reading both paragraphs. The "regular" audits and the descriptions of several specific actions indicate a systematic approach addressing specifically two Item requirements: "how the company maintains a safe work environment" and "how employee well-being factors such as . . . safety . . . are included in improvement activities."

The Area for Improvement comment repeats the words in the Criteria. It states that "it is not clear" because safety (a key measure) data for only U.S. locations are reported, and there is no explanation for the apparent omission of foreign locations (which we know exist from the Business Overview). This is a *deployment* issue. This comment recognizes that there are linkages among the Criteria and that information from other parts of the application can be used to improve the value of both Strength and Area for Improvement comments.

Step 4 (continued):   Write comments.
Answer: See Table 6.2.

Step 5:   Denote the scoring dimensions and (sub)Areas to which the comment applies (see Table 6.2). Both comments in Step 4 refer to Area 5.3a. The Strength comment addresses the Item requirements, so the relevant scoring dimension is SY (Systematic). The Area for Improvement comment addresses the lack of deployment of the approach, so the relevant scoring dimension is DE (Deployment).

Step 6:   Check that the set of comments addresses the Item in its entirety and nothing else.
Answer: All comments address a specific (sub)Area to Address, which can be noted by the words from the Criteria in the comments. Every (sub)Area receives at least one comment. There does not appear to be any irrelevant comment. So, this set of comments meets the condition of addressing the Item in its entirety and nothing else.

Critique   Note that all other conditions for being value added and nonprescriptive occur.

- The comments are legible.
- The comments are complete sentences.
- The comments identify the Area and subArea to Address.

Table 6.2   Comments to Example: Item 5.3

<u>Purposes</u> how work environment/climate supports employee well-being, satisfaction, motivation

<u>Work Units\~~Key Areas~~</u> all categories of employees; all sectors and locations

5.3 Employee Well-Being and Satisfaction *(30 pts)*

Score Dim.	Area to Address	STRENGTHS
SY	a	To proactively prevent accidents or incidents, Safety Awareness Teams regularly audit each plant and improvement teams are assigned to find root causes. All hazardous materials are identified, "red flagged," and their reduction measured and tracked, aiming for 45% reduction in solvent-based incidents by 1998, elimination of ozone-depletion compounds by 1999, 50% hazardous waste reduction by 1998, and 60% reduction of cumulative trauma injuries by 1997.
SY	a	The Safety Improvement Team fosters and directs the quality of environment, health, and safety (EHS), including championing improvements through equipment vendors and publication of performance standards. EHS issues include illness, injury, and ergonomics.
SY/ DE	b	CFI has implemented various programs worldwide to improve employee well-being and satisfaction, e.g. an extensive EAP that includes mental health, chemical dependency, child-care, 100% tuition reimbursements, financial support; recreational facilities; nine-week sabbaticals. These vary by location following local laws and customs.
SY	c(1)	Employee satisfaction is determined through regular surveys, focus groups, one-to-one interviews, BUMs, and other assessment and feedback tools.
CI	c(2)	The HRET, a multi-sector team, assesses how human resource strategies and practices contribute to business performance. They have shown involvement reduced turnover by 14% and increased employee satisfaction by 43%, contributed 67% of cycle time improvements, and 83% of quality improvements.
Score Dim.	Area to Address	AREAS FOR IMPROVEMENT
DE	a	It is not clear that the EHS efforts are applied to all locations since data in Figure 7.3-1 (Lost Work Day Cases) refer only to U.S. locations and the ergonomic improvements may be only in Boston.
SY\ DE	c(1)	There is no description of the key factors that affect employee well-being, satisfaction, and motivation nor how CFI assesses its work climate. There is no mention of how well-being and motivation are determined.
CI	c(2)	There does not appear to be any correlation between employee well-being and motivation and business results. It is not clear how these relations lead to identifying improvement activities.

Comment and Scoring Work Sheet   Percent Score _____

- The comments use the applicant's words in descriptions of Strengths (e.g., Strength comments for 5.3a include measures and targets from the application).
- The comments use the Criteria's words to identify to what they apply or what is missing or unclear, such as, 5.3c(1).
- The comments explicitly identify a scoring dimension. Since this is an Approach-Deployment Item, the relevant scoring dimensions are Systematic (SY), Deployment (DE), and Continuous Improvement (CI). Look at the Areas for Improvement comments to see how they identify the scoring dimension:

Areas for Improvement comment to 5.3a identifies one aspect that makes the approach not fully *deployed* or not used by all areas or work units (different employee groups may be excluded).

Areas for Improvement comment to 5.3c(1) indicates that the approach does not address all requirements (*Systematic*) because complete descriptions are missing.

Areas for Improvement comment to 5.3a(2) addresses the Continuous Improvement scoring dimension.

EXAMPLE   Write comments to the response to Item 7.2 in Appendix C.

Step 1:   Identify the type of Item.
Answer: This is a Result Item. The scoring dimensions are Key Areas (KA), current Levels (LE), Trends (TR), and Comparisons (CO).

Step 2:   List the primary purposes of the Item.
Answer: Item 7.2's primary purposes are to summarize the company's financial and marketplace results.

Step 3:   Since this is a Results Item, identify what constitutes the key measurement areas and cross out *Work Units*.
Answer: CFI identifies as financial measures ROI (return on investment) ROI for shareholders (a key stakeholder) and profit margins (for themselves) and identifies market share as a marketplace measure.

Step 4:   Write value-added and nonprescriptive Strength and Area for Improvement comments.
Answer: See Table 6.3.

Step 5:   Identify the applicable scoring dimensions for each comment.
Answer: See Table 6.3. The two Strength comments indicate performance for the current year (Level). The second Strength comment also includes Trend and Comparison performance. Each Area for Improvement comment addresses a different scoring dimension: the first is for Key Areas (KA) (missing), the second for Levels versus goals (LE) (below), the third is for Trends (TR) (adverse), and the last is for Comparisons (CO) (missing).

Step 6:   Check that the set of comments addresses the Item in its entirety and nothing else.
Answer: All comments address a specific Area to Address, either satisfaction or dissatisfaction measures. Every Area to Address has at least one comment. There does not appear to be any irrelevant comment. There are

Table 6.3   Comments to Example: Item 7.2

<u>Purposes</u> summary of key financial and marketplace results
~~Work Units~~/<u>Key Areas</u> financial: ROI (shareholders), profit margins (CFI); marketplace: market share, sales
7.2 Financial and Market Results *(130 pts)*

Score Dim.	Area to Address	STRENGTHS
LE	a	Profit margins for CPS are above '97 goal.
LE/ TR/ CO	a	All four sectors have excellent, sustained current levels and trends for %TAM compared to best competitors. Profit margins show improving trends for CAS and CPS.
Score Dim.	**Area to Address**	**AREAS FOR IMPROVEMENT**
KA/ LE	a	There are no data for shareholders' ROI, a critical stakeholder requirement.
LE	a	Current profit margins are below '97 goal for NSS and substantially below '97 goal for CAS and DAS.
TR	a	Profit margin trends are unfavorable for DAS (due to increased pressures from government and competitors) or flat for NSS during past five years.
CO	a	There are no comparisons of profit margins to competitors or benchmarks.

Comment and Scoring Work Sheet   Percent Score ____

comments on Levels for key measures, Trends, and Comparisons. So, this set of comments meets the condition of addressing the Item in its entirety and nothing else. The comments are value added and nonprescriptive because

- The comments are legible.
- The comments are complete sentences.
- The comments identify the Area and subArea to Address.
- The comments use the applicant's words in descriptions of Strengths and the Criteria's words to identify to what the comments apply or what is missing or unclear.
- The comments explicitly identify a scoring dimension.

Critique   The Strength comments identify first those measures with favorable current Levels and then those measures with favorable Trends and Comparisons. The Area for Improvement comments identify first those key measures without results, then those measures with unfavorable current Levels, and last those measures with unfavorable Trends and Comparisons. This is one way of ensuring that all scoring dimensions are addressed, and it will make scoring easier (see next chapter).

Use "favorable" or "unfavorable" rather than "increasing" or "decreasing." Since for some measures increasing is better and for others it is worse, the words *favorable* and *unfavorable* reduce the possibility of confusion or error. Judgment is sometimes required for determining whether Levels are poor, good, or excellent. You can typically make this judgment by comparing to goals and not just the absolute level. Comparisons to internal goals cannot be used as comments addressing the Comparison scoring dimension. This internal comparison differs from comparisons made to external targets (e.g., industry average, best competitors, best in class, or benchmarks).

Result Items' titles state the performance area that the results must reflect. Results Items have only one Area to Address, which states that current Levels, Trends, and Comparisons should be included when appropriate. Appropriate Comparisons for responses to Item 7.1 are major customers or customer groups, to Item 7.3 major suppliers or supplier groups, and to the other Items, major competitors or competitor groups.

Exercise 6.2   Make copies of the scorebook Comment and Scoring Worksheet (Table 6.1) and write comments for the case study using all the Criteria. You should have one Worksheet per Item, or 20 Worksheets. *Do not score.* The first time you write comments, you may spend about 60 to 90 minutes per Item. The upper limit will depend on how good a job you did reading the case study and taking notes and how well you understand the Criteria. As you become more familiar with the Criteria, gain experience in writing comments, and improve your ability to interpret the application and take notes, you should be able to maintain about 30 to 45 minutes per Item for comment writing and about the same for reading and taking notes. This will mean about 20–30 hours total to produce a complete set of comments for the entire application, including reading and taking notes.

Evidence of your improved abilities consists of spending less time reading the Criteria and rereading the application and more time fine-tuning your comments. You may also feel less frustrated when searching for information for formulating your comments.

7

Scoring Comments

OVERVIEW Ideally, well-trained examiners would give the same score to the same set of value-added, nonprescriptive comments for an Item (see Figure 7.1). Even with examiner training, this task is not easy or straightforward. Examiners must combine the three scoring dimensions for an Approach-Deployment or the four scoring dimensions of a Results Item to produce a single score. The Criteria do not have a specific procedure for combining these dimensions. In fact, these dimensions are not as clearly delineated in the *1997 Criteria* as they are in Chapter 6. Readers with the skills to write value-added, nonprescriptive comments should have less scoring variation than readers without these skills.

In this chapter, we show how to reduce scoring variation when scoring under the Baldrige guidance for examiners. After reading Chapter 12, we show how to reduce scoring variation further when scoring applications for a three-level award.

OBJECTIVES By completing the exercises in this chapter, the reader will be able to

- explain how the scoring dimensions play a role in scoring,
- score an application based on value-added and nonprescriptive comments, and
- justify a score for an Item based on its comments and their relation to the scoring dimensions.

INTRODUCTION Recall that the scoring guidelines shown in Table 4.1 (page 27) were modified to look like those in Table 4.2 (page 28) to reveal the dimensions of each row:

- Row 1 represents a score of 0%.
- Row 2 represents scores from 10% to 30%.
- Row 3 represents scores from 40% to 60%.
- Row 4 represents scores from 70% to 90%.
- Row 5 represents a score of 100%.

Individual examiners always score using multiples of 10%. So, for the three middle rows—Rows 2, 3, and 4—the examiner must then choose whether the score is at the low, middle, or high end of the row to convert the row selection to a score. To help examiners score to the nearest 10%, other authors have expanded the Scoring Guidelines (see Brown's and Blazey's books, for example). This makes it easier and more consistent to select a score to the nearest 10%. Table 7.1 is another expansion of the Scoring Guidelines. It differs from the others by including specific definitions for

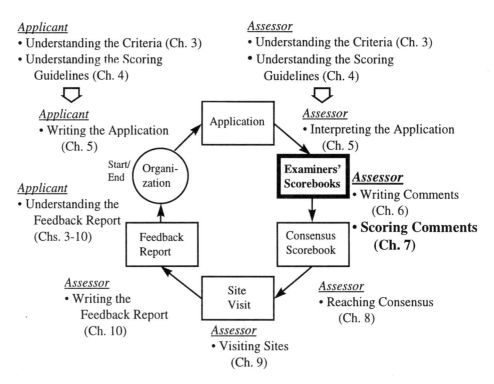

Applicant
• Understanding the Criteria (Ch. 3)
• Understanding the Scoring
   Guidelines (Ch. 4)

Assessor
• Understanding the Criteria (Ch. 3)
• Understanding the Scoring
   Guidelines (Ch. 4)

Applicant
• Writing the Application
   (Ch. 5)

Assessor
• Interpreting the Application
   (Ch. 5)

Applicant
• Understanding the
   Feedback Report
   (Chs. 3–10)

Assessor
• Writing Comments
   (Ch. 6)
• **Scoring Comments
   (Ch. 7)**

Assessor
• Writing the
   Feedback Report
   (Ch. 10)

Assessor
• Reaching Consensus
   (Ch. 8)

Assessor
• Visiting Sites
   (Ch. 9)

Start/End — Organization — Application — Examiners' Scorebooks — Consensus Scorebook — Site Visit — Feedback Report

Figure 7.1 The Feedback Process: Scoring comments.

every 10% score on every scoring dimension. We use this table in this chapter and recommend it or a modification of other such tables to include the scoring dimensions defined in Chapter 4.

Because each Item is scored, the task of scoring is complicated by integrating the information on all Areas to Address for the Item with the relevant scoring dimensions of the Scoring Guidelines. For this reason, value-added comments identify the specific Area to Address and, if applicable, the sub-Area to Address. In addition, value-added Area for Improvement comments identify a weakness by referencing both a particular scoring dimension (e.g., Systematic or Continuous Improvement for an Approach-Deployment Item or Trend for a Results Item) and a scoring row. The more explicit this reference, the greater the value of the comment to the applicant and others (e.g., other examiners and judges).

BALDRIGE SCORING GUIDELINES

Assignment of Scores to Applicants' Responses
Baldrige Award examiners observe the following guidelines in assignment of scores to applicants' responses:

■ All relevant Areas to Address should be included in the Item response. Also, responses should reflect what is relevant and important to the applicant's business.

■ In assigning a score to an Item, an examiner first decides which scoring

Table 7.1 Expanded Scoring Guidelines with Scoring Dimensions

APPROACH-DEPLOYMENT ITEMS

Score	Systematic	Deployment	Continuous Improvement
0%	No system evident	No evidence of deployment	No evidence of continuous improvement
10%	Beginning of systematic approach to some primary purposes of the Item	Some deployment, but excludes major areas/units	Beginning to recognize problems
20%	Beginning of systematic approach to half the primary purposes of the Item	Deployment to some major areas/work units	General orientation to correcting problems but still reactive
30%	Beginning of systematic approach to all the primary purposes of the Item	Deployment to most major areas/work units	Transition from reacting to problems to a general improvement orientation
40%	Sound system responsive to some primary purposes of item	Deployment to all major areas/work units; most in early stages	More emphasis on improvement than reaction
50%	Sound system responsive to half the primary purposes of item	Deployment to all major areas/work units; some in early stages	Fact-based improvement process in place
60%	Sound system responsive to all the primary purposes of item	Deployment to all major areas/work units; few in early stages	Preventive orientation integrated with corrective action; some evidence of refinement through one or two cycles
70%	Sound system responsive to some overall purposes of item	Deployment to all major and some nonmajor areas/work units	Evidence of refinement, integration, and maturity; two or more cycles and analyses
80%	Sound system responsive to half of overall purposes of item	Deployed to all major and half nonmajor areas/work units	Clear evidence of refinement and improved integration from cycles and analyses
90%	Sound system responsive to almost all purposes of Item	Deployment to almost all areas/work units: major or otherwise	Improvement process shows evidence of innovation and integration to major areas/work units
100%	Sound system fully responsive to all Item requirements	Fully deployed without significant gaps or weaknesses	Key management tool: strong integration and excellent analyses

RESULTS ITEMS

Score	Levels and/or Trends	Comparisons
0%	None to few levels and/or trends reported in key areas	No comparisons in key areas
10%	No favorable levels or trends reported in key areas	Few fair comparisons in key areas
20%	In some key areas, early good [favorable] performance levels and/or early stages of setting trends; most levels poor [unfavorable]	Some fair comparisons in key areas
30%	In many key areas, early good [favorable] performance levels and/or early stages of setting trends with some adverse trends and/or poor [unfavorable] performance levels	In some key areas, performance levels and/or trends show good comparisons
40%	In some key areas, improvement trends and/or good [favorable] performance levels with few adverse trends and/or poor [unfavorable] performance levels	In many key areas, performance levels and/or trends show good comparisons
50%	In many key areas, improvement trends and/or good [favorable] performance levels with few adverse trends and/or poor [unfavorable] performance levels	In most key areas, performance levels and/or trends show good comparisons
60%	In most key areas, improvement trends and/or good [favorable] performance levels with no adverse trends and/or no poor [unfavorable] performance levels	In some key areas, performance levels and/or trends show very good comparisons
70%	In many key areas, good [favorable] performance levels and/or sustained trends with no adverse trends and/or no poor [unfavorable] performance levels	In key areas, many levels and/or trends show very good and leadership comparisons
80%	In most key areas, good to excellent performance levels and/or sustained trends with no adverse trends and/or no poor [unfavorable] performance levels	In key areas, most levels and/or trends show very good and leadership comparisons
90%	Sustained excellent performance levels and/or excellent improvement trends in some key areas	Industry and benchmark leader in some key areas
100%	Sustained excellent performance levels and/or excellent improvement trends in most key areas	Industry and benchmark leader in many key areas

range (e.g., 40% to 60%) best fits the overall Item response. Overall "best fit" does not require total agreement with each of the statements for that scoring range. Actual score *within the range* depends on an examiner's judgment of the closeness of the Item response in relation to the statements in the next higher and next lower scoring ranges.

■ An Approach-Deployment Item score of 50% represents an approach that meets the *basic* objectives of the Item and that is deployed to the principal activities covered in the Item. Higher scores reflect maturity (cycles of improvement), integration, and broader deployment.

■ A Results Item score of 50% represents clear indication of improvement trends and/or good levels of performance in the principal result areas covered in the Item. Higher scores reflect better improvement rates and comparative performance, as well as broader coverage.

SCORING PROCEDURE

The examiner takes five simple steps to score.

Step 1: Score each relevant scoring dimension of an Item to the nearest 10%.

Step 2: When all scoring dimensions have been scored, combine them to produce a single score for the Item to the nearest 10%.

Step 3: Multiply each Item's percentage score by the number of points it is worth to produce a point score. You may round to the nearest whole number.

Step 4: Calculate Category point totals by summing points for all Items of that Category.

Step 5: Calculate an application total point by summing points for all Items.

The purpose of Step 1 is to reduce the variability at Step 2. There are several ways to combine scores. Two are described here. First, you can take the arithmetic mean. This reduces inconsistency but does not take into account different values or weights for each scoring dimension. Second, you can look at the Scoring Guidelines to select the row that "best" matches your scores for the scoring dimensions and comments and then, for the middle rows, determine whether the score is at the low, middle, or high end of the row. This is what the Baldrige Criteria say examiners do.

Scoring Results Items could be easier except for gaps in the scoring row definitions. We saw in Table 4.2 that the four scoring dimensions collapse into three for purposes of scoring because performance is judged by Levels and/or Trends. So, the higher score of the two determines the score for these two dimensions. In addition, if you reread the Scoring Guidelines (Table 4.1), you should notice that Key Areas is a limiting factor. That is, to score in the 70% to 90% range on Levels and/or Trends, the good-to-excellent performance must be in Key Areas. Thus, the first step for combining Results scores on the scoring dimensions is to determine the score on the scoring dimension Key Areas. The combined score cannot be any higher than the score on this dimension. From there, we need only combine the other three scoring dimensions, which amounts to combining only two scores: one for Levels and/or Trends and one for Comparisons.

Table 7.1 makes all this easy. It closes the gaps and incorporates the Key Areas scoring dimension into the Level/Trends and Comparison scoring dimensions. Using Table 7.1 directly, Key Areas is automatically included as a limiting factor, and there are definitions for each 10% score on these dimensions. Thus, scoring results consists of looking at two columns.

TIPS FOR SCORING

- If you do not have any Area for Improvement comments—you must score the Item 100%.
- If you do not have any Strength comments—you must score the Item 0%.
- To determine which row to select for a combined score, look at the definitions of each row. It is unlikely that a set of comments corresponds exactly to the definition, so you will have to choose the row that best corresponds to it.
- The dimension scores place bounds on the combined Item score. For example, if for an Approach-Deployment Item one dimension is scored 90%, another 50%, and the third 40%, the Item score cannot be higher than 90% or lower than 40%.
- To select the low or high end of the chosen row, compare the definitions and your comments to see whether the comments imply scoring lower or higher.

EXAMPLE: STEPS 1–3 FOR AN APPROACH- DEPLOYMENT ITEM

Step 1

This is a simple example (see Table 7.2). It is an Approach-Deployment Item. The scoring dimensions are Systematic (SY), Deployment (DE), and Continuous Improvement (CI). Use the expanded Scoring Guidelines in Table 7.1 that show the scoring dimensions. Some people laminate these tables and use washable or erasable markers to write their scores on the table for each Item (as shown in Table 7.3), transfer them to a summary score sheet, erase the scores, and reuse the table.

The primary purposes of Item 5.3 are how the company maintains a work environment and work climate that supports the well-being, satisfaction, and motivation of all employees. From the titles of the three Areas of Item 5.3, we see that Areas 5.3a (Work Environment) and 5.3b (Employee Support Services) focus on the primary purposes of this Item. Addressing Area 5.3c would go beyond the primary purposes of the scoring dimension Systematic and include the Continuous Improvement scoring dimension.

The Area to Address 5.3b is missing entirely. So, on the Systematic dimension, the comments imply a score less than 40%, the lowest score for a systematic approach. It is not a 0% score because there is a specific response to Area to Address 5.3a: ''how the company *maintains* a work environment and climate.'' The Strength and Area for Improvement comments together

Table 7.2 Comments to Item 5.3 for Scoring: Simple Case

<u>Purposes</u> how work environment/climate supports employee well-being, satisfaction, motivation

<u>Work Units\Key Areas</u> all categories of employees; all sectors and locations

5.3 Employee Well-Being and Satisfaction *(30 pts)*

Score Dim.	Area to Address	STRENGTHS
SY	a	Colony Fasteners has a process for maintaining a safe work environment through the reduction and elimination and safe use of hazardous materials in its DAS and NSS plants.

Score Dim.	Area to Address	AREAS FOR IMPROVEMENT
DE	a	It is unclear whether the process for maintaining a safe work environment through the reduction and elimination and safe use of hazardous materials applies to all four sectors.
SY	a	The response does not address the key measures and targets for each important factor.
DE	a	The response does not distinguish among different work environments and different employee groups, which would indicate the extent of deployment of the process to maintain a safe and healthful work environment.
SY	b	The response does not describe how the company supports the well-being, satisfaction, and motivation of employees via services, facilities, activities, and opportunities.
SY	c(1)	The response does not describe how the company determines employee satisfaction, well-being, and motivation.
CI	c(2)	The response does not describe how it relates employee well-being, satisfaction, and motivation results to key business results and/or objectives to identify improvement activities.

SY = 10   DE = 20   CI = 0

Comment and Scoring Work Sheet   Percent Score <u>10</u>

imply a score of 10% because less than half the primary purposes are addressed according to the comments.

Deployment means applying the approach to all employee categories. Since it appears that two of four sectors (major work units) are not included, there is a major gap in deployment. Since a score of 40–60% implies no major gaps, we know the score must be 30% or less. While half the sectors are mentioned, the approach is not systematic. This implies a score of 20% on Deployment.

The score for Continuous Improvement is 0% because there is no response to Area to Address 5.3c(2), which is the continuous improvement element of this Item.

Once you become familiar with scoring guidelines or if you do not have a reusable set of tables, you can write each dimension's score below your comments on the worksheet using the following abbreviations: for Approach-Deployment Items, use SY for Systematic, DE for Deployment, and CI for Continuous Improvement; for Results Items, use KA for Key Areas, LE for Levels, TR for Trends, and CO for Comparisons. For this example, you would write SY = 10, DE = 20, CI = 0, as shown in Table 7.2.

Table 7.3 Scoring Example of an Approach-Deployment Item: Item 5.3 (Simple Case)

APPROACH-DEPLOYMENT ITEMS

Score	Systematic	Deployment	Continuous Improvement
0%	No system evident	No evidence of deployment	No evidence of continuous improvement
10%	Beginning of systematic approach to some primary purposes of the Item	Some deployment, but excludes major areas/units	Beginning to recognize problems
20%	Beginning of systematic approach to half the primary purposes of the Item	Deployment to some major areas/units	General orientation to correcting problems but still reactive
30%	Beginning of systematic approach to all the primary purposes of the Item	Deployment to most the major areas/units	Transition from reacting to problems to a general improvement orientation
40%	Sound system responsive to some primary purposes of Item	Deployment to all major areas/units; most in early stages	Evidence of improvement from facts although no systematic improvement process in place
50%	Sound system responsive to half the primary purposes of Item	Deployment to all major areas/units; some in early stages	Fact-based improvement process; more emphasis on improvement than reaction
60%	Sound system responsive to all the primary purposes of Item	Deployment to all major areas/units; few in early stages	Preventive orientation integrated with corrective action; some evidence of refinement through one or two cycles
70%	Sound system responsive to some overall purposes of Item	Deployment to all major and some nonmajor areas/units	Evidence of refinement, integration, and maturity; two or more cycles and analyses
80%	Sound system responsive to half of overall purposes of Item	Deployed to all major and half nonmajor areas/units	Clear evidence of refinement and improved integration from cycles and analyses
90%	Sound system responsive to almost all purposes of Item	Deployment to almost all areas/units: major or otherwise	Improvement process shows evidence of innovation and integration to major areas/units
100%	Sound system fully responsive to all Item requirements	Fully deployed without significant gaps or weaknesses	Key management tool: strong integration and excellent analyses

Step 2   The first way to combine these scores yields a mean of 10%. The rationale for the Baldrige approach is as follows. By comparing the full definitions of the 0% row and the 10–30% row, we can identify Row 2 (10–30%) as the overall row that most closely matches the scores: "beginning of a systematic approach to the primary purposes of the Item . . . with major gaps existing in deployment" (Table 4.1). To determine whether the score is at the low, middle, or high end of Row 2, we note the lack of Continuous Improvement and the lack of approach to one primary purpose. This supports a score at the low end of Row 2, which is 10%, for this set of comments. Place this number at the bottom right-hand side of the worksheet.

Step 3   This Item is worth 30 points. So, the point score is 10% of 30, or 3 points.

EXAMPLE: STEPS 1–3 FOR AN APPROACH-DEPLOYMENT ITEM

Now, let us score a more difficult case; the set of comments recognizes many Strengths and Areas for Improvement. Score the same Item 5.3 but now let us use the comments from the first example in Chapter 6. Refer to the full set of comments in Table 6.2 in that example.

Step 1   Score the scoring dimensions (see Table 7.4). The response addresses the primary purposes (what is asked at the Item level) and addresses some

Table 7.4 Scoring Example of an Approach-Deployment Item: Item 5.3 (Full Case)

APPROACH-DEPLOYMENT ITEMS

Score	Systematic	Deployment	Continuous Improvement
0%	No system evident	No evidence of deployment	No evidence of continuous improvement
10%	Beginning of systematic approach to some primary purposes of the Item	Some deployment, but excludes major areas/units	Beginning to recognize problems
20%	Beginning of systematic approach to half the primary purposes of the Item	Deployment to some jaor areas/units	General orientation to correcting problems but still reactive
30%	Beginning of systematic approach to all the primary purposes of the Item	Deployment to most the major areas/units	Transition from reacting to problems to a general improvement orientation
40%	Sound system responsive to some primary purposes of Item	Deployment to all major areas/ units; most in early stages	Evidence of improvement from facts although no systematic improvement process in place
50%	Sound system responsive to half the primary purposes of Item	Deployment to all major areas/ units; some in early stages	Fact-based improvement process; more emphasis on improvement than reaction
60%	Sound system responsive to all the primary purposes of Item	Deployment to all major areas/ units; few in early stages	Preventive orientation integrated with corrective action; some evidence of refinement through one or two cycles
70%	Sound system responsive to some overall purposes of Item	Deployment to all major and some nonmajor areas/units	Evidence of refinement, integration, and maturity; two or more cycles and analyses
80%	Sound system responsive to half of overall purposes of Item	Deployed to all major and half nonmajor areas/units	Clear evidence of refinement and improved integration from cycles and analyses
90%	Sound system responsive to almost all purposes of Item	Deployment to almost all areas/ units: major or otherwise	Improvement process shows evidence of innovation and integration to major areas/units
100%	Sound system fully responsive to all Item requirements	Fully deployed without significant gaps or weaknesses	Key management tool: strong integration and excellent analyses

overall purposes (what is asked at the Area to Address level), so I give it a 70% on the Systematic dimension. The evidence that it is not addressing half or most of the overall purposes comes in part from the Area for Improvement comment 5.3a, but mostly from the Area for Improvement comment 5.3c(1). To be responsive to most overall purposes would require addressing well-being and motivation in Area to Address 5.3c(2) and identifying some factors affecting all three—well-being, satisfaction, and motivation—in 5.3c(1).

I give the response based on my comments 50% on Deployment because there are no obvious major gaps from the response to Area to Address 5.3a. However, what may not be deployed (environmental, health, and safety [EHS] efforts) is a small part of the systematic approach described and is deployed to all four sectors. The Strength comment to 5.3b clearly says all locations. The 50%, rather than 60%, comes from the doubts denoted by ''it is not clear'' and from the fact that other employee groupings are clearly not distinguished. These Area for Improvement comments suggest that, for EHS, some locations may still be in the early stages. A site visit (see Chapter 9) should clarify the extent of deployment.

My reason for giving these comments 40% on Continuous Improvement is because improvements are based on facts with more emphasis on improvement. These comments cannot receive higher than 50% because there is no history of "cycles and analyses." The 40%, rather than 50%, comes from the lack of specific steps to link these results to the next improvement activities (indicating lack of specific improvement process), and it appears that well-being and motivation are not correlated with business results.

The scores for this example can be written as follows: SY = 70, DE = 50, CI = 40

Step 2   This one is easier to combine. Either way of combining scores should yield 50%. Place this number in the box at the bottom right-hand side of the score sheet (Table 6.2).

Step 3   This Item is worth 30 points. So, the point score is 50% of 30, or 15 points.

EXAMPLE: STEPS 1–3
FOR A RESULTS ITEM   Let us score the set of comments for Item 7.2, from Chapter 6, Table 6.3.

Step 1   This is a Results Item, so the scoring dimensions are Areas, Levels, Trends, and Comparisons (Table 7.5). There are two Key Areas that need measures: financial and marketplace performance. The financial area must include measures that are important to the business and to its key stakeholders/

Table 7.5   Scoring Example of a Results Item: Item 7.2

RESULTS ITEMS

Score	Levels and/or Trends	Comparisons
0%	None to few levels and/or trends reported in key areas	No comparisons in key areas
10%	No favorable levels or trends reported in key areas	Few fair comparisons in key areas
20%	In some key areas, early good [favorable] performance levels *and/or* early stages of setting trends; most levels poor [unfavorable]	Some fair comparisons in key areas
30%	In many key areas, early good [favorable] performance levels *and/or* early stages of setting trends with some adverse trends *and/or* poor [unfavorable] performance levels	In some key areas, performance levels *and/or* trends show good comparisons
40%	In some key areas, improvement trends *and/or* good [favorable] performance levels with few adverse trends *and/or* poor [unfavorable] performance levels	In many key areas, performance levels *and/or* trends show good comparisons
50%	In many key areas, improvement trends *and/or* good [favorable] performance levels with few adverse trends *and/or* poor [unfavorable] performance levels	In most key areas, performance levels *and/or* trends show good comparisons
60%	In many key areas, improvement trends *and/or* good [favorable] performance levels with no adverse trends *and/or* no poor [unfavorable] performance levels	In some key areas, performance levels *and/or* trends show very good comparisons
70%	In most key areas, good [favorable] performance levels *and/or* sustained trends with no adverse trends *and/or* no poor [unfavorable] performance levels	In key areas, many levels *and/or* trends show very good and leadership comparisons
80%	In most key areas, good to excellent performance levels *and/or* sustained trends with no adverse trends *and/or* no poor [unfavorable] performance levels	In key areas, most levels *and/or* trends show very good and leadership comparisons
90%	Sustained excellent performance levels *and/or* excellent improvement trends in some key areas	Industry and benchmark leader in some key areas
100%	Sustained excellent performance levels *and/or* excellent improvement trends in most key areas	Industry and benchmark leader in many key areas

partners (e.g., shareholders). Results for these measures should be reported for the whole organization and/or by sectors.

- Key Areas: All Key Areas except ROI have measures by sector.
- Levels: To be higher than 50%, there must be no poor Levels. The Area for Improvement comments identifies profit margins for NSS as below the 1997 goal and for CAS and DAS substantially below the 1997 goal, which I interpret as poor. Since "in many key areas . . . good performance levels," I score this dimension 50%.
- Trends: To be higher than 50% there must be no adverse Trends. Profit margins for DAS and NSS are flat or poor. However, since "in many key areas, [there are] improvement trends," I score this dimension 50%.
- Comparisons: The Comparisons of %TAM by sector are excellent, but there are no Comparisons for the other key measures. For the score to be higher than 70% requires comparisons for most Key Areas. The score is 70%.

We could write the scores as: LE = 50, TR = 50, CO = 70.

Step 2   We are interested in Levels, Trends, and Comparisons for Key Areas (areas of importance to the applicant). Recall that we pick whichever is better, Levels or Trends, because the Scoring Guidelines say Levels *and/or* Trends. Since both Levels and Trends are 50%, they yield 50% for these two scoring dimensions. Now, we need only combine 50% for Levels and/or Trends with 70% for Comparisons. The arithmetic mean is 60%.

Step 3   This item is worth 130 points. So, the point score is 60% of 130, or 78 points.

BENEFIT OF THE DOUBT   If you are "torn" between two scores, you may give the applicant the higher score. This is called "giving the benefit of the doubt." The reason for this is that if the applicant scores high enough, it may receive a site visit to resolve issues of clarity or missing information in the application. Without a high enough score, the applicant may not receive the site visit under some award processes, including the Baldrige (see also Chapter 12 on three-level awards). Thus, the chance to discover an organization that is actually better than what the application describes is lost.

Giving the benefit of the doubt can be done when converting comments to scores. If something is not clear, say so in an Area for Improvement comment. Depending on the evidence and overall application, that comment may not be weighted as heavily as others. Thus, the approach to scoring using a straight arithmetic mean of scores denies giving the benefit of the doubt. The Baldrige approach allows for this option by being less specific on how the scores are combined. So, the Baldrige approach gains this option at a loss of consistency because of greater subjectivity.

When combining scores, it is more important to find agreement on the scoring row of the Scoring Guidelines than it is to agree to the nearest 10%. Two reasons for this are: if the score is too low further distinction may not be valuable from a feedback perspective, and if the score is high a site visit will resolve any differences. This is discussed further in the chapters on consensus and site visits.

Table 7.6 Summary Score Sheet for Items Using the Scoring Dimensions

CRITERIA						
APPROACH-DEPLOYMENT						
Item	SY	DE	CI	Score	Pts	Total
1.1					80	
1.2					30	
2.1					40	
2.2					40	
3.1					40	
3.2					40	
4.1					25	
4.2					15	
4.3					40	
5.1					40	
5.2					30	
5.3					30	
6.1					60	
6.2					20	
6.3					20	
RESULTS						
Item	LE	TR	CO			
7.1					130	
7.2					130	
7.3					35	
7.4					25	
7.5					130	
TOTALS					1000	

SCORING DIMENSIONS

SY = Systematic   DE = Deployment   CI = Continuous Improvement
LE = Levels   TR = Trends   CO = Comparisons

Application Score

The last two steps in scoring are to produce a total point score for each Category and a single point score for the entire application. This is a simple task. Multiply each Item's percentage score by the number of points to get a point score. Then, total the points by Category and for all Items. Table 7.6 contains a worksheet for doing this.

Exercise 7.1: Application

Score the answer comments (use the answer to Exercise 6.2 in Appendix B) for the case study (make copies of the worksheet in Table 7.6) and calculate a total application point score. This should take no more than one to two hours. Compare your scores to those provided in Appendix B. Because you may combine your scores for scoring dimensions differently, you should consider our scores equivalent if they are within 10%. By now, you should understand why there is variation in scoring.

REFERENCES

Mark Blazey. *Insights to Excellence 1997: An Inside Look at the 1997 Baldrige Award Criteria.* Milwaukee: Quality Press, 1997.

Mark Graham Brown. *Baldrige Award Winning Quality: How to Interpret the Malcolm Baldrige Award Criteria* (Seventh Edition). New York: Quality Resources, 1997.

8

Reaching Consensus

OVERVIEW   Examiner teams must produce a single scorebook (consensus scorebook) from individual scorebooks. The better written the individual scorebooks are, the easier the tasks of reaching consensus (see Figure 8.1) will be: preparing for consensus, reaching consensus on comments, and reaching consensus on scores for those consensus comments. The success of this chapter in teaching you examiner consensus skills depends on the skills you gained from the previous chapters. With the added skills from this chapter, you can help reduce variation in the consensus process and its outcome.

You will learn more from this chapter if you work with others to form a team and do consensus. If that is not possible or feasible, you can still learn about consensus by doing the exercises described here.

OBJECTIVES   By completing the exercises in this chapter, the reader will be able to

- explain why consensus is needed;
- prepare for consensus, given comments from other examiners;
- participate in consensus to produce consensus comments and scores; and
- resolve conflicts arising during consensus.

PURPOSE OF CONSENSUS   Ideally, we would like all well-trained and educated examiners to produce the same set of comments from which they would agree on the scores for each Item. This was my objective in writing this workbook. In practice, this will not always happen. So, this is one reason for having training on consensus: to have skilled examiners in this area for when it does occur.

A second reason for having consensus is that some applicants may have site visits (see Chapter 9). Since no single examiner can do justice to a site visit, it makes sense to have several examiners with full knowledge of the applicant. These examiners can ensure they have common and complete knowledge through a short and effective consensus.

The purpose of consensus as part of the Feedback Process is to produce the most value-added, nonprescriptive feedback report possible. This is better accomplished when the individual examiner *scores* from the score books are discarded and never used again by examiners (except as data for process improvement).

PREPARING FOR CONSENSUS   At consensus, the examiners are in a different situation than when they individually produced a score book. Now, each examiner has the advantage

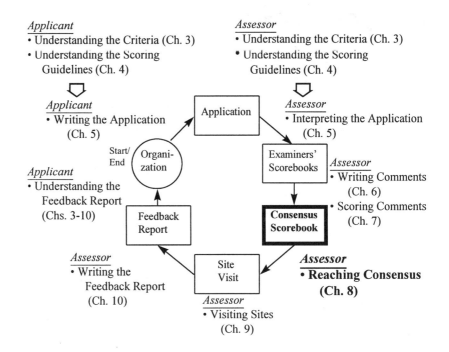

Figure 8.1 The Feedback Process: Reaching Consensus.

of knowing what others were able to extract from the application. So, the first step to consensus is to prepare for it by collating all examiners' comments by Item.

This can be done by assigning Categories and Items to individual examiners. Each examiner collates the comments of all examiners for their assigned Items. The results for collating are the same as for originally producing comments. So, the following Consensus Preparation Procedure can be used:

1. For each Area to Address, identify comments that are value added and nonprescriptive.
2. If there are comments in common but they are not exactly the same, prepare the "best" value-added, nonprescriptive comment possible.
3. If there are comments that only one examiner identified, include them in the collation if and only if such comments individually address the Item and only the Item and they are not prescriptive.
4. Identify Areas or subAreas to Address for which there are no comments.
5. Prepare the collated comments using the form in Table 6.1. You may have to add, delete, modify, or combine comments to do this. *Do not include scores.*
6. Distribute to all other examiners before consensus.

EXAMPLE   A team of four examiners (A, B, C, and D) individually comment and score the case study in Appendix C. Their comments to the case study response to Item 6.2 are shown in Table 8.1.

Critique   Note that Examiner A's comments are not value added since they are not complete sentences. Failure to write in complete sentences makes the task more difficult for other examiners during consensus and will not be accepted

Table 8.1 Example of Four Examiners' Comments to Item 6.2 Using the Case Study

Examiner A

<u>Purposes</u> support service design, management, and improvement

<u>Work Units\</u>~~Key Areas~~ all support functions' key processes (see Figure 0-2 in BOV); all sectors

6.2 Management of Support Processes *(20 pts)*

Score Dim.	Area to Address	STRENGTHS
SY	a(1)	Service departments determine process and principal requirements to establish priorities.
SY	a(2)	Teams flowchart, compare, document processes.
DE	a(3)	Key support processes identified in BOV.
Score Dim.	Area to Address	AREAS FOR IMPROVEMENT
CI	a(5)	CFI does not evaluate and improve its support processes.

Comment and Scoring Work Sheet   Percent Score ____

Examiner B

<u>Purposes</u> support service design, management, and improvement

<u>Work Units/</u>~~Key Areas~~ all support functions' key processes (see Figure 0-2 in BOV); all sectors

6.2 Management of Support Processes *(20 pts)*

Score Dim.	Area to Address	STRENGTHS
SY	a(2)	Key support processes have an assigned process team. Processes are flowcharted, compared to similar processes, and documented.
SY	a(4)	Support processes are managed using process control. This includes a measurement plan with identified parameters and sampling frequency.
Score Dim.	Area to Address	AREAS FOR IMPROVEMENT
SY	a(1)	There is no evidence that internal customers are involved or even consulted in the design of support processes.
DE	a(3)	Support processes and their principal requirements are not described.
CI	a(5)	Although some examples of improvements are given, it is not evident that there is a systematic approach to evaluate and improve support service processes.

Comment and Scoring Work Sheet   Percent Score ____

(Continued on next page)

Table 8.1 Continued

Examiner C

<u>Purposes</u> support service design, management, and improvement

<u>Work Units\Key Areas</u> all support functions' key processes (see Figure 0-2 in BOV); all sectors

6.2 Management of Support Processes *(20 pts)*

Score Dim.	Area to Address	STRENGTHS
SY	a(1)	Planning teams set priorities in the order of importance to the business sectors. Most sectors have regular meetings with their internal customers and suppliers to discuss mutual needs and services.
SY	a(2)	Planning teams set priorities then flow chart the processes, compare them to similar processes, and document them.
SY/ DE	a(3)	CFI identifies eight key support areas (Figure 0-2 and Item 7.5), each having defined processes for which they are responsible. Each process is measured and expected to attain a process capability of $C_p \geq 2$.
SY	a(4)	The eight key support areas have performance measures on cycle time, accuracy, and costs.
CI	a(5)	CFI uses various techniques to evaluate and improve its support processes.
Score Dim.	Areas	AREAS FOR IMPROVEMENT
SY	a(2)	It is unclear if there are members of all business sectors on the planning teams of the support sectors.
CI	a(5)	It is not clear in the application how the evaluation and improvement of support processes achieves better performance.

Comment and Scoring Work Sheet   Percent Score ____

(Continued on next page)

for feedback reports. Second, notice that even when examiners follow the writing procedures, they will not write the exact same sentences. But, to the extent the sentences follow the rules for being value added and nonprescriptive, they will be easier to collate (see Table 8.2).

Examiner A's comments also do not address the whole Item since there is no comment for Area to Address a(4). Examiner B's comments are better; they are complete sentences and address the Item in its entirety and nothing else. However, Examiner B appears not to want to have both Strengths and Areas for Improvement comments for the same subArea. Thus, no Strengths were listed for a(1), a(3), and a(5); no Areas for Improvement comments were listed for a(2) and a(4). Some examiners believe that having both Strengths and Areas for Improvement comments to the same subArea is, if not contradictory, confusing to the applicant. In the Comment and Scoring Worksheet used in this workbook we include a column to identify the scoring dimension(s). This additional information eliminates contradictions and confusions.

Examiner C's comments are more detailed than B's and allow for both Strength and Areas for Improvement comments to the same subArea. Examiner C, however, misplaced Areas for Improvement comment a(4), and Areas for Improvement comment a(2) goes beyond the requirements.

Table 8.1   Continued

Examiner D

<u>Purposes</u> support service design, management, and improvement
<u>Work Units</u>/~~Key Areas~~ all support functions' key processes (see Figure 0-2 in BOV); all sectors
6.2 Management of Support Process *(20 pts)*

Score Dim.	Area to Address	STRENGTHS
SY	a(1)	Each support service department determines its key process and principal requirements from information supplied by the strategic planning process. Process teams work with internal customers to set limits for each process step.
SY	a(2)	Using the strategic plan, planning teams set priorities for process teams who flowchart processes and structure them with specific limits for each step.
SY/ DE	a(3)	CFI's key support areas are identified in Figure 0-2. All processes must have C_p's $\geq$ 2 to maintain cycle time, accuracy, and costs requirements. For example, FDS requirements include accuracy, time to generate reports, containment of costs and revenues, and timely reports. Other examples are cited in Item 7.5.
SY	a(4)	Support processes are managed through process control applications in paper handling and administration.
CI	a(5)	Support processes are evaluated and improved through process analysis and research for new techniques and equipment, benchmarking in the goal-setting mode, alternative technology for personal computers and communications, and information from customers at regular meetings. This approach has significantly improved time to pay invoices and days to close the books.

Score Dim.	Area to Address	AREAS FOR IMPROVEMENT
SY	a(1)	There are no descriptions of how key requirements are determined or set.
SY	a(4)	The response does not describe *how* processes are managed.
CI	a(5)	The descriptions do not suggest a systematic approach to support service process evaluation and improvement through analysis and research, benchmarking, alternative technologies, and customer input to achieve better performance.

Comment and Scoring Work Sheet   Percent Score ____

The best comments come from Examiner D. These have even more detail than C's; for example, compare Strength comments to a(5). Examiner D also uses more applicant words in Strength comments and more Criteria words in Areas for Improvement comments. Still, there are obvious similarities among all four that come from a well-written application and good interpretation.

Exercise 8.1   1. Apply the Consensus Preparation Procedure to the set of comments in Table 8.3.

CONSENSUS   At the end of consensus, all comments should be value added and nonprescriptive (Chapter 6), and you should have a consensus score for each Item based on the consensus comments (Chapter 8). This can be accomplished using the following Consensus Standard Operating Procedure:

Table 8.2 Example Collation of Examiner A, B, C, and D's Comments in Table 8.1

6.2 Management of Support Processes *(20 pts)*

Score Dim.	Area to Address	STRENGTHS
SY	a(1)	Each support service department determines its key process and principal requirements from information supplied by the strategic planning process. Most sectors have regular meetings with their internal customers and suppliers to discuss mutual needs and services. Process teams work with internal customers to set limits for each process step.
SY	a(2)	Using the strategic plan, planning teams set priorities for process teams who flowchart processes and structure them with specific limits for each step.
DE/ SY	a(3)	CFI's key support areas are identified in Figure 0-2. All processes must have C_p's ≥ 2 to maintain cycle time, accuracy, and costs requirements. For example, FDS requirements include accuracy, time to generate reports, containment of costs and revenues, and timely reports. Other examples are cited in Item 7.5.
SY	a(4)	Support processes are managed through process control applications in paper handling and administration with performance measures on cycle time, accuracy, and costs.
CI	a(5)	Support processes are evaluated and improved through process analysis and research for new techniques and equipment, benchmarking in the goal-setting mode, alternative technology for personal computers and communications, and information from customers at regular meetings. This approach has significantly improved time to pay invoices and days to close the books.

Score Dim.	Area to Address	AREAS FOR IMPROVEMENT
SY	a(1)	There are no descriptions of how key requirements are determined or set.
SY	a(4)	The response does not describe *how* processes are managed.
CI	a(5)	The descriptions do not suggest a systematic approach to support service process evaluation and improvement through analysis and research, benchmarking, alternative technologies, and customer input to achieve better performance.

Comment and Scoring Work Sheet   Percent Score ____

For each Item

1. Review the collated comments.
2. Agree on the Strength and Area for Improvement comments.
3. Check that the comments address the Item in its entirety and nothing else.
4. Check that the comments are value added and nonprescriptive.
5. Individually score the Item according to the appropriate scoring dimensions but using the consensus comments.
6. Reach consensus on a single score for the Item.

When all the above are done, for the application

7. Convert the individual percentage scores to a single percentage score.
8. Calculate total point scores for each Category and for the whole application.

Table 8.3 Four Examiners' Comments to Item 7.4 for Exercise 8.1

Examiner A

<u>Purposes</u> summary of supplier and partner performance

~~Work Units~~/Key Areas supplier level; delivery, price, and quality (C_{pk}s and corrective action); Cost of Doing Business

7.4 Supplier and Partner Results *(25 pts)*

Score Dim.	Area to Address	STRENGTHS
LE	a	Of the top 155 suppliers by dollar volume, 148 were certified in 1994.
CO	a	G&A and materials delivery levels are excellent compared to bic.
TR	a	The trends for all measures shown are favorable.
Score Dim.	Area to Address	AREAS FOR IMPROVEMENT
KA	a	No results are shown for price, one of the three principal requirements for key suppliers.
CO	a	Only three measures had bics or '97 goals. No results met goals or bic.

Comment and Scoring Work Sheet　　　　　　　　　　　　　　Percent Score ____

Examiner B

<u>Purposes</u> summary of supplier and partner performance

~~Work Units~~/Key Areas supplier level; delivery, price, and quality (C_{pk}s and corrective action); Cost of Doing Business

7.4 Supplier and Partner Results *(25 pts)*

Score Dim.	Area to Address	STRENGTHS
LE	a	Ninety-five percent of suppliers that deliver 80% of supplies by dollar volume are certified. The number of suppliers has decreased.
LE/ TR	a	CFI has a number of measures with good to excellent levels and favorable trends for suppliers.
Score Dim.	Area to Address	AREAS FOR IMPROVEMENT
KA	a	In Item 6.3, CFI indicates that price is a key measure, but there is no measurement of the price of raw materials and/or services from suppliers.
CO	a	Comparison data against industry standards and/or benchmark organizations are not provided.

Comment and Scoring Work Sheet　　　　　　　　　　　　　　Percent Score ____

(Continued on next page)

Table 8.3 Continued

Examiner C

<u>Purposes</u> summary of supplier and partner performance

~~Work Units~~/Key Areas supplier level; delivery, price, and quality (C_{pk}s and corrective action); Cost of Doing Business

7.4 Supplier and Partner Results *(25 pts)*

Score Dim.	Area to Address	STRENGTHS
LE/ CO	a	Supplier performance data shown have excellent levels and positive trends. Both certified and noncertified Supplier Quality Results show dramatically improving performance trends and on-time deliveries are near bic.
LE	a	The number of certified suppliers, and the percent of business they represent, has increased since 1992 to 1996 in all four product sectors (Table 7.4-1).
Score Dim.	Area to Address	AREAS FOR IMPROVEMENT
KA	a	No performance results are given for Cost of Doing Business, a key measure of supplier performance (6.3).
CO	a	Supplier Receiving History and SCAR performance falls far short of best-in-class.
CO	a	With two exceptions, no comparison information is provided, making assessment difficult.

Comment and Scoring Work Sheet   Percent Score ____

Examiner D

<u>Purposes</u> summary of supplier and partner performance

~~Work Units~~/Key Areas supplier level; delivery, price, and quality (C_{pk}s and corrective action); Cost of Doing Business

7.4 Supplier and Partner Results *(25 pts)*

Score Dim.	Area to Address	STRENGTHS
TR	a	CFI results for suppliers shows good to excellent results in trend data over the past ten years.
Score Dim.	Area to Address	AREAS FOR IMPROVEMENT
KA	a	The principal requirement of price for supplier management identified in 6.3 is not reflected in the results.
CO	a	Of the six graphs showing key measurements of supplier performance, only two have comparable data to best-in-class and none have benchmarks. In both comparisons to bic, CFI lags behind its competitors and no explanation is given.

Comment and Scoring Work Sheet   Percent Score ____

If you have done the exercises in the previous chapters, the only additional education and training you need are for Step 6. There are two rules to follow when converting individual team members' scores on the consensus comments (not the individual score book scores) to a single score: (1) if the range (highest individual score minus lowest individual score for consensus comments) of scores is 30% or less, then the single score is the arithmetic mean; (2) if the range is more than 30%, continue discussion or use Option 1.

The purpose of further discussion in Option 2 is to reduce the range to 30% or less so the mean can be used. Progress can often be made by first focusing on the scoring dimension with the difference among the team members that is greater than 30% and then focusing on the relevant comments according to the Scoring Dimension references in the Comment and Scoring Worksheet. Usually, this leads to refining, modifying, adding, or deleting comments so that the scores are within 30%. When this happens, you are confirming that scores are derived from specific comments and not vice-versa.

Should it happen that, although there is complete agreement on the comments and the scoring dimensions to which they apply, the individual team members' scores are not within 30% after much discussion, you may choose just to calculate the arithmetic mean of all scores. This should readily be decided for Items with low point values.

CONFLICT RESOLUTION

If Option 2 reaches a stalemate because of conflicting views, the conflict needs to be resolved. There are five places at which conflicts can arise with this procedure. They are at Steps 1–4 and Step 6. These five steps require the team members to agree. That agreement is reached using consensus.

The first step to reduce or prevent conflict is to become aware of where it may occur and what form it may take. With this awareness, you can take the second step of preventing it or you have the means to reduce it.

Types of Conflicts

Conflict occurs in the following forms:

A. One or more members come with unprepared or poorly prepared comments.
B. Two or more members cannot agree on whether to write a comment to an Area to Address as a Strength or an Area for Improvement comment.
C. Two or more members cannot agree on whether the set of comments addresses the Item in its entirety and nothing else.
D. Two or more members cannot agree on whether one or more comments are value added and nonprescriptive.
E. Two or more members cannot score the Item any closer than 40%.

Exercise 8.2

1. For each type of conflict (A–E above), develop ways to resolve the conflict, assuming it is occurring during consensus. This is called corrective action.
2. For each type of conflict (A–E) above, develop ways to stop it from occurring. This is called preventive action.

Table 8.4 Conflict Resolution: Corrective and Preventive Actions

Issue	CORRECTIVE ACTION	PREVENTIVE ACTION
A		
B		
C		
D		
E		

Use the form in Table 8.4 to write your proposals. Then, compare with the suggested answers in Appendix A.

Prevention-Orientation

From Table 8.4, it should be apparent that preventing conflicts is far better than trying to resolve them once they occur. A critical first step for preventing conflicts is to discuss several possible issues before the first session starts:

- domination of conversation by one person
- unprepared team members
- unwillingness to consider other views
- leaving before all the work is done
- failure to respond to assignments
- specific issues such as those listed in Exercise 8.2

Raise these issues and have the team decide how they will be handled should they arise. By talking about them, you create awareness and a seriousness about the tasks. This may be sufficient to prevent them. By agreeing on how to handle them, you avoid wasting time and energy developing ideas on your own and wondering what to do about them. The agreement also prepares everyone for the actions taken and the consequences.

9

Visiting Sites

OVERVIEW   The purpose of the site visit is to collect information so that the examiners' interpretation of the application can be clarified and verified and to discover any additional and relevant information (see Figure 9.1). Variation in this collection procedure leads to variation in the feedback report. The purpose of this chapter is to help examiners on site visits reduce the effects of site visit variation by describing a procedure for preparing for site visits. Preparation is greatly facilitated when examiners are skilled in understanding the Criteria and Scoring Guidelines, interpreting an application, writing and scoring comments, and reaching consensus.

OBJECTIVES   By completing the exercises in this chapter, the reader will be able to

- explain the purposes of a site visit,
- prepare for visiting sites,
- conduct a site visit that achieves its purposes, and
- analyze and synthesize information collected during a site visit.

PURPOSE OF SITE VISITS   For some award processes, the judges decide whether an application receives a high enough score to warrant a site visit. For other processes, which applicants receive site visits may be automatic. In either case, the examiners assigned to the application must prepare for the site visit.

There are two customers of the feedback report: the judges, who make a decision on whether to recognize the applicant, and the applicant, who we hope uses it to progress along its quality journey. Because of these two customers, there are three purposes for a site visit:

1. To clarify: Any comments that state, "It is unclear," must have the Items they reference become clear during the site visit.
2. To confirm: Strength comments should be confirmed as strengths, and Area for Improvement comments should be confirmed as weaknesses.
3. To discover: The site visit should create opportunities to discover information not supplied by the applicant that answers an Area to Address. (See Chapter 1 for possible reasons for this to occur.)

PREPARING FOR A SITE VISIT   The team of examiners must prepare for a site visit. If you have value-added, nonprescriptive comments, the task of preparing site visit issues is greatly

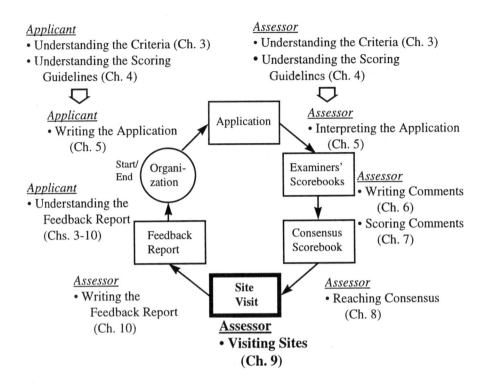

Figure 9.1   The Feedback Process: Visiting sites.

simplified. In addition, since the purposes of the site visit do not include collecting non-value-added information or changing comments so they are prescriptive, the site visit issues are primarily the Area for Improvement comments. These were the comments that prevented the examiner from giving the application a higher score. To these issues raised by the Area for Improvement comments, you need only add key Strength comments for confirmation and, if the application is for a multiple-level award (see Chapter 12), comments that address critical aspects of the relevant award level.

The simplest way to develop site visit issues to meet the purposes of the site visit is to use exactly the wording in the comments. If this wording is not good enough for you to understand what to ask during a site visit, it probably will not be good enough for the applicant to understand what to do with the comment in a feedback report. What may not be clear from both the comment and the application is whom to ask questions about the site visit issues. So, preparing for a site visit means

- having a list of issues by Item,
- knowing who you want to talk to about each issue,
- knowing what you want to ask, and
- knowing how you will record the information you collect.

The following Site Visit Preparation Procedure reduces variation in preparing for a site visit. It is based on the form illustrated in Table 9.1. Since a single sheet is used for each issue, you will have many such sheets. Each sheet will have the Item number, an issue (Step 1, 2, or 3), whom to ask (Step 4), and what to ask (Step 5).

Table 9.1 Site Visit Issues Worksheet

Site Visit Issues Worksheet

Examiner Initials_____ Applicant Number_____

Item No. _____ Issue:

Strategy (Person to Interview, Evidence)

Findings:

Effect of Findings on Score (indicate the scoring dimension before each effect-SY, DE, CI, KA, LE, TR, and CO): Total: ☐ raise ☐ lower ☐ no effect

___ ☐ raise ☐ lower ☐ no effect   ___ ☐ raise ☐ lower ☐ no effect

___ ☐ raise ☐ lower ☐ no effect   ___ ☐ raise ☐ lower ☐ no effect

Record only one issue per page

1. List all Area for Improvement comments as issues. Indicate, with the two-letter abbreviation, the associated scoring dimension(s): SY for Systematic, DE for Deployment, CI for Continuous Improvement, KA for Key Areas, LE for Levels, TR for Trends, and CO for Comparisons.
2. Identify key Strength comments as issues to confirm for the appropriate award level and/or to confirm in their own right. (See Chapter 12 for further information on how award levels may be defined.) Indicate the associated scoring dimension(s).
3. Identify critical and/or repeating themes by scoring dimension from all Area for Improvement comments from all Categories as issues. Indicate the associated scoring dimension(s). For example, if two or more Items appear to be lacking Continuous Improvement, this would be both a critical and a repeating theme.
4. For each issue, determine the person(s) to ask concerning the issue. You will need to use the organization chart or its equivalent (if not supplied, ask for one from the applicant) to identify specific people or job titles.
5. For each issue, list questions to ask. There are two types of questions you can use. The first consists of forming the comment into a question or questions. The second is asking for evidence. Evidence can consist of reports, minutes, corroboration from others, and the like.

TIPS

It makes it easier to trace your work if you also include the Area to Address reference in identifying your issues, such as A. [1.1a(1)] *comment*.

Assign questions to pairs of examiners if possible. While one examiner asks and interacts with the person being interviewed, the other examiner takes notes.

EXAMPLE

Prepare a Site Visit Issues Worksheet for Category 1 using the answer scorebook (see Exercise 6.2) for the case study in Appendix C.

Step 1: Areas For Improvement

For Item 1.1:

- *A. It is unclear the extent to which each senior executive is involved to [a(1)] set direction and seek opportunities; [a(3)] communicate and reinforce values, directions, expectations, customer focus, and continuous learning; and [a(4)] review overall performance, reinforce company direction, and improve the leadership system. (Deployment)*
- *B. [a(2)] There is no description of a system for how senior leaders seek future opportunities. (Systematic)*
- *C. [a(4)] There is no clear evidence of leadership system refinement and improved integration from cycles and analyses (e.g., number of improvement cycles the management by planning (MBP) process has gone through). (Continuous Improvement)*

For Item 1.2:

- *D. [a(1)] There are no measures and targets for legal and ethical requirements and for risks. (Systematic)*
- *E. [a(2)] There are no descriptions of systems for anticipating public concerns and for addressing these issues in a proactive manner. (Systematic)*

- *F. [b] It is unclear whether the company and employee support extends to major sites and all locations, especially in non-U.S. communities. (Deployment)*

Step 2: Strengths
Let us consider the scoring dimension Continuous Improvement as critical.

- *G. [1.1a(4)] The leadership system is improved through the continuous learning (e.g., an annual 360° review of all senior managers, system effectiveness assessments, and the use of several personality and behavior assessment tools) of its senior leaders (Continuous Improvement).*
- *None for Item 1.2.*

Step 3: Critical/Repeating

- *With only one Category and two Items, there are no repeating themes.*

Steps 4 and 5: Site Visit Issue Worksheets
For issues A and B, completed worksheets are shown in Table 9.2.

Exercise 9.1   Apply the Site Visit Preparation Procedure to Category 3, using the answer scorebook (Exercise 6.2) in Appendix B, for the case study in Appendix C. Write your answers on copies of the Site Visit Issues Worksheet in Table 9.1.

RECOMMEN-DATIONS

After you have made a site visit, you will integrate the information you collected and update the consensus score book. Whether you rescore de-

Table 9.2   Step 4 of Example for Site Visit Issues Worksheet: Item 1.1, Issues A and B

Site Visit Issues Worksheet Examiner Initials *KCM* Applicant Number *CS*

Item No. *1.1*   Issue:
A. [a(1),a(2),a(4)] Determine each senior leader's involvement in 1) setting direction; 2) seeking opportunities; 3) communicating and reinforcing values, directions, expectations, customer focus, and continuous learning; 4) reviewing overall performance; 5) reinforcing company direction; and 6) improving the leadership system. [SY]

Strategy (Person to Interview, Evidence)
A. Who to ask: Senior management — select 3 or 4 senior leaders
A. What to ask: Would you please define/describe CFI's leadership system? What is your involvement in the leadership system, i.e., what specific activities do you do (check parts 1-6 from Issue statement)? Do you have minutes or records showing your involvement and achievements?

Site Visit Issues Worksheet Examiner Initials *KCM* Applicant Number *CS*

Item No. *1.1*   Issue:
B. Determine how often the leadership system has been improved through continuous learning. [CI]

Strategy (Person to Interview, Evidence)
B. Who to ask: Senior management — select 3 or 4 senior leaders
B. What to ask: How do you continuously learn? How has the leadership system improved as a result of your learning? How has the leadership system improved as a result of the learning of the other senior leaders? How do you know the leadership system improved as a result of the learning?

pends on the policy for the award—the national Baldrige Award does not rescore. For self-assessments, it may be better to rescore based on the new information to maintain a consistent and complete document. If you do not rescore the comments, you can make recommendations about changes to scores for particular Items. These changes are noted at the bottom of the Site Visit Issues Worksheet. Your recommendation will be to not change, raise, or lower the Item's consensus score.

EXAMPLE   For the site visit worksheet prepared above for Item 1.1 using the case study, suppose the findings were the following:

Findings [from notes you took during the site visit]:   Sheila Anne A. Leadership system consists of processes for determining CFI's plans and deriving senior leaders' assignments. MBP with annual cycle sets stage. Senior leaders all involved in MBP. Once COs [corporate objectives] set, then senior leaders know what to continually communicate and reinforce. COs based on six values. Sheila Anne also involved in ensuring that HR plan is derived from strategic plan and that there are clear goals and objectives for employee satisfaction. Claims to spend about 1/4 to 1/3 time on specific leadership activities; remaining time on other job responsibilities, including community activities. Note: Each senior leader responsible for their sector or area (e.g., support function) being included in strategic plans. Note (for Category 2): Complete strategic plan [shown to us] includes resources assigned to COs but no specific targets for years other than current.

Findings: B. Sheila Anne's 360° reviews and employee feedback led to her changing her communication methods to more personal and small group sessions. Believes MBP's whole process has not changed since implemented but sees changes in other vice presidents' manners and attitudes, with some being more involved than others.

CRITIQUE   These findings come from interviewing Sheila Anne, Vice President of Human Resources and Organizational Learning. One examiner asked questions while the other took notes. When Sheila Anne mentioned the strategic plan, the examiner interviewing asked for a copy of it, which Sheila Anne showed the examiners. This led to Sheila Anne providing information beyond this Category. The interviewer pursued this momentarily to capture this information. A note was made to include it when reviewing Category 2.

The notes indicate that, in fact, all senior leaders are involved in the leadership system, primarily through their own sector/area responsibilities. Thus, this would indicate a change in the first Area for Improvement comment to Item 1.1. Since each leader's involvement varies, then a more appropriate comment might be: *The senior leadership system includes all senior leaders, with varying involvement for each.* This reflects a Deployment score in the 70% to 90% range, which is an increase. The corresponding Strength comment should be adjusted to reflect this, too.

After the site visit, the examiners realize they never addressed the second Area for Improvement comment to Item 1.1: *There is no description of a system*

Table 9.3 Documenting Effects of Findings from a Site Visit on Scoring Dimension Scores

Effect of Findings on Score (indicate the scoring dimension before each effect-SY, DE, CI, KA, LE, TR, and CO):   Total: ☐ raise   ☐ lower   ☑ no effect

SY	☐ raise	☐ lower	☑ no effect	DE	☑ raise	☐ lower	☐ no effect
CI	☐ raise	☑ lower	☐ no effect		☐ raise	☐ lower	☐ no effect

Record only one issue per page

for how senior leaders seek future opportunities. Failure to get answers for every issue can and will occur. Examiners and organizations have limited re-sources, in this case time. This comment should then be changed to: *It is unclear whether, and if so, how, senior leaders seek future opportunities.* The examiners agree that there is no change in the Systematic scoring dimension.

The last Area for Improvement comment to Item 1.1 can also be changed since the examiners discovered that there have been no improvements to the leadership system per se. A more appropriate comment might be: *The leadership has not undergone refinement and improved integration as a result of improvement cycles and analyses.* The corresponding Strength comment can be changed to reflect that individual leaders have improved, but the leadership system has not. These findings clarify that the score on Continuous Improvement is in the 10% to 30% range. This lowers the score.

From this analysis, we can determine the effects of our findings on our consensus score and record them at the bottom of the Site Visit Issues Worksheet as shown in Table 9.3.

10

Writing the Feedback Report

OVERVIEW

Once you have developed the final scorebook that includes updated consensus comments, consensus scores, and recommended changes to scores, you now have to produce the product the applicant gets: the feedback report (see Figure 10.1). National examiners take their final scorebook and eliminate all references to Areas to Address. Applicants value this information. So, in our version of the final scorebook—the Feedback Report—we retain them. The finishing touch on the feedback report is a summary. This summary includes a reference to the applicant's total score and may also include scores by Category or Item.

OBJECTIVES

By completing the exercises in this chapter, the reader will be able to

- explain the purposes of a feedback report,
- prepare the information needed for a feedback report, and
- write a complete feedback report.

INTRODUCTION

The feedback report consists of all the comments associated with each Item's Areas to Address so that the set of comments addresses the Item in its entirety and nothing else. In addition, the feedback report has a summary that highlights key strengths and weaknesses with respect to the Criteria in a way that identifies where along the Baldrige journey the applicant is.

WRITING THE FEEDBACK REPORT

You have almost completely written the feedback report if you have done everything according to the recommendations in the previous chapters. In fact, the easiest and shortest way to write a feedback report is to have value-added, nonprescriptive comments

- that address the Items in their entirety, and nothing else
- developed in your individual scorebook,
- prepared for consensus,
- agreed on during consensus, and
- for clarified, confirmed, and discovered information from the site visit.

There are two additions that convert a scorebook into a feedback report: (1) add an executive summary and (2) identify, using a scoring range, how far along the Baldrige journey the applicant is. Depending on the feedback process for the award for which you are an examiner, it is also possible that scores for individual Items and subtotals by Categories are eliminated.

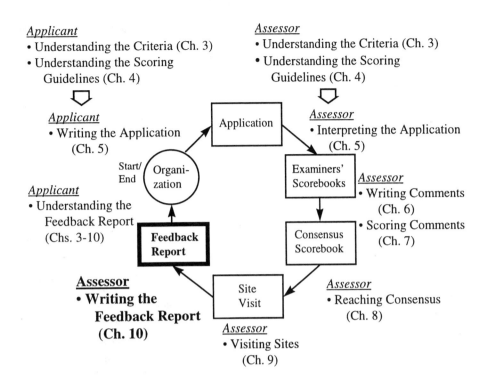

Figure 10.1 The Feedback Process: Writing the feedback report.

Table 10.1 contains eight scoring range bands. (The title of this table says it is for Award Level III in anticipation of Chapter 12, in which a three-level award is defined. Ignore this information for now.) When you have a total point score for an applicant, determine which scoring band it is in. Use the information describing that band to check your final comments and executive summary.

At the Baldrige and other state award levels, the feedback report does not contain references to the Areas to Address. Because the purpose of the feedback report is to provide information, deleting this information devalues the feedback report. The customer wants the references to the Areas to Address, so the feedback report in this workbook requires that you retain references to the Areas to Address. In the feedback report, we also retain references to the scoring dimensions.

The executive summary is a single page that summarizes the critical comments. Therefore, the executive summary should

- identify a scoring range for the entire application (see Table 10.1),
- summarize at the Category level consistent with the scoring range assigned, and
- use words from the Criteria (at the appropriate award level), the scoring range description and the scoring guidelines to highlight Strengths and highlight Areas for Improvement.

EXAMPLE   For Category 1 (see the critique in Chapter 9 of the example of Site Visit Findings), the first step is to look at the comments after the site visit. Use the suggestions from the critique in Chapter 9.

Table 10.1   Scoring Range Information for Award Level III

Range	No.	Comments
0-250	1	Early stages of developing and implementing approaches to Category requirements. Important gaps exist in most Categories.
251-350	2	Beginning of a systematic approach to the primary purposes of the Items, but major gaps exist in approach and deployment in some Categories. Early stages of obtaining results stemming from approaches.
351-450	3	A systematic approach to the primary purposes of most Items, but deployment in some key Areas to Address is still too early to demonstrate results. Early improvement trends in some areas of importance to key requirements.
451-550	4	Effective approaches to many Areas to Address, but deployment in some Areas is still at early stages. Further deployment, measures, and results are needed to demonstrate integration, continuity, and maturity.
551-650	5	A sound, systematic approach responsive to many Areas to Address with fact-based improvement process in place in key Areas. No major gaps in deployment. Improvement trends and/or good performance reported for most areas of importance.
651-750	6	Refined approaches, including key measures, good deployment, and good results in most Areas. Some outstanding activities and results clearly demonstrated. Good evidence of continuity and maturity in many Areas. Basis for further deployment and integration is in place. May be "industry" leaders or benchmark leaders in some Areas.
751-875	7	Refined approaches, excellent deployment, and good to excellent improvement and levels demonstrated in most Areas. Good to excellent integration. "Industry" leadership and some benchmark leadership.
876-1000	8	Outstanding approaches, full deployment, excellent and sustained results. Excellent integration and maturity. National and world leadership.

"Industry" refers to other organizations performing substantially the same functions thereby facilitating direct comparisons.

Executive Summary

Consolidated Fasteners, Incorporated (CFI), scored in Band 5 as a result of a Consensus review and site visit. See Table 10.1 for an explanation of the scoring bands.

There is evidence of sound, systematic approaches that are well deployed and responsive to many Areas to Address. The leadership system, while in the early stages of refinement, does involve all leaders, who are individually improving.

CFI's approach to its public responsibilities and citizenship do not appear well deployed to non-U.S. communities. In addition, there is little evidence of a proactive systematic approach that addresses public concerns.

Critique

The Band 5 assignment is determined in this example by calculating that 63 points is 57% of 110. The 57% was used to select the band range as if it had been on a 1000-point scale. The actual total score may not be given by an external award. However, for self-assessments, this information is readily conveyed, along with Item and Category scores.

Exercise 10.1

Write an executive summary for the case study using the comments in the answer scorebook in Appendix B containing the Comment and Scoring Worksheet to Exercise 6.2. You will not have the benefit of a site visit as in the example.

IV

THE ORGANIZATION'S TASK

11

Writing the Application/Documentation

UNDERSTANDING THE CRITERIA, SCORING GUIDELINES, AND APPLICATION

There are two kinds of organizations that need to develop applications or equivalent documentation: those organizations applying for an award and those organizations doing a self-assessment. The former will be governed by the award rules for applicants. The latter are free to develop their own guidelines. The value of using a format consistent with an application is twofold: (1) the documentation can readily be converted to an application, which may be beneficial to an organization because most states have Baldrige-based awards; and (2) the self-assessment report based on the documentation can follow the guidelines recommended in this workbook, thereby providing the same benefits.

Figure 11.1 shows how writing the application fits into the Feedback Process. This figure should clarify to organizations writing an application or documenting their systems why understanding the examiner's tasks in the Feedback Process will help them maximize the value of the feedback report by making the feedback report easier to understand (Chapters 3–10).

Applications

When an organization applies for a quality award based on the Baldrige Criteria, the writers of the application must

- understand the Criteria,
- understand the Scoring Guidelines,
- understand the application process, and
- understand their own organization.

Writers can accomplish the first two by using this workbook, especially reading the chapters in Part II. They can develop further understanding by doing all the exercises in Part III so they prepare an application that is more amenable to an examiner's perspective. Understanding how an examiner views an application helps significantly in writing a clear, concise, and complete application. But, more importantly, it will help you better understand what to look for in your own organization and how to use the feedback report from the examiners for continuous improvement.

The application process is usually described in the award's application. After understanding the process, plan to have at least one writer attend any awareness and how-to-apply workshops given by the award. The more people that understand the Criteria, especially the linkages among the Items and Areas to Address, the easier it will be to integrate all information collected.

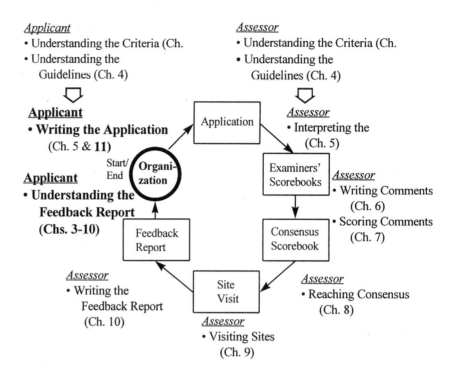

Figure 11.1 The Feedback Process: Writing the application based on the feedback report.

The most difficult part could very well come from trying to understand your own organization. By having one or more employees of the organization be examiners or use this workbook before collecting the information, you will be in a better position to understand your organization with respect to the Criteria. Plan ahead to make sure you meet all award deadlines with sufficient time to review and emend earlier drafts of the application.

Another source aimed more at applicants than this workbook is Mark Graham Brown's *Baldrige Award Winning Quality* (New York: Quality Resources, 7th Edition, 1997). The seventh edition addresses the *1997 Criteria*.

Self-Assessment

The same advice is applicable to organizations wishing to do a self-assessment. The organization's internal assessors must have knowledge of the Criteria, Scoring Guidelines, and their own organization. This book can be a valuable tool to gain that knowledge, to decide what Criteria to use, to write a description of the organization (or collect and organize that data on the organization), and to write the feedback report. We strongly recommend that any self-assessment be made from a written description of the organization and not from conversations or interviews. There is no reliable and valid way of retracing and recollecting the data on which such a self-assessment is based when the description of the organization comes from oral reports. Writing the description (''application'') has several advantages:

- It is documentation of the data on which the assessment is made.
- It can be verified.

- It can be emended or corrected.
- It is the basis for improvements when combined with the assessment.

PREPARATION

Teamwork

No one person can plan, collect the data, prepare the information, and write the application unless it is done full time and the organization is quite small. Organizations typically assign teams to do the work.

Different people recommend different ways to prepare for writing the application. Some emphatically do not want teams assigned to different Categories. The reason is that these Categories—more accurately, the Items and Areas to Address—are linked. Separating the Categories could (and apparently does) result in missing the connections. This makes it difficult for the examiners to understand the organization because the application will not read as an integrated description of a single organization. This is true even when the examiners are from the same organization and perform a self-assessment.

However, if the cause of the linkages not being evident is that the writers do not understand the Criteria, then the recommendation of not using Category-assigned teams does not get at the root cause. Assuming that you have a superior understanding of the Criteria and the Scoring Guidelines because you have read the previous chapters, assigning teams to Categories need not be a mistake and can be advantageous. Several Baldrige winners have used teams assigned to Categories.

In any case, regardless of how the information is collected, you will need to check on the linkages. The overall links are as follows:

- results asked for in Categories 1 and 3–6 are included in responses to Category 7,
- Category 2 should list all key performance areas, especially Area to Address 2.2a, and
- Category 4 should contain all measures and/or indicators, especially Areas to Address 4.1a(1) and 4.3a.

Approach-Deployment Areas to Address for Strategic Planning, Human Resources, Process Management, and Customer Focus and Satisfaction ask for results. The specific measures and/or indicators should be stated in the responses to these Approach-Deployment Areas to Address. Table 5.4 identifies the Results Item where these results should appear. Results should include current and past levels and competitive comparisons or benchmarks. Table 4.3 defines ''areas'' or ''work units'' for determining extent of Deployment for all Approach-Deployment Items. Exercises 3.5 and 3.6 also identify other linkages implied by the terms, notes, and integration of core values.

Business Overview

The Business Overview sets the stage for the examiner. Use the Criteria description and instructions to develop the Business Overview. Then, use Table 5.3 to ensure that the connections are there.

WRITING

Notation

For the feedback report to have the most value to you, every comment, whether a Strength or an Area For Improvement, will have the specific (sub)Area to Address to which it refers (see Table 6.2). This is sufficient reason for you to identify in your application the specific (sub)Areas to Address. There is another reason why you should do this. It ensures that you have a complete and comprehensive application. If any Area to Address is missing, it means you either do not have a response or you have not collected the information to respond. If the latter, it is easier to discover this when you use (sub)Areas to Address.

The specific suggestions below are based on the distinction between Approach-Deployment Items, which require descriptions, and Results Items, which require summaries. The phrases after Description or Summary refer to scoring dimensions for these two classes of Items (see Chapter 3 for more detailed explanations).

Descriptions: Systematic

Remember that Approach-Deployment Items ask for descriptions of systems and processes. To the extent you can list the steps or phases, you are more likely to have a system or process. **Do not just cite an example** of what you did. It gives the appearance that you only did it once, it was probably reactive, and therefore it was not systematic.

If possible, include diagrams of systems and process (e.g., flow charts).

Do not just say you do "it," with "it" repeating the Criteria. For example, 4.2a(3) asks for a description of "how comparative information and data are used to set stretch targets and/or to encourage performance breakthroughs." A poor response would be: *We set stretch targets using competitive and benchmarking comparisons for many processes.* A good response would list the procedure's steps for setting stretch targets, identify the competitors, and list the processes.

Descriptions: Deployment

Whether or not you include definitions of deployment for all Categories in the Business Overview, you should state the extent of deployment in your responses to Items. The Items that need definitions of what constitute deployment are listed in Table 4.3. Use this table to specifically identify the deployment units so that in your response you can state which work units use the approaches and which do not.

Descriptions: Continuous Improvement

Most Approach-Deployment Items have one Area to Address (see Table 12.1 for a complete listing) that focuses on the continuous improvement scoring dimension (see Chapter 3). Describe the process you use to continuously improve the specific processes asked for in these Areas to Address. Do not just cite an example or say that you continuously improve. Responses to these Areas to Address require descriptions just as Approaches do. They also require evidence of cycles of refinement. Here is where you can give examples.

Summaries: Key Areas

Results Items have four features: Key Areas, Levels, Trends, and Comparisons. In the Business Overview (especially Parts 2 and 4) and Items 2.2, 4.1 and 4.3, you should have defined the Key Areas. There should be five, unless you can provide reasons for excluding them: customer related, operational (including product and service quality), human resource related, financial, and supplier related. You should only provide results for key measurement areas.

Summaries: Levels

In Items 2.2, 3.1–4.3, 5.3, and 6.1–6.3, you will list measures and/or indicators for the Key Areas you identified above. The results for these measures and/or indicators will go in your responses to Category 7. "Measures and indicators refer to numerical information that quantify (measure) input, output, performance dimensions of processes, products, and services. Measures and indicators might be simple (derived from one measurement) or composite" (*1997 Criteria*, page 4). You must report the current level of all critical measures and indicators or show a sample and summarize the remaining ones. Graphs and tables are convenient ways to do this.

Summaries: Trends

You should clearly state when your cycle is something other than a year and explain why. For trends, examiners are looking for a minimum of three cycles worth of data to show (1) that there is improvement and/or (2) good

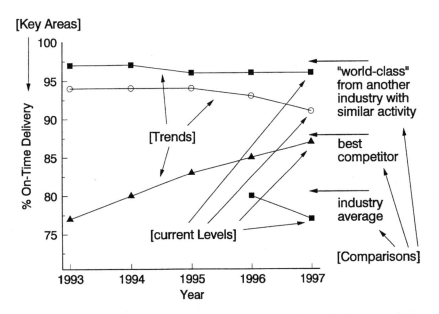

Figure 11.2 An example of a complete graph of results for an application showing Key Area, current Levels, Trends, and Comparisons.

performance is sustained. You should explain, as best you can, erratic performance.

Summaries: Comparisons

There are two kinds of comparisons: competitive and benchmarks. "Benchmarking refers to processes and results that represent best practices and performance for similar activities, inside or outside the company's industry. Competitive comparisons refer to performance relative to direct competitors [who you listed in the Business Overview] in the company's markets" (*1997 Criteria*, page 10, Note to Item 4.2). This distinction between competitive comparisons and benchmarks is critical and one that is being lost by the general use of the word benchmark.

One reason for this distinction is that a benchmark's role is to drive breakthrough performance. Recall that one aspect of evaluating Approach is "evidence of innovation. This includes significant and effective adaptation of approaches used in other types of applications or businesses" (*1997 Criteria*, page 24). This is evaluated indirectly through the company's results relative to benchmarks.

All four Results dimensions can easily be included in a graph as shown in Figure 11.2.

V

INFORMATION FOR AWARD COMMITTEES AND SELF-ASSESSING ORGANIZATIONS

12

Three-Level Quality Awards

INTRODUCTION

Some state awards distinguish themselves from the national Baldrige Award in that their purpose is not primarily to recognize the "best" quality organizations, but to help organizations become better by adopting a total quality management framework. To do this, several states now have more than one award level. Tennessee, for example, has four award levels, while Texas, Connecticut, and others have three. The use of multiple levels for state awards is a way of encouraging organizations to continue in their quality journey, especially when they are unfamiliar with the Criteria or are not as far along as the top quality-oriented organizations.

Having more than one award level is consistent with the major premise of this workbook: the feedback report is to be valuable and nonprescriptive. If the feedback report is to maximize its value to applicants, it should give different information to an organization at the beginning of its quality journey than it gives to one much further along. Organizations need to learn how to stand up first and then to walk before they can run. Information on running refinements given to someone who does not know how to walk is not as valuable as it is to a runner. This chapter includes an approach to maximize the value of the feedback report through a three-level award (see Figure 12.1).

THREE AWARD LEVELS

Since organizations at different stages along the quality journey need different information, the feedback report must be tailored to these stages. These stages can be the basis for different award levels. One way to define different levels is by using the three levels of the Criteria: Categories, Items, and Areas to Address. This is an intuitive way to define award levels—some states do it this way. At first blush, it appears logical. Not the least significant reason is that the Criteria have been difficult to understand initially in their entirety.

However, there are more compelling reasons for choosing another way to define the award levels. Both the Criteria and the Scoring Guidelines provide the basis for this other way. First, notice that scoring is done at the Item level, which asks for descriptions and summaries. The Categories only state what is examined. Scoring at the Category level without substantially more work on the scoring guidelines will create greater variation because of greater subjectivity in all aspects: applications, comments, scoring, consensus, feedback reports, and value to the applicant. Because Items are scored, we can see that three areas are automatically defined: Approach, Deployment, and Results. We recommend defining three award levels using the Approach, Deployment, and Results distinction.

The second reason for these award levels is that these three areas—Approach, Deployment, and Results—describe exactly the order in which one

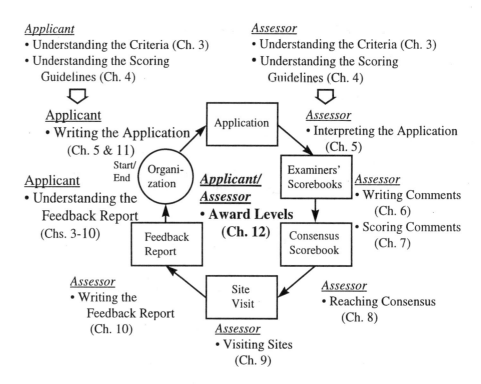

Figure 12.1 The Feedback Process: Three-level Awards.

progresses: first develop an approach (system or process), then deploy the approach to where it is intended to apply, and finally collect results on the approach's effectiveness.

The third reason is that getting results is not enough—many organizations have results but are not strong quality organizations, let alone Baldrige "winners." To emphasize a core value of the Baldrige framework, Continuous Improvement and Learning,[1] it is imperative that we make this sequence of Approach → Deployment → Results a cycle (Figure 3.2, page 19). Baldrige winners have continuous improvement cycles in their processes.

The scoring dimensions of Approach-Deployment and Results further refine this continuous improvement cycle, which in turn define three award levels. To collect data one needs to know what to measure; for continuous improvement, one needs to use the results to show improvement. So, three award levels can be defined with respect to the seven scoring dimensions that are the basis of Approach-Deployment-Results (Table 12.1).

Level I

Figure 12.2 depicts Award Level I, Systematic (Approach-Deployment) and Key Areas (Results). In Chapter 4, we learned that the scoring dimension

---

[1]The Baldrige Criteria have 11 core values and concepts (see Chapter 3). One is continuous improvement and learning. "Achieving the highest levels of performance requires a well-executed approach to continuous improvement. The term 'continuous improvement' refers to both incremental and 'breakthrough' improvement. The term 'learning' refers to adaptation to change, leading to new goals and/or approaches. Improvement and learning need to be 'embedded' in the way the company operates. Embedded means improvement and learning: (1) are a regular part of daily work; (2) seek to eliminate problems at their source; and (3) are driven by opportunities to do better, as well as by problems that must be corrected" (1997 Criteria, p. 39). "Action-oriented learning takes place via feedback between processes and results via learning cycles [with] four, clearly defined stages: planning [Approach], execution [Deployment], assessment [Results], and revision [new Approach and/or goal]" (1997 Criteria, p. 43).

Table 12.1 Using the Approach-Deployment-Results Characteristics to Define the Three Award Levels

AWARD LEVEL:	LEVEL I	LEVEL II	LEVEL III
AREAS TO ADDRESS *EXCLUDED*	1.1a(4), 1.2a(2), 1.2b, 2.1b, 2.2b(1), 3.1a(3), 3.2a(1), 4.1a(4), 4.2a(4), 4.3b, 5.1b 5.2a(5), 5.3c(2), 6.1b(3), 6.2a(5), 6.3a(3)	1.1a(4), 1.2a(2), 1.2b, 2.1b, 2.2b(1), 3.1a(3), 3.2a(1), 4.1a(4), 4.2a(4), 4.3b, 5.1b 5.2a(5), 5.3c(2), 6.1b(3), 6.2a(5), 6.3a(3)	NONE
APPROACH/ DEPLOYMENT DIMENSIONS *EXAMINED*	• Systematic	• Systematic • Deployment (defined by the Business Overview)	• Systematic • Deployment • Continuous Improvement
RESULTS DIMENSIONS *EXAMINED*	• Areas	• Areas • Levels	• Areas • Levels • Trends • Comparisons

NOTE: The excluded Areas To Address apply to both the applicant in preparing the application and the examiners in preparing the scorebooks and feedback reports. These Areas To Address focus on continuous improvement, which is required by these definitions only by the award level III applications. See Tables 4.1-4.2 for an explanation of the Approach-Deployment-Results dimensions.

Systematic included both methods and measures. So, at Level I, the applicant must have systematic approaches, not just a "beginning of a systematic approach" (Tables 4.1 and 4.2). To encourage the development of a continuous improvement orientation, the applicant must also identify its key measures. This is automatic when the applicant successfully provides a Business Overview and responds to Items 2.2, 3.2, 4.1, 4.3, 5.3, and 6.1–6.3 of the 1997 Criteria. These Items request measures in the three performance areas of customer satisfaction and dissatisfaction, financial and marketplace success, and operations, including supplier/partner and human resource relations.

Award Level I

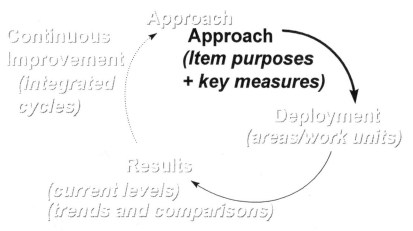

Figure 12.2 Defining Award Level I as companywide Approaches meeting the purposes of the Item with Key Areas for measurement identified.

The idea behind recognition at Level I is to promote a total quality management effort. Sometimes state and other awards recognize organizations that excel in one Category. This is valuable encouragement but can send misleading messages: It suggests both that the Categories are not linked and that organizational quality is not total. This definition of Award Level I requires an organization to have approaches in all six Approach-Deployment Categories (Categories 1–6 in the 1997 Criteria).

The requirement of Key Areas, a Results scoring dimension, sends the message to the applicant that approaches without any intention of measuring their effectiveness are not systematic or quality oriented. Quality means measurement. The requirement of identifying an organization's key measures forces the organization to plan for continuous improvement to close the Approach → Deployment → Results sequence into a cycle (as in Figure 3.2).

Level II   Figure 12.3 depicts Award Level II, which is Level I plus Deployment (Approach-Deployment) and Levels (Results). To move to Level II, the applicant must show that the systematic approaches (methods and measures) developed and described in Level I are deployed to the relevant and critical areas. In addition, the applicant must show current results for its key measures. There is no requirement at Level II that the results reflect good performance, although this can be a decision made by the award committee or judges.

The idea is to promote the expansion of the approaches to principal areas of the organization. This sends the message that organizations that focus too narrowly or fail to apply their quality efforts to areas important to the organization are not considering the total picture and understanding the linkages. The requirement of Results' Levels prepares the organization for

Award Level II

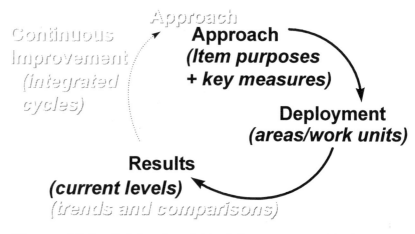

Figure 12.3 Defining Award Level II as companywide Approaches meeting the purposes of the Item, with sufficient Deployment in appropriate areas or work units with current Levels for Key Areas.

the next award level and strengthens the continuous improvement and learning cycle value.

Level III (Full Baldrige)

Figure 12.4 depicts Level III (full Baldrige), which is **Level II Plus Continuous Improvement (Approach-Deployment), Trends (Results), and Comparisons (Results)**. At Level III, the applicant must show that results lead to improvement by showing that the key approaches have "embedded" a continuous improvement process that includes planning, execution, assessment, and revision. The execution and evaluation will show improvement when the results for two or more cycles (trends) show absolute or relative improvement (comparisons of levels).

Together, these three award levels have the following advantages over the Category-Item-Areas to Address way of defining award levels:

- Feedback reporting is consistent across all levels because it always comments to Areas to Address. Thus, it adds value at the most detailed level of the Criteria and supports the applicant's understanding of the Criteria (Categories, Items, and Areas to Address; Approach-Deployment and Results) and Scoring Guidelines (seven scoring dimensions).
- Examiner training (see Chapter 13) is consistent because the same Criteria framework and Scoring Guidelines are used.
- Applicants do not need to learn different Criteria and Scoring Guidelines or apply in different ways depending on the award level.
- This three-level award emphasizes the "total" in total quality management. By defining award levels by Category, Items, and Areas to Address, "winners" at the Category level may be good in only two or three Catego-

Award Level III

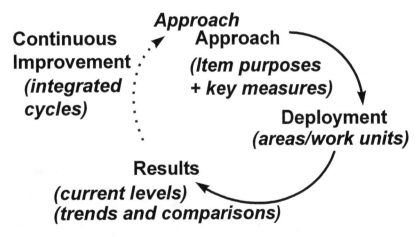

Figure 12.4 Defining Award Level III as companywide Approaches meeting the purposes of the Item, with sufficient Deployment in appropriate areas or work units with current Levels and Trends for Key Areas showing favorable Comparisons.

ries. Such winners model a contrary impression to other organizations: you only need to be good in parts of your organization, not all of it.

COMMENTING AND SCORING THE THREE-LEVEL AWARD

Commenting and scoring for the three-level award can be changed to overcome a weakness in a single-level award. Because there are three dimensions to Approach-Deployment Items and four-dimensions to Results Items, single scores for Items are ambiguous. Consider a score of 50% on an Approach-Deployment Item with a continuous improvement Area to Address (e.g., Item 1.1). There are numerous ways of getting to a total Item score of 50%. Six ways are based on an equal weighting of Systematic, Deployment, and Continuous Improvement, with each dimension getting a score of 0%, 50%, or 100%, without duplication of scores. The seventh way is when all three dimensions receive a score of 50%. (Two cases cannot occur: a 0% on Systematic and either 50% for Deployment and 100% for Continuous Improvement or vice-versa. Without an approach, it cannot be deployed or have been improved.) Other ways of getting 50% are by having unequal weightings of these three dimensions.

The Criteria do not have guidelines for deciding how to weight these dimensions, and these dimensions are typically not so clearly identified in examiner training as they are in this workbook. Thus, examiners do a mental weighing of these components, which means sometimes they include all three and sometimes not, sometimes they do it equally and, sometimes not. As a consequence, variation in scoring increases in part because the comments do not reflect all three dimensions.

This weakness is reduced with a three-level award, with Level III the full Baldrige Criteria and Scoring Guidelines. Making the award levels cumulative reduces the applicable scoring dimensions for Levels I and II and makes scoring easier and less variable. So, at Award Level I, only Systematic and Key Areas scoring dimensions are considered. At Award Level II, Deployment and current Levels are added. At Award Level III, Continuous Improvement, Trends, and Comparisons are added. At the first two award levels, scoring does not require combining any dimensions because the dimensions apply to different types of Items.

Another advantage results from applying the lowest scoring dimension to score the Item. For example, the comments in Table 7.2; if the lowest scoring dimension determines the score, this application for Award Level III would receive a percentage score of 0% because it received 0% on Continuous Improvement. If it were an application for Award Level II, it would receive a 10% because we would exclude the Continuous Improvement scoring dimension and Systematic would be the lower scoring dimension. This would also be the score if it were an application for Award Level I because the score of 20% on Deployment would be excluded.

This method of scoring creates three scales, one for each award level, that range from 0 to 1000 points. Thus, a score of 300 at Level III is not the same as a score of 300 at Level I. To keep the 0-to-1000 range for all three Award Levels, Level I scores must be adjusted. Since Level I excludes Results, which have 450 points (Category 7), there are only 550 points possible. By multiplying the total application score by 1000/550, the Level I scores are normalized to a 0-to-1000 range.

An analogy may help explain this. Consider the grade a student receives. A sixth grader, tenth grader, and college senior all can receive a grade on the same scale. Yet, getting an ''A'' for sixth-grade math does not mean the student has the same mathematical ability and understanding as the student getting an ''A'' for precalculus, which is not the same as receiving an ''A'' for advanced calculus.

This way of scoring also increases the value of comments if they match the award level. At Award Level I, comments will focus exclusively on the Systematic and Key Area dimensions. At Award Level II, Area for Improvement comments will focus primarily on the Deployment and Levels dimensions, while Strength comments should support the Systematic and Key Area dimensions. At Award Level III, Area for Improvement comments will focus primarily on the Continuous Improvement, Trends, and Comparison dimensions, while Strength comments will support the organization's progress on Systematic, Deployment, Key Areas, and Levels dimensions.

This does not mean that there will be no comments on Systematic and Deployment dimensions at Level III. Rather, it means that an examination of the Continuous Improvement scoring dimensions should quickly reveal whether Level III is the appropriate award level for the applicant.

To ensure that this occurs, applications are reassigned to lower award levels based on their scores. Thus, an applicant for Award Level III that does not score high enough on the Continuous Improvement dimension of Approach-Deployment and/or the Trends and Comparison dimensions of Results can be ''reassigned'' as an Award Level II applicant by the examination process. If the applicant does not score high enough on the Deployment dimension of Approach-Deployment and/or the Levels dimension of Results, the applican can be reassigned as an Award Level I applicant by the examination process. Fortunately, this does not mean rescoring an entire application. It only means recalculating each Item score by combining the scores already given for the fewer applicable scoring dimensions.

This gives applicants an opportunity to receive recognition at the appropriate level in a less ambiguous way. It also alters the product of the examination process, the Feedback Report, so that it better ''fits'' the applicant's stage in its quality journey.

It might be asked, Could an applicant's score be high enough so that its application is reassigned to a higher award level? In theory, the answer is yes, but in the next section we explain why this may not occur in practice.

A multilevel award provides examiners a tool to identify at which stage along the quality journey the applicant is so that the site visit and feedback report can be better suited to the applicant. If, as we have presented the purpose of this workbook, we want to provide value-added feedback, then the primary goal is meaningful comments with valid scores, not subjective scores or unique consensus scores based on highly variable individual scores.

EXAMPLE   Consider the site visit findings for Category 1 in the example of Chapter 9. There was no net effect for Award Level III. According to the information the team members collected, there was no effect on Systematic, an increasing effect on Deployment, and a decreasing effect on Continuous Improvement. The increasing and decreasing canceled each other.

However, this is not true if the application is considered for Award Level II. For Award Level II, the Continuous Improvement dimension is eliminated. Since the Deployment dimension score is increased as a result of the site visit, the total score for the Item is also increased when combining no effect on Systematic with an increase on Deployment. This site visit would support the premise that the organization is at the Level II phase in its journey but not yet at the Level III phase. The three award levels help the applicant (and the examiner) appreciate the distinction among the scoring dimensions.

To clarify further these issues in the feedback report, the Connecticut Award for Excellence strives for giving all applicants, regardless of award

Table 12.2 Three-Level Award Summary Scoresheet for Items Using the Scoring Dimensions

CRITERIA				AWARD LEVELS								
APPROACH-DEPLOYMENT				LEVEL I			LEVEL II			LEVEL III		
Item	SY	DE	CI	Score	Pts	Total	Score	Pts	Total	Score	Pts	Total
1.1					80			80			80	
1.2					30			30			30	
2.1					40			40			40	
2.2					40			40			40	
3.1					40			40			40	
3.2					40			40			40	
4.1					25			25			25	
4.2					15			15			15	
4.3					40			40			40	
5.1					40			40			40	
5.2					30			30			30	
5.3					30			30			30	
6.1					60			60			60	
6.2					20			20			20	
6.3					20			20			20	
RESULTS												
Item	LE	TR	CO									
7.1				NA	130			130			130	
7.2				NA	130			130			130	
7.3				NA	35			35			35	
7.4				NA	25			25			25	
7.5				NA	130			130			130	
TOTALS					550			1000			1000	

SCORING DIMENSIONS

SY = Systematic   DE = Deployment   CI = Continuous Improvement
LE = Levels   TR = Trends   CO = Comparisons

level, a site visit. The advantages should be clear. By clarifying issues according to the scoring dimensions, the applicant receives not only a feedback report that is based on more information, but the feedback information is more definitive on issues related to the scoring dimensions. This makes it clearer for the applicant how to continue along the Approach-Deployment-Results-New Approach cycle (see Figure 3.2).

Normally, an application submitted at Award Level I will not contain sufficient information for examiners to evaluate it at Award Level II. Similarly, Award Level I and II applications will normally be insufficient for evaluation at Award Level III. This prevents applications from being submitted to higher levels than for what they applied. We saw that the reverse is perfectly possible and will occur. On a rare occasion, an applicant may submit a "full" application yet apply to Level I or II. In that case, examiners can enhance their feedback report by commenting to the Award Level III scoring dimensions and requirements but not scoring the comments applicable only to Level III.

This means that one approach to scoring is to identify quickly whether the applicant is far enough along the appropriate scoring dimensions for the award level of the application and, if not, then reevaluate at the next lower level.

- Check Continuous Improvement, Trends, and Comparisons for Award Level III applicants. If these are inadequate or missing, reevaluate at Award Level II.
- Check Deployment and Levels for Award Level II applicants. If these are inadequate or missing, reevaluate at Award Level I.
- Check Systematic and Key Areas for Award Level I applicants.

To facilitate this sequence, a summary score sheet can be used that includes both the scoring dimensions and the award levels (Table 12.2).

Table 12.3 Scoring Ranges for Award Level I

Range	No.	Comments
0-250	1	Early stages of developing and implementing approaches to Category requirements. Important gaps exist in most Categories.
251-350	2	Beginning of a systematic approach to the primary purposes of the Items, but major gaps exist in approach in some Categories.
351-450	3	A systematic approach to the primary purposes of most Items.
451-550	4	Effective approaches to many Areas to Address. Further measures are needed to demonstrate integration, continuity, and maturity.
551-650	5	A sound, systematic approach responsive to many Areas to Address.
651-750	6	Refined approaches and/or key measures in most areas of importance. Good evidence of continuity and maturity in many Areas. Basis for further integration is in place.
751-875	7	Refined approaches demonstrated in most Areas. Good to excellent integration.
876-1000	8	Outstanding approaches. Excellent integration and maturity.

Table 12.4 Scoring Ranges for Award Level II

Range	No.	Comments
0-250	1	Early stages of developing and implementing approaches to Category requirements. Important gaps exist in most Categories.
251-350	2	Beginning of a systematic approach to the primary purposes of the Items, but major gaps exist in approach and deployment in some Categories. Early stages of obtaining results stemming from approaches.
351-450	3	A systematic approach to the primary purposes of most Items, but deployment in some key Areas to Address is still too early to demonstrate results.
451-550	4	Effective approaches to many Areas to Address, but deployment in some Areas is still at early stages. Further deployment and measures are needed to demonstrate integration, continuity, and maturity.
551-650	5	A sound, systematic approach responsive to many Areas to Address with fact-based improvement process in place in key Areas. No major gaps in deployment. Good performance reported for most areas of importance.
651-750	6	Refined approaches, including key measures, good deployment, and good results in most Areas. Some outstanding activities and results clearly demonstrated. Good evidence of continuity and maturity in many Areas. Basis for further deployment and integration is in place.
751-875	7	Refined approaches, excellent deployment, and good to excellent levels demonstrated in most Areas. Good to excellent integration.
876-1000	8	Outstanding approaches, full deployment, excellent and sustained results. Excellent integration and maturity.

THE FEEDBACK REPORT FOR THE THREE-LEVEL AWARD

All the education and training you have completed is completely valid and appropriate for the three-level award. You must make four minor adjustments when considering applicants for Award Levels I and II:

1. You only need write comments to the Areas to Address for the award level according to Table 12.1.
2. You only need score the Areas to Address for the award level according to Table 12.1. Scoring for Award Levels I and II is easier because fewer scoring dimensions are used.
3. Site visits need only focus on the Areas to Address for the award level for which the applicant is being considered according to Table 12.1.
4. Write the Executive Summary using the appropriate scoring bands. Tables 12.3 and 12.4 define scoring bands for Award Levels I and II, respectively, to complement Table 10.1.

Exercise 12.1

1. Score the answer comments to the case study (answer to Exercise 7.1 in Appendix B) at Award Levels I and II.
2. Write an executive summary for the case study at Award Level I. Use the answer scores in Appendix B to the previous exercise (12.1, number 1).

13

Training Examiners for Three-Level Awards

INTRODUCTION When possible, training of examiners for three-level awards (and even single-level awards) should be done on nonconsecutive days so that trainees have learning cycles to develop maturity in understanding and applying what they learn. Each learning cycle should consist of the following:

1. Introduction and explanation of material
2. Examples of the material presented
3. Exercises to practice material learned
4. Review and discussion of the exercises
5. Application of material learned
6. Review and discussion of the assignment

Each chapter in Parts II and III of this workbook follows this approach.

Thus, this workbook serves as the basis for training examiners. The benefits of training examiners using the sequence are

- learning is developmental: examiners learn in blocks, each one covering a specific topic in a way that prepares for the next block;
- learning is just in time: rather than receiving all materials at once, examiners receive only what they will immediately learn and apply;
- learning is instructive and constructive: what must be applied is defined, explained by examples, taught through exercises, and reinforced through discussion before it must be applied; and
- learning is comprehensive: there is no need for additional training on different award levels.

Additional material during the training would include, as appropriate and applicable, information on the specific award/self-assessment process; expectations and coordination of the award/self-assessment process, reference materials; and list of contacts, members of the board of examiners, and other people involved in the process.

THREE-DAY COURSE In the following example of a three-day course, the three workshop days should be scheduled one or two weeks apart. Assignments are given prior to each workshop day, which are referred to as "pre-days" in Figure 13.1. This results in six "sessions": three pre-day sessions and three day sessions.

To prepare for the course, use a three-ring binder about 1.5-inch thick with an eight-tab divider. Three tabs are used for the three workshop days and three for the pre-day assignments. The two extra tabs can be used for additional materials. Materials are disbursed on a just-in-time basis. So, trainees get only the material for the Pre-Day 1 homework prior to Day 1. When possible, make worksheets available on disk so that it is easier for

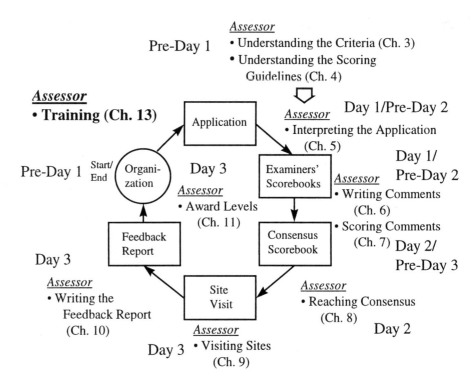

Figure 13.1 The Feedback Process: Training examiners.

trainees to do assignments, there is greater consistency in trainee-produced formats, and it is easier for others to review and critique assignments because it is easier to read printer-written than handwritten work.

In the outline below, use the learning objectives from the chapters as the basis for creating your own learning objectives for your training program.

Pre-Day 1

Homework due on Workshop Day 1.
• *Lesson 1:* Understanding the Criteria
Assignment: Read Chapter 3. Do all exercises, 3.1–3.6.
• *Lesson 2:* Understanding the Scoring Dimensions
Assignment: Read Chapter 4. Do all exercises, 4.1–4.9.
Materials: Introduction (greetings and an explanation of the training process), instructions (including course objectives, time commitment required, expectations and what happens if they are not met), full Criteria book, worksheets on disk (if possible), case study.

Note: You can vary the course by selecting exercises and/or redesigning exercises similar to those in the chapters. For example, you may only send the Business Overview, one passage (say from one Item or Area to Address), and one related figure from the case study for Exercises 4.2 and 4.5–4.7.

Day 1

(Schedule one to two weeks after trainees receive Pre-Day 1 materials.)
Collect/check assignments.
• Review exercises
• *Lesson 1:* Interpreting the Application
Exercises 5.1 and 5.2 from Chapter 5: For Exercise 5.1, assign one section

(there are five) and for Exercise 5.2 assign one Item per person (or group of trainees).

- Present and discuss.
- *Lesson 2:* Writing Comments

Exercises 6.1 and 6.2 from Chapter 6: For Exercise 6.2, use the same Item chosen for Exercise 5.2.

- Present and discuss.

Materials: Overheads, instructions, exercise sheets, case study, audiovisual equipment for presentations by instructors and trainees, flip charts, markers, tape.

Pre-Day 2   Homework due on Workshop Day 2.

- *Lesson 3:* Application of Interpreting the Application to the Case Study

Assignment: Exercise 5.2 (entire case study per trainee). Bring an original and two copies of your work for an Item selected for you by the instructor. Assign Items to groups of trainees.

- *Lesson 4:* Application of Writing Comments to the Case Study

Assignment: Exercise 6.2 (entire case study per trainee). Bring an original and two copies of your work for an Item selected for you by the instructor. Assign Items to groups of trainees.

Materials: Instructions, case study, Comment and Scoring Worksheets (Table 6.1), Scoring Dimensions (Table 4.2).

Day 2   (Schedule two weeks after Day 1.) Collect/check assignments.

- Review Exercise 5.2.
- *Lesson 5:* Scoring Comments

Exercise 7.1 from Chapter 7: for Exercise 7.1, assign one Item to each trainee or group of trainees.

- Present and discuss.
- *Lesson 6:* Preparing for Consensus

Exercise 8.1 from Chapter 8: for Exercise 8.1, use the Items selected for Pre-Day 2 assignments. Have individuals prepare for consensus using the comments of other trainees for the same Item (see example in Table 8.1).

- Present and discuss.
- *Lesson 6:* Reaching Consensus

Have groups reach consensus on comments for the Item they prepared.

- *Lesson 7:* Scoring Comments

Have groups score consensus comments and compare to their individual scores prior to consensus.

Materials: Overheads, Consensus Preparation Procedure (Chapter 8), forms (Table 6.1), examples, instructions, exercises, Scoring Dimensions (Table 4.2), Summary Score Sheet (Table 7.5), audiovisual equipment for presentations by instructors and trainees, flip charts, markers, tape.

Pre-Day 3   Homework assignment for Workshop Day 3.

- *Lesson 8:* Application of Scoring Comments to the Case Study

Assignment: Exercise 7.1 (entire case study per trainee).

Materials: Instructions, case study, scorebook, Summary Score Sheet (Table 7.5).

Day 3   (Schedule two weeks after Day 2.) Collect/check assignments.
- Review Exercise 7.1.
- *Lesson 9:* Visiting Sites

Exercise 9.1: Assign one Category to each trainee or group of trainees. They are to use their own comments from the case study.
- Present and discuss.
- *Lesson 10:* Writing the Feedback Report

Exercise 10.1: Have each trainee or group write an executive summary for the Category for which they prepared site visit issues.
- *Lesson 11:* Understanding the Award Levels

Exercise 11.1: Have each trainee or group score and then write an executive summary at Award Levels I and II for the Category for which they prepared site visit issues.

Materials: Overheads, Site Visit Preparation Procedure (Chapter 9), forms (Table 9.1), executive summary sheet (Chapter 10), summary scoring bands (Tables 10.1, 12.3, and 12.4), instructions, exercises, application, audiovisual equipment for presentations by instructors and trainees, flip charts, markers, tape.

VI

APPENDICES

Appendix A—Glossary

Application.   A written document describing an organization relative to the Baldrige (or state) Award Criteria.

Approach.   (1) A method that addresses Criteria requirements. (2) With Deployment, a type of Item. (3) One of four elements of the basic concept of the Criteria, the other three being Deployment, Results, and Continuous Improvement.

Area for Improvement.   One of two types of comments, the other being Strengths. Area for Improvement comments occur in a scorebook and feedback report to identify areas in which the applicant/organization does not comply with the Criteria based on the information available to the examiner.

Area to Address.   Also known as Area. The third level of detail of the Criteria. A subpart of a Criteria Item denoted by letters (a, b, c) and numbers in parentheses, such as 2.1a(3) refers to Area ''a(3)'' of Item 2.1 of Category 2.

Award Level.   Some awards have different levels for recognizing different levels of maturity relative to the Criteria. Three award levels described in this workbook are Award Level I, which recognizes approaches in the six Categories, with Approach-Deployment Items and key measures for those approaches; Award Level II, which recognizes deployment of those approaches with identified measures and their current performance levels; and Award Level III, which recognizes favorable trends and comparisons of the key measures in addition to what Level II recognizes.

Category.   The first level of detail in the Criteria. There are seven Categories, each with one or more Items.

Comment.   A statement summarizing the examiner's interpretation of the information provided by an organization on approaches, deployment of approaches, and results of measures on the approaches according to the Criteria, Core Values, Key Business Factors, and Scoring Guidelines.

Comment and Scoring Worksheet.   The form used by examiners to record Strength and Area for Improvement comments and scores for each Item. In this workbook, the form includes the Areas to Address and scoring dimensions to which the comments apply and provides space for listing of deployment units (for Approach-Deployment Items) or Key Areas (for Results Items).

Comparisons.   A scoring dimension for Results Items that refers to performance on measures identified by the organization in Key Areas and how good the performance is relative to external targets such as industry average, best competitors, and benchmarks.

Consensus.   The process by which examiners review individual scorebooks and agree on a set of comments and a score for each item to produce a single scorebook.

Continuous Improvement.   (1) A scoring dimension for Approach-Deployment Items that refers to whether an approach addressing Criteria requirements has a fact-based process for improving the method and the degree of integration and maturity of the method through cycles of learning and improvement. (2) One of four elements of the basic concept of the Criteria, the other three being Approach, Deployment, and Results.

Criteria.   The set of requirements identified through Categories, Items, Areas to Address, Notes, and glossary. The Criteria also can refer to these requirements plus the Core Values, Scoring Guidelines, Response Guidelines, and Scoring System.

Deployment.   (1) The extent to which approaches addressing Item requirements are used consistently in all appropriate areas or work units of the organization. (2) With Approach, a type of Item. (3) One of four elements of the basic concept of the Criteria, the other three being Approach, Results, and Continuous Improvement. (4) A scoring dimension for Approach-Deployment Items.

Feedback Process. The process by which an organization reviews itself relative to the Criteria, documents the observations, and submits the documentation to an assessment that culminates in a feedback report. The six critical examiner tasks are interpreting the application, writing comments, scoring comments, reaching consensus, visiting sites, and writing the feedback report. To do these tasks, the examiner must have knowledge of the Criteria and Scoring Guidelines.

Feedback Report. The final set of comments, scores, and executive summary provided an organization as a result of the Feedback Process. The feedback report may also include additional information about processes and other organizations (e.g., the award process, the Feedback Process, distribution of scores).

Key Areas. A scoring dimension for Results Items that refers to whether performance results reported by the organization address areas of importance to the organization as identified in the responses to the Criteria and in the Business Overview.

Levels. A scoring dimension for Results Items that refers to the performance for the current period on measures identified by the organization in Key Areas, how good the performance is on an absolute scale or relative to internal targets, and whether the performance is sustained.

Nonprescriptive. Refers to comments that refrain from describing how the organization could or should comply with Criteria requirements.

Overall purposes of an Item. The Item requirements identified in the Areas to Address of the Item that extend beyond the primary purposes of the Item.

Primary purposes of an Item. The Item requirements identified in the Item description.

Results. (1) One of four elements of the basic concept of the Criteria, the other three being Approach, Deployment, and Continuous Improvement. (2) One of two types of Items, the other being Approach-Deployment.

Scorebook. The examiner's written assessment of an organization based on the information provided from an application and, possibly, a site visit. There are two kinds of scorebooks: the examiner's scorebook is done independently by each examiner assigned to an application and the consensus scorebook is done by several examiners using consensus.

Scoring dimension. Seven elements of the Scoring Guidelines three components: Approach, Deployment, Results. Approach has two scoring dimensions: Systematic (SY) and Continuous Improvement (CI). Deployment has one scoring dimension: Deployment (DE). Results has four scoring dimensions: Key Areas (KA), Levels (LE), Trends (TR), and Comparisons (CO).

Scoring Guidelines. The numerical scale as scoring rows and definitions of the scoring rows used to assign points to Items based on the maturity of the approaches, extent of deployment, and strength and duration of performance results. The Scoring Guidelines have two parts, one for Approach-Deployment Items and another for Results Items.

Scoring range band. The eight groups of total points assigned an applicant that describe the maturity of the organization relative to the Criteria's requirements on Approach, Deployment, and Results. In this workbook, each Award Level has a set of scoring range bands based on the scoring dimensions applicable to the Award Level.

Scoring row. One of five groups of scores assigned Items using the Scoring Guidelines.

Site visit. A process for enhancing the application by interviewing, observing, and reviewing documents at one or more applicant locations. The purpose of the site visit is to clarify and verify the examiners' interpretation of the application and to discover additional information addressing the Criteria but not included in the application.

Strength. One of two types of comments, the other being Area for Improvement. Strength comments occur in a scorebook and feedback report and identify areas in which the applicant/organization complies with the Criteria based on the information available to the examiner.

Systematic. A scoring dimension for Approach-Deployment Items that refers to whether a method exists to address the Criteria requirements consistent with the organization's key business factors, how closely the method addresses all requirements, and whether there are key measures associated with the method.

Trends. A scoring dimension for Results Items that refers to performance on measures identified by the organization in Key Areas for two or more periods and whether the performance trend is favorable.

Value added. Refers to comments that are legible, use complete sentences; include an explicit reference to a (sub)Area to Address; use the words of the application when the comment is a Strength and use the words of the Criteria when the comment is an Area for Improvement; implicitly identify a scoring row and dimension; and, when combined with all Strength and Area for Improvement comments for the same Item, address the Item requirements in their entirety and nothing else.

Appendix B—Answers to Exercises

CHAPTER 3

Exercise 3.1   Category 2, Strategic Planning, examines

- how the company sets strategic direction,
- how the company determines key action plans, and
- how action plans are translated into a performance management system.

Category 3, Customer and Market Focus, examines

- how the company determines requirements and expectations of customers and markets,
- how the company enhances relationships with customers, and
- how the company determines customer satisfaction.

Category 4, Information and Analysis, examines

- how management of data and information support key company processes and the performance management system, and
- how effective use of data and information support key company processes and performance management system.

Category 5, Human Resource Development and Management, examines

- how the workforce is enabled to develop and use its full potential, aligned with the company's objectives, and
- the company's efforts to build and maintain an environment conducive to performance excellence, full participation, and personal and organizational growth.

Category 6, Process Management, examines

- key aspects of process management: customer-focused design, product and service delivery processes, support processes, and supplier and partnering processes.
- how key processes are designed, effectively managed, and improved for better performance.

Category 7, Business Results, examines

- the company's performance, improvement, and levels relative to competitors in five areas: customer satisfaction, financial and marketplace performance, human resources, supplier and partner performance, and operational performance.

Exercise 3.2   1. How the company addresses its responsibilities to the public and how the company practices good citizenship.
2. 2.1: How the company sets strategic directions and how the strategic development process leads to action plans. 2.2: The company's strategic and action plans, how they are deployed, and how performance projects into the future.
3. 3.1: How the company determines longer term requirements, expectations, and preferences of customers and markets. 3.2: How the company determines and enhances its customers' satisfaction.
4. 4.1: Company's selection, management, and use of information and data. 4.2: Company's

123

selection, management, and use of comparative information and data. 4.3: How the company analyzes and reviews overall performance.

5. 5.1: How the company's work and job design and its compensation and recognition approaches enable and encourage employees to contribute. 5.2: How the company's education and training address key company plans and needs. 5.3: How the company maintains a work environment and work climate that support employee well-being, satisfaction, and motivation.

6. 6.1: How new, significantly modified, and customized products and services are designed and how production/delivery processes are designed, implemented, and improved. 6.2: How the company's key support processes are designed, managed, and improved. 6.3: How the company's supplier and partnering processes, relationships, and performance are managed and improved.

Exercise 3.3

1. The company's key financial and marketplace performance results.
2. The company's human resources results, including employee well-being, satisfaction, development, and work system performance.
3. The company's supplier and partner performance results.
4. The company's key operational performance results that significantly contribute to key company goals.

Exercise 3.4

1. 1.2: 2; 2.1: 2; 4.1: 1; 5.2: 1; 6.3: 1; 7.1: 1.
2. 1.2a: 2; 3.1b: 0; 4.3b: 0; 5.3c: 2; 6.2a: 5; 7.5a: 0.
3. • 2.1b: How strategy is translated into action plans, including a clear basis for communicating and aligning critical requirements and tracking performance relative to plans.
   • 3.2b(3): How the company determines customer satisfaction, including how the company obtains objective and reliable information on customer satisfaction relative to its competitors.
   • 4.3a(2): The principal financial and nonfinancial measures integrated and analyzed to determine operational performance, including product and service performance.
   • 5.2a(5): How education and training are evaluated and improved, taking into account company performance, employee development objectives, and costs of education and training.
   • 6.3a(2): How the company ensures that these [overall performance] requirements for suppliers and partners) are met; include key measures, expected performance levels, and how performance is fed back to suppliers and partners.

4. • 7.1a: Current levels and trends in key measures and/or indicators of customer satisfaction and dissatisfaction, including satisfaction relative to competitors.
   • 7.2a(2): Marketplace performance, including market share, business growth, and new markets entered, as appropriate.
   • 7.3a: Current levels and trends in key measures and/or indicators of employee well-being, satisfaction, development, work system improvement, and effectiveness, including appropriate comparative data.
   • 7.4a: Current levels and trends in key measures and/or indicators of supplier and partner performance, including company cost and/or performance improvements attributed to supplier and partner performance, as appropriate, including appropriate comparative data.
   • 7.5a: Key company-specific current levels, trends, and appropriate comparative data derived from product and service quality and performance; key process performance; productivity, cycle time, and other effectiveness and efficiency measures; regulatory/legal compliance; and other results supporting the company's strategy.

Exercise 3.5

1. Alignment refers to consistency of processes, actions, information, and decisions among company units in support of key companywide goals. Effective alignment requires common understanding of purposes and goals and use of complementary measures and information to enable planning, tracking, analysis, and improvement at three levels: the company level, the key process level, and the work unit level. When translating strategy

into action, critical requirements must align. Deployment of action plans must align goals to actions.

2. Measures and indicators refers to numerical information that quantifies (measures) input, output, and performance dimensions of processes, products, services, and the overall company. Measures must be stated for two-to-five-year strategic projections; methods for determining customer satisfaction; analysis of company-level data; methods for determining employee satisfaction; and production/delivery, support, and supplier/partnering processes.

3. Performance refers to output results information obtained from processes, products, and services that permits evaluation and comparison relative to goals, standards, past results, and to others. The Criteria address three types of performance: operational (including product and service quality), customer related, and financial and marketplace. Category 7 asks for performance results on measures of importance to the company. In Category 7, operational performance is separated into three areas: human resource (Item 7.3), supplier and partnering (Item 7.4), and internal measures of product and service quality (Item 7.5).

4. Strategy development process refers to the company's approach to a future-oriented basis for major business decisions, resource allocations, and companywide management. The strategy development process should include revenue growth, as well as cost reduction thrusts.

5. Leadership system refers to how leadership is exercised throughout the company—the basis for and the way that key decisions are made, communicated, and carried out at all levels. An effective leadership system includes mechanisms for the leaders' self-examination and improvement. The leadership system should incorporate values, company direction, high-performance expectations, a strong customer focus, and continuous learning.

6. Cycle time refers to time performance—the time required to fulfill commitments or to complete tasks. Work, information and data, and support processes in particular should be designed with fast cycle times. Cycle time improvements should be reported in Item 7.5.

7. Work design refers to how employees are organized and/or organize themselves in formal or informal, temporary or longer term units, including work, problem-solving, and cross-functional teams and functional or departmental units. Job design refers to responsibilities, authorities, and tasks assigned to individuals.

8. Appropriate indicators of employee well-being, satisfaction, and motivation include safety, absenteeism, turnover, turnover rate for customer-contact employees, grievances, strikes, worker compensation, innovation and suggestion rates, courses completed, cross-training, and employee survey results.

9. Process refers to linked activities with the purpose of producing a product or service for a customer (user) within or outside the company. In some situations, processes might require adherence to a specific sequence of steps. In services, processes spell out what must be done. In knowledge work such as strategic planning and research and analysis, process does not necessarily imply formal sequences of steps. Category 6 examines the key aspects of process management. Together, Items 6.1, 6.2, and 6.3 should cover all key operations, processes, and activities of all work units.

10. Action plans refer to principal company-level drivers, derived from short-and long-term strategic planning. Action plans are set to accomplish those things the company must do well for its strategy to succeed. Action plan development represents the critical stage in planning when general strategies and goals are made specific so that effective companywide understanding and deployment are possible. Deployment of action plans requires analysis of overall resource needs and creation of aligned measures for all work units. Action plan summaries should include key performance requirements, key performance measures and/or indicators, and how plans, resources, and measures are deployed.

Exercise 3.6

1. Customer requirements are essential in each Area, from strategic planning, leadership system, and work design to process management.
2. Leaders create, deploy, and improve the leadership system in part by reviewing company-wide performance.
3. Each Area asks how methods are evaluated and improved and tracked for identifying improvement activities; or, how they reinforce other objectives.
4. Employees and the company have a mutually beneficial relationship: employees contrib-

ute to the company's success through the work systems designed for their performance, and the company in turn seeks to satisfy employees through work environment, climate, and facilities conducive to employee well-being and satisfaction. One critical method for accomplishing both is through education, training, and development of employees.

5. Responsiveness to market changes and customer, employee, and business needs requires processes to be fast and flexible.

6. Certainly for production/delivery processes and products and services, designing quality in reduces problems, waste, environmental impact, and customer complaints. Less obvious, perhaps, is that this also applies to the designs for work systems, education and training programs, and information systems. A prevention orientation leads to designing in quality.

7. Strategy planning must distinguish between the short and long term. Thus, the Criteria ask for two-to-five-year projections of key measures and how they would compare to key competitors' performance on these measures.

8. Critical to management by fact is the selection of performance measures that best represent factors that lead to customer, operational, and financial success (see Results focus core value).

9. Partnerships can increase the company's capabilities and opportunities when they include customers, suppliers, educational organizations, labor groups, and community groups.

10. The focus here is on the expectations of the business through ethical behavior and protection of the public health and safety and environment.

11. By explicitly including all stakeholders' (e.g., customers, stockholders, suppliers, partners, the public, and communities) requirements, it becomes easier to balance conflicting and changing aims.

CHAPTER 4

Exercise 4.1

1. The primary purposes of Item 2.2 are to describe how the company sets strategic directions and how the strategic development process leads to action plans. The primary purposes of Item 4.3 are to describe how the company analyzes overall performance and how the company reviews overall performance.

2. The full requirements of Area 2.2b are to provide a brief summary of key human resource plans derived from overall strategy that include (1) changes in work design and/or organization to improve knowledge creation/sharing, flexibility, innovation, and rapid response; (2) employee development, education, and training; (3) changes in compensation, recognition, and benefits; and (4) recruitment, including critical skill categories and expected or planned changes in demographics of the workforce. The full requirements of Area 5.1b are to describe how the company's compensation and recognition approaches for individuals and groups reinforce overall work systems, performance, and learning objectives.

Exercise 4.2

1. 11 leaders: 1. Don Blackwell, Chairman of the Board; 2. Philip Ruben, Chief Executive Officer; 3. Eugene Farmer, President and Chief Operating Officer; 4. Jack Harvey, VP, Consumer Products Sector; 5. Jason Tommas, Senior VP, Commercial and Automotive Sector; 6. Todd Charleson, VP, Defense and Aerospace Sector; 7. George Jefferson, VP, Nuclear and Specialty Sector; 8. Hiro Miyazaki, Senior VP, Corporate R&D and Site Services; 9. Sheila Anne A., VP, Human Resources and Organizational Learning; 10. Brenda Taylor, Advisory VP, Sales and Marketing and Product Distribution; 11. Thomas Anthony, VP, Administration and Information Systems.

2. Two classification methods: U.S. (56%) and non-U.S. (44%); hourly (61%), nonexempt (18%), and salaried contributors (21%).

3. There are seven major suppliers: Southern States Steelmill, Tilken Steel Supply, Alacon Aluminum Foundry, Nippon National Mill, Precise Explosive Corporation, Wilmont Wire, Inc., and Northern Rod & Bar Distributor; five levels: nonqualified, conditional, qualified, pass through partnerships (PTP), and certified.

4. Special Performance Products, Critical Life Components, Worldwide Pins Corp., and Top Flight Hardware.

Exercise 4.3

In Category 1: 1.1a(3), how senior leaders communicate and reinforce . . . commitment to learning throughout workforce; 1.1a(4), how senior leaders *review* the company's overall performance and use the review process to reinforce company directions and *improve* the leadership system; 1.2a(2) how the company *anticipates* public concerns, *assesses* potential impacts on society, and *addresses* these issues in a *proactive* manner; 1.2b how the company and its employees *support* and *strengthen* their key communities.

In Category 2 (these are not as clear as in other Items): 2.1b, how strategy is translated into action plans, including a clear basis for communicating and aligning critical requirements, and *tracking performance* relative to plans; 2.2b(1), changes . . . to *improve* knowledge creation/sharing, flexibility, innovation, and rapid response.

In Category 3: 3.1a(3), how the company's approach to listening to and learning from customers and markets is *evaluated, improved,* and kept current with changing business needs; 3.2a(1), how the company determines customer contact requirements. Deploys the requirements to all employees who are involved in meeting the requirements and *evaluates and improves* customer contact performance.

In Category 4: 4.1a(4), how information and data, their deployment, and effectiveness of use are *evaluated, improved,* and kept current with changing business needs; 4.2a(4), how comparative information and data, their deployment, and effectiveness of use are *evaluated, improved,* and kept current with changing business needs; 4.3b, how company performance and capabilities are *reviewed* to assess progress relative to goals, plans, and changing business needs. Describe how review findings are translated into *improvement* priorities and deployed through the company and, as appropriate, to the company's suppliers and/or business partners.

In Category 5: 5.1b, how the company's compensation and recognition approaches . . . *reinforce the overall work systems, performance, and learning objectives*; 5.2a(5), how education and training are *evaluated and improved*, taking into account company performance, employee development objectives, and costs of education and training; 5.3c, how the company relates employee well-being, satisfaction, and motivation results to key business results and/or objectives to *identify improvement activities*.

In Category 6: 6.1b(3), how product and service processes are *evaluated and improved* to achieve better performance including improvements to products and services, and the transfer of learning to other company units and projects; 6.2a(5), how the processes are *evaluated and improved* to achieve better performance including cycle time; 6.3a(3), how the company *evaluates and improves* its management of supplier and partnering processes to achieve better performance.

Exercises 4.4

1. Regulatory/legal compliance, environmental improvements, or use of ''green'' technology should be reported as Company-Specific Results (Item 7.5) (Note N1, Item 1.2).
2. Key performance measures from the company's action plans and appropriate comparisons with competitors and/or key benchmarks. Report in Item 7.5 (see its note N1).
3. Area 3.2a(1) asks for customer contact requirements, which should be reported in Item 7.5 (see note N3, Item 3.2). Area 3.2b(2) asks for measurements for customer satisfaction determination, which are reported in Item 7.1 (see its note N1).
4. Performance results are required in four areas: customer related, operational, competitive, financial and market related, which should be reported in Items 7.1–7.5, depending on the area (see note N2).
5. Work system improvement and effectiveness, which should be reported in Item 7.3 (see its note N1).
6. Education, training, and development, which should be reported in Item 7.3 (see its note N1).
7. Employee well-being and satisfaction, which should be reported in Item 7.3 (see note N3, Item 5.3).
8. Product and service design and delivery processes, product and service quality, and product and service performance. These should be reported in Item 7.5 (see note N5).
9. Support process and performance. These should be reported in Item 7.5 (see note N3).
10. Supplier and partnering processes and supplier/partner performance. These should be reported in Item 7.4 (see Note).

Exercise 4.5

1. Suppliers have three requirements: quality, delivery, and price. Certified suppliers must also meet six sigma capability and control requirements. Area 6.3a(3) identifies another supplier requirement: the cost of doing business.
2. Key process requirements include quality, cycle time, and cost. Area 7.5a suggests yield, productivity, and scrap and waste are also requirements. Item 6.1 says all critical processes must comply with the six sigma program.

Exercise 4.6

1. The 1997 levels for *delivery* as measured by percentage received on time are 99% for G&A, 98% for material, and 93% for services.
2. The 1997 process *yield* levels are 93% for rivets, 98% for pins and bolts, and 100% for screws.

Exercise 4.7

1. The trends for percentage materials and G&A received on time are favorable and/or sustained. The trend for percentage services received on time is sustained.
2. Except for percentage yield of bolts and pins, percentage yield of all other six trends for yield are favorable. Quality from operations and as warranty returns have all favorable trends. The eight productivity trends are split equally between favorable and sustained (NSS product and all nonproduct except CPS). Cycle time trends are all favorable and/or sustained. Scrap/waste trends are all favorable and/or sustained.

Exercise 4.8

1. The 1997 goal and best-in-class (bic) performance is 99.2% received on time. The three types of supplies—services, materials, and G&A—are all below bic. While services on-time delivery is currently near bic, its 10-year trend wavers between 97% and 99%.
2. There are no comparisons—competitors, best in class, or benchmarks—for percentage yield by fastener.

Exercise 4.9

1. SY because 1.2 is an Approach-Deployment Item, and ethical conduct is a required Area to Address. Failure to address a basic purpose results in a lower score on Approach.
2. TR because 7.3 is a Results Item, and trends are based on more than one year's results.
3. CI because 4.2 is an Approach-Deployment Item, and Area to Address 4.2a(4) is the continuous improvement element of it. By definition, CI requires improvement to be fact based.
4. CO because 7.1 is a Results Item, and comparisons are made to competitors.
5. KA because 7.5 is a Results Item, and support services, 6.2a, is a required Area to Address. Failure to include it means a Key Area is missing. Of course, Levels, Trends, and Comparisons are also missing.
6. DE because 1.1 is an Approach-Deployment Item, and deployment for this Item means all senior executives use the Approach.
7. LE because 6.3 is a results Item, and while specific measures/indicators exist (Key Area), their current levels do not. Of course, Trends and Comparisons are also missing.

CHAPTER 5

Exercise 5.1

Key Business Factors Worksheet

1. Basic Description of the Company

   ■ World leader in the design and manufacture of fasteners—pins, bolts, rivets, screws, and specialty fasteners; four product sectors: Consumer Products Sector (CPS), Commercial and Automotive Sector (CAS), Defense and Aerospace Sector (DAS), and Nuclear and Specialty Sector (NSS); a fifth sector is the Corporate Support Sector (CSS). Business Overview. [BOV]

   ■ Nearly $1 billion in sales: CPS $250 million, CAS $400 million, DAS $200 million, NSS

$50 million; 21 sites: manufacturing plants in Asia, Central and South America, and Europe; Philadelphia, PA, is world headquarters. 56% of total employee base and 70% of sales in United States. Publicly traded on New York Stock Exchange. [BOV]

- For CAS, the U.S. "Big 3" and Japan's "Big 2" automotive manufacturers—commercial and automotive; for DAS, all major airframe manufacturers and top defense contractors; for NSS, nuclear and specialty; for CPS, distributors, wholesalers, jobbers, retailers, and end customer. [3.1a(1)]
- Of the 9941 employees worldwide, 56% are in the United States; 61% are hourly, 18% salaried nonexempt, 21% salaried; 92% of hourly employees have high school diplomas, 56% of salaried nonexempt employees have some college, and 83% of salaried exempt employees have college degrees; there is a 20% virtual workforce. [BOV]
- No major equipment, facilities, and technologies used.

2. Customer Requirements

- Customer requirements: delivery, quality, price, responsiveness, ease of doing business [BOV]; service, satisfaction, value [BOV, 1.1a: Credo]; technology leader [1.1a(2)]; CPS: low price; CAS: automotive requirements; DAS: high quality, extensive testing; NSS: complicated designs.

3. Supplier Relationships

- 788 suppliers, 420 suppliers of raw materials and distributors [BOV]; 158 deliver 80% by volume [7.4a]; top seven: Southern States Steelmill, Tilken Steel Supply, Alacon Aluminum Foundry, Nippon National Mill, Precise Explosive Corporation, Wilmont Wire, Inc., Northern Rod & Bar Distributor. [BOV]
- Five levels: unqualified, conditional, qualified, pass through partner (PTP), certified; PTP/certified have reduced inspection; delivery/price assessed by purchasing [6.3a(2)]; requirements: quality, delivery; price: critical process $C_{pk} \geq 1.5$. [BOV]
- Included in product design, verification, qualification, and field failure analyses. [BOV]

4. Competitive Factors

- Leader overall [BOV] and in all sectors with growth in all sectors. [7.2]
- Major competitors: Special Performance Products, Critical Life Components, Worldwide Pins Corp., and Top Flight Hardware. [BOV]
- Principal factors that determine competitive success such as productivity growth, cost reduction, and product innovation varies by sector.
- For DAS, decrease in defense spending; for CAS, long-time competitors challenging. [BOV]

5. Other Factors Important to the Applicant

- No major new thrusts for the company such as entry into new markets or segments
- No new business alliances
- No introduction of new technologies
- Highly regulated: environment, safety; Fastener Quality Act of 1990. [BOV]
- Started quality movement with focus on Baldrige initiated by customer and six sigma program.
- No unique factors.

Notes for Exercises 5.1 and 5.2

1 Leadership

1.1 11 Senior leaders (BOV, Figure 0-1). Consolidated Fasteners, Incorporated (CFI) is committed to meeting stakeholder expectations: Shareholders expect a fair return on their investment; customers expect advanced performance solutions with superior quality and service, competitive pricing, on-time delivery, and organizational responsiveness; employees expect challenging jobs, the means to be successful, and recognition for their contributions and accomplishments (1.1).

1.1a(1) Set direction: active customer relations; quality visits; monthly, weekly, meetings; sponsor benchmark studies; review competitive information; evaluate government directions [1.1a(1)]. Seek opportunities ??.

1.1a(2) CFI's credo is "To All Customers, We Promise Service, Satisfaction, and Value." It has six values: Results, Risk Taking, Customer Orientation, Quality, Great Place To Work, Discipline (Table 1.1-1).; MBP (Figure 2.1-1) to identify five key strategies and objectives (world-class performance); mirror customer organizations and dialog at several levels; 360° review 100% employee surveys; system effectiveness assessments; personality and behavioral assessments [1.1a(2)].

1.1a(3) Communicate: new-hire orientation; courses on values/culture; BUMs; printed media [1.1a(3)]. Reinforce: all-employee survey; retraining; customer focus groups; external surveys; third party assessments [1.1a(3)].

1.1a(4) Senior leaders actively participate in periodic corporate/sector reviews; new proprietary product review [1.1a(3)]; also participate in personal assessments, e.g., 360° reviews, employee evaluation of leadership effectiveness, system effectiveness assessments, that improve leadership system. [1.1a(2); continuous learning].

1.2a(1) Sectors hold annual planning sessions for next 2, 5, 10 years; Code of Ethics handbook; annual review; 4 hours for new-hires and 40 hours for senior management, procurement and customer contact personnel, project managers legal training on ethical behavior.

1.2a(2) Formalized product/process for risk assessment; new business return on investment (ROI); product market assessment various simulations.

1.2b 45th Annual Fastener Reliability Testing Institute Conference; 1996 employees presented over 235 quality-oriented papers; CFI donated > $500,000 in grants; CFI principal sponsor of Pennsylvania's quality award.

2 Strategic Planning

2.1a Management By Planning (MBP) process (Figure 2.2-1) and annual planning cycle-six steps (Figure 2.2-2).

2.1a(1)–a(5) Factors considered: ✓ customer/market requirements, ✓ competitive environment, ✓ risks, ✓ company capabilities, ✓ supplier/partner capabilities.

2.1b Actions occur at project level, derived from "catchball" process to link project goals to tactics and strategic objectives (Figure 2.1-3).

2.2a CFI has five key business strategies and goals: (1) to deliver products to customers on time and defect free (6 sigma levels); (2) to be recognized as the producer of highest value fasteners; (3) to be the technology leader in the introduction of revolutionary fastener products; (4) to protect the environment at all worldwide locations and set benchmark levels of compliance; and (5) to be recognized as number on in employee satisfaction at all worldwide locations [2.1(a)]. Table 2.2-1 contains goals for 1997, with a 100% accomplishment of objectives.

2.2b(1)–b(4) Human resource strategic long-range plan (HR SLRP) derived from SLRP: changes in work systems (increase work teams and self-audits, reduce management layers, increase core competencies, achieve 20% virtual workforce); changes in development (expand skills, specialist cadre, develop/publish long-term skills needs, develop "buy" skills, increase number of managers attending core management development [2.2b(1)]; changes in compensation/recognition (merit performance appraisal system with 50% greater weight on quality v. quantity, Bonus Programs; individual and team reward/award systems); changes in recruitment (doubling key external hires, decrease cost per hire, increase offer and acceptance rates, improve GPTW tactics and goals).

2.2c Table 2.2-1 contains only three-year projections although not clear what the goals are for the years 1998–2000; targets to meet or exceed competitive benchmarks.

3 Customer and Market Focus

3.1a [1.1a] stakeholders (ROI need), customers (delivery, quality, price, responsiveness, ease of doing business [BOV]), employees (challenging jobs, means to succeed, recognition [1.1a]).

3.1a(1) Sales representatives trained to listen; CFI continually monitors business and physical environment; regular searches; listening posts; Customer Expectation Determination (CED) process (Figure 3.1-1); engineers follow publications and patent filings, attend trade shows [3.1a(1)].

3.1a(2) Five features: delivery, quality, price, responsiveness, ease of doing business; three from credo: service, satisfaction, and value [BOV]; by sector: CPS (higher end, excellence: competition, growth); CAS (daily use, high volume, short lead time, special design needs); DAS (military specs, low price bidder); NSS (nuclear regulations, safety, unique requirements and specifications) [3.1a(1)–a(2)]. Engineering, sales, production, administration team determines important features [3.1a(2)].

3.1a(3) CFI uses several methods to evaluate and improve adequacy, timeliness, reliability of information received and used for decision making including changing training program for customer contact personnel, soliciting comments from nonrespondents to surveys [3.1a(3)].

3.2a Customers can access CFI and receive information through toll-free telephone and FAX, E-mail, and electronic data interchange (EDI) 24 hours/day every day; receive facility manager's phone number; postage-paid, self-addressed cards [3.2a].

3.2a(1) Service standards include response time to answer phone; time to respond to problem; time to resolve critical/urgent problem; problem escalation to manager [3.2a(1)]. Three steps: inputs (feedback, comments, field sales engineer [FSE] information), action (focus groups), results (possible changes in standards or additional training) [3.2a(1)].

3.2a(2) All complaints logged in to marketing data system (MDS); with formal comments sent to service center and customer contact personnel; complaints categorized as critical (FSE responds within 2 hours) or urgent (FSE responds within 24 hours); daily reporting of status at service personnel meetings [3.2a(2)].

3.2b(1) Follow-up: special surveys, monthly private visits, mail-back cards, call-backs from service center managers [3.2b(1)].

3.2b(2) Through follow-up procedures; surveys; Industrial Fastener Institute (IFI) surveys total industry; contracts with nine universities/three colleges; CFI does one or two yearly; mail-back cards [3.2b(1)-b(2)].

3.2b(3) Competitor information from IFI surveys, surveys from contracted universities and colleges [3.2b(3)].

4 Information and Analysis

4.1a(1) CFI collects data on measures and indicators derived for each business strategy. Specific measures/indicators in each performance area as follows:

- ✔ customer requirements: delivery, quality, price, responsiveness, ease of doing business [BOV]; service, satisfaction, value [BOV, 1.1a: Credo]; technology leader [1.1a(2)]
- ✔ financial/market: ROI [shareholders, 1.1a]; profit margin; market share [7.2a]
- ✔ human resource performance: great place to work, employee satisfaction [1.1a]; lost work days, workers' compensation, turnover, years of service, hours of training, team/individual awards, team involvement, implemented suggestions [7.3a]
- ✔ supplier qualifications: quality, delivery, price [6.3a(1)]; cost of doing business [6.3a(3)]
- ✔ product/service characteristics and operational performance: quality, cycle time, cost [6.1b]; accuracy [6.2a(3)]; yield, productivity, scrap/waste, availability, responsiveness [7.5a]

4.1a(2) World-wide information system, access to five major databases [4.1a(2)]

4.1a(3) Sector teams meet weekly with users, developers, customers, suppliers [4.1a(3)].

4.1a(4) Semiannual. Top-down reviews including analysis of "Has current data enabled us to make decisions and set priorities?" "Are data actionable?" "Do data enable us to determine performance of processes?" [4.1a(4)]; example of improvement (Figure 7.5-16).

4.2a(1) Each sector benchmarks critical processes for 2 to 3 specific functions. CFI usually adds 5 more for each sector based on business conditions, for a total of 10–15 [4.2a(1)].

4.2a(2) Identifying benchmark partners having most effect, competitor performance, better performance outside industry [4.2a(2)].

4.2a(3) Criteria for stretch goals: benchmark team's data, costs, process, disruption, criticality, impact [4.2a(3)].

4.2a(4) Change from selecting benchmark partners based on convenience to potential impact; also noted benefit of public domain searches prior to benchmarking tour [4.2a(4)].

4.3a(1) Market Database System (MDS): market share, customer satisfaction, complaints, survey results, etc. [4.3a(1)].

4.3a(2) Operations data system (ODS): operational performance/capabilities; human resources data system (HRDS): human resource (HR) data; technical data system (TDS): technical specs [4.3a(2)].

4.3a(3) MDS for competitive data [4.3a(3)].

4.3a(4) Financial Database System (FDS): sales, inventories, profits, cash flow [4.3a(4)].

4.3b Reviews include customer related (MDS data, e.g., surveys, complaints), operational (ODS data, e.g., C_{pks}; TDS data, e.g., specs), competitive (price and product from MDS), and financial/market related (e.g., sales, inventories, profits, cash flow from FDS) [4.3a(1)–a(4)]. Annual reviews on yearly performance and long-range plans; quarterly on cost and annual plans; monthly performance to productivity, design, annual plans, and goals; weekly/daily reviews external inputs, internal quality, corrective actions; vendor of choice reviews for performance against customer requirements; sector operation reviews on annual and corporate plans at sector level [4.3b, Table 4.3-1].

5 Human Resource Development and Management

5.1a(1) CFI uses different types of teams (over 550 active teams in 1997): uses self-directed work, self-audit, self-sustained, Product Development Team (PDT), project, Natural Work Team (NWT), Process Improvement Team (PIT), problem solving, task force, review board [5.1a(1)].

5.1a(2) Fostered through education/learning to develop multiskilled employees, reduce management layers; CFI deployed 91% of Macon operations [5.1a(2)].

5.1a(3) Communications: business update meetings (BUMs), written publications, E-mail, voice mail [5.1a(3)].

5.1b Different kinds of awards for individuals and teams: CFIAA, SRA, departmental; profit sharing started in 1988 (50/50 split); bonus and stock option programs; incentive pay and promotion plans for quality over quantity [2.2b(3), 5.1b].

5.2a(1) Four methods for training: functional area training departments, CFI University, Corporate Education and Development, external consultants [5.2a(1)].

5.2a(2) Employees update career enhancement forms: recommendations for education, training, and work assignments [5.2a(2)].

5.2a(3) Four methods for delivery: functional area training department; CFI University; Corporate Education and Development; external training consultants; tracking done through Training and Education Support System (TESS); four-tier deployment process (Figure 5.2-1) [5.2a(1)–a(3)].

5.2a(4) Three-step process for on-the-job reinforcement; post-tests, simulation practice; TESS tracks progress on skills, knowledge, capabilities [5.2a(4)].

5.2a(5) New-hire training revised to meet new philosophy [5.2a(5); training department annually analyzes course effectiveness and changes curricula, instruction, delivery [5.2a(4)].

5.3a Safety Awareness Teams audit plants; improvement teams find root causes: hazardous materials "red-flagged"; goals: 45% reduction of solvent-based incidents (1998), elimination of ozone-depletion compounds (1999), 50% hazardous waste reduction (1998), 60% reduction cumulative trauma injuries (1997). Differences between groups not noted [5.3a].

5.3b Worldwide but varying by local laws/customs: Employee Assistance Program (EAP) includes 24-hour treatment/referrals for mental health, chemical dependency, general living problems; recreational facilities/showers (domestic sites) including aerobic classes, sports, wellness programs, stress management workshops; child care, parental leave of absence; 100% tuition reimbursement; financial support (loan mortgage program) [5.3b].

5.3c(1) Satisfaction determined through surveys, focus groups, one-to-one interviews, BUMs, various other assessment tools [5.3c(1)]; nothing on well-being and motivation.

5.3c(2) Multisector team (Human Resources Evaluation Team, HRET) assesses HR strategies and practices: involvement reduces turnover 14%, increased employee satisfaction 43%, cycle time improvement 67%, quality improvement 83%. Nothing on well-being/motivation and business results [5.3c(2)].

6 Process Management: Core Business

6.1a(1) Listening posts and FSEs provide customer information; customers provide designs [6.1a(1)].

6.1a(2) Design process: Concept/feasibility, Engineering and Validation Test, Production Validation Test, and Product Maturity Acceptance [Figure 6.1-1]; differences in sector products not accounted for in design process.

6.1a(3) Various departments included in reviews: Preliminary Design Review, Final Design Review, Product Acceptance Review, Design for Quality and Reliability [Figure 6.1-1; 6.1a(3)].

6.1b(1) Key production processes: receiving materials check, drawing and upsetting, machining and threading, heat transfer, chemical processing, product review for release, shipping and distribution [6.1b(1)]; key requirements: quality, cycle time, cost at $C_{pk} \geq 1.5$ [6.1a(1)].

6.1b(2) Periodic audits, performance sampling, chemical/physical audits [6.1b(2)].

6.1b(3) Departments within sector teams review processes and use process analysis and research, benchmarking, alternative technology, customer information [6.1b(3)]; no specific improvements as evidence of cycles.

Support

6.2a(1) Reliance on strategic plan: no details provided.

6.2a(2) Process teams flow chart, compare to similar processes, document; use CI methodology to establish and change processes [6.2a(2)]; get priorities from strategic plan [6.2a(1)].

6.2a(3) Operations, Corporate R&D, Site Services, Human Resources, Organizational Learning, Sales, Marketing, Product Distribution, Information Systems, Administration [Figure 0-1]. Requirements: cycle time, accuracy, costs with $C_{pk} \geq 1.5$ and $C_p \geq 2$ [7.5a]; example FDS requirements: accuracy, time to generate reports, containment of costs/revenues, timely reports that are clear and understandable [6.2a(3)]. Other than generation of reports by the Financial Data System, the application does not mention any specific support processes.

6.2a(4) Process control applications; focus on paper handling/administration [6.2a(4)].

6.2a(5) Process analysis and research, benchmarking, alternative technology, customer information; planning teams establish method for review [6.2a(5)].

Suppliers/Partners

6.3a(1) Five levels: unqualified, conditional, qualified, Pass Through Partner (PTP), certified; PTP/certified have reduced inspection; delivery/price assessed by Purchasing [6.3a(2)]; requirements: quality, delivery, price: critical process $C_{pk} \geq 1.5$ [BOV].

6.3a(2) Process capability and control requirements; incoming inspection if noncertified; purchasing reviews price and delivery; cost of doing business factor [6.3a(2)].

6.3a(3) Cost of doing business factor used to trigger action plans for reduced inspection costs; CFI asks suppliers to evaluate them through Preferred Customer Certification Program (PCCP) [6.3a(3)].

7 Results

7.1a *Key Areas:* There are five key customer requirements: *delivery, quality, pricing, responsiveness,* and *ease of doing business* [BOV]. The company is also committed to its credo: "To All Customers, We Promise *Service, Satisfaction,* and *Value*" [1.1a]. CFI's third strategy is "To be the *technology leader*" [1.1a(2)]. The measurable goal for these requirements is no more than 3.4 parts per million (ppm) defects or the six sigma program [6].

Levels: CFI measures *customer satisfaction* with delivery, quality, pricing, responsiveness, and ease of doing business. Satisfaction is measured on a five-grade scale (A–D, and F). The 1996 levels are as follows [Figures 7.1-4 to 7.1-7]: delivery between D and C for CPS and between B and A for Commercial and Automotive Sector (CAS), Defense and Aerospace Sector (DAS), and Nuclear and Specialty Sector (NSS); price between C and B for Consumer Products Sector (CPS) and DAS, B for CAS and NSS; quality between B and A for CPS, DAS, and CAS, A for NSS; responsiveness between B and A for CPS, CAS, and DAS and between C and B for NSS; and ease of doing business between D and C for CPS, B for CAS, between C and B for DAS, and between B and A for NSS. The 1997 levels for perceived *value* were 7 for CPS, 7.5 for CAS, 8.5 for DAS, and 9 for NSS [Figure 7.1-8]. CFI got 14 patents in 1997 as an indicator of technology leadership [Figure 7.1-9]. *Customer complaints* below 0.1/$000 sales.

Trends: The trend for number of patents issued is flat. Operations quality trends for CPS were improving; for NSS and DAS were improving except for 1992; for CAS were improving except for 1993. Operations yield trends were somewhat improving for all four sectors. C_{pk} trends were flat for CPS, CAS, and DAS at high levels and improving for NSS. On-dock performance trends were flat for CAS and CPS (at high levels), improving then flat for DAS, and flat then improving significantly for NSS. Trends for problem calls resolved within 24 hours improving for all four sectors. Trends for time to resolve critical and urgent calls, problem escalation, and times to answer calls and respond to problem calls are all improving. There are no trend results for satisfaction with product cost, perceived value satisfaction, and only 1996 results are shown for satisfaction with delivery, price, quality, responsiveness, and ease of business. For all sectors' customer satisfaction and for CAS composite satisfaction, the trends are flat.

Comparisons: CAS Composite Customer Satisfaction and the survey results on price, delivery, quality, responsiveness, and ease of business have both benchmarks and best competitor results. Patents issued have competitor results. The remaining measures/indicators do not have benchmarks or competitor results. For CAS composite customer satisfaction, the comparison is unfavorable. For the surveys, CPS 1996 results are no better than the best competitor on two of five indicators, with 1997 goals for these two set below the competitor results; CAS 1996 results are no better than the competitors on two of five indicators; for DAS, results are no better than the competitor on three of five indicators; and for NSS, results are no better than the competitor on one of five indicators. For patents issued, the comparison is favorable. No comparisons for 13 of 33 indicators shown; remaining 9 of 20 no better than best competitor.

7.2a *Key Areas:* financial—ROI (missing), profit margins; marketplace—market share, sales.

Levels: CPS profit margins above 1997 goal; others below.

Trends: % Total Available Market (TAM) excellent, sustained; CAS, CPS improving; unfavorable for DAS.

Comparisons: %TAM excellent versus best competitors; no comparisons for profit margins.

7.3a *Key Areas:* Survey measures, team/individual involvement, training, turnover, safety, worker's compensation; three employee groups: HRL (hourly), SE (salaried-exempt), SNE (salaried nonexempt).

Levels: Training (HRL, SE, SNE), turnover (SE, SNE), lost work days, Great Place To Work better than 1997 goals; worker's compensation, ratings, HRL turnover, team growth, HRL and SE team involvement, suggestions worse than 1997 goals.

Trends: 18 of 24 measures shown favorable; 3 of 6 values from survey unfavorable.

Comparisons: SE turnover better than benchmark (same industry); no comparisons or goals for service years, surveys, team awards; only six indicators had comparisons: 5 worse.

7.4a *Key Areas:* Suppliers have three requirements: quality, delivery, and price [6.3a(1)], and a cost-of-doing-business indicator [6.3a(3)]. Certified suppliers must also meet six sigma capability and control requirements [6.3a(1)].

Levels: CFI measures supplier *quality* using ppm defect rates: 1997 level of incoming material was between 0 and 250 ppm [Figures 7.4-3, 7.4-4]; 1997 level of supplier corrective action requests is 0.25% of receipts [Figures 7.4-5, 7.4-6]; no 1997 results are provided for supplier certification, but 1996 levels were 80 of 83 for CAS, 30 of 33 for CPS, 27 of 28 and 11 of 11 of the top 155 by dollar volume suppliers were certified [Table 7.4-1]. The 1997 levels for *delivery* [Figure 7.4-2] as measured by percentage received on time are 99% for G&A, 98% for material, and 93% for services. There are no *price* results.

Trends: The trends for number of suppliers, number of suppliers that are PTP and that are certified, percentage materials and G&A received on time, certified and noncertified supplier quality, Supplier Corrective Action Requests (SCARs), and percentage Corrective Action Request (CAR) closures are favorable and/or sustained. The trend for percentage services received on time is sustained.

7.5 *Key Areas:* Key process requirements include yield, quality, productivity, cycle time, scrap and waste [7.5a]. All critical processes must comply with the six sigma program [6.1].

Levels: The 1997 levels for on-dock *delivery* [Figure 7.5-6] are 100% for CAS, 99.8% for DAS, 99.2% for CPS, and 99% for NSS. The 1997 levels for *quality* are operations quality of 100% for CPS, 98% for DAS, 95% for NSS, and 82% for CAS [Figure 7.5-10]; warranty returns approximately 40 $PM for CPS, 70 $PM for DAS and NSS, and 80 $PM for CAS [Figure 7.5-4]; percentage of critical process with $C_{pk} > 1.5$ [Figure 7.5-1] 100% for CPS, CAS, and DAS, and 95% for NSS. There are no *pricing* results. Lead time to order fulfillment is one measure of *responsiveness*, with 1997 levels of 1 day for CAS and CPS, 18 days for DAS, and 114 days for NSS [Figure 7.5-7]. Other responsiveness measures could include problem calls resolved within 24 hours (1997 levels are CPS 98%, CAS 95%, NSS 90%, DAS 75%) [Figure 7.5-5], time to resolve critical problems (1997 CFI level is 98% within 2-hour specification) [Figure 7.5-22], time to resolve urgent problems (1997 CFI level is 94% within 24-hour specification) [Figure 7.5-23], problem escalation to manager (1997 CFI level is 2.2%) [Figure 7.5-24], telephone rings before answer (1997 CFI level is 71% within 2-hour specification) [Figure 7.5-20], and time to respond to problem calls (1997 CFI level is 90% within 2-hour specification) [Figure 7.2-21]. There are no *ease-of-doing-business* results.

The 1997 process *yield* levels are 93% for rivets, 98% for pins and bolts, and 100% for screws; and for operations, yield levels are 100% for CPS and CAS, 90% for DAS, and 85% for NSS. *Quality* levels for 1997 measured by warranty returns are 35 $PM for CPS, 75 $PM for CAS and NSS, and 100 $PM for DAS; and for sector operations quality are 99% for CPS and DAS, 77% for CAS, and 95% for NSS. The 1997 *productivity* levels are as follows, using product operations in $000 revenue/product employee: 230 for CPS, 190 for CAS, 185 for DAS, and 175 for NSS; using nonproduct operations in $000 revenue/product employee: 365 for CPS, 340 for CAS, 330 for DAS, and 220 for NSS. *Cycle time* 1997 levels are, for product design: 1 week for CPS and CAS, 3 weeks for DAS, and 18 weeks for NSS; and for setup, 1 minute for CPS and CAS, 17 minutes for DAS, and 100 minutes for NSS. *Scrap/ waste* is measured by solid waste, with 1997 levels of 8 tons for CPS and NSS, 5 tons for CAS, and 7 tons for DAS; by percentage reclaimed material, with 1997 levels of 0.5 for CPS, 2.5 for CAS and DAS, and 1.2 for NSS; and by percentage material wastage, with 1997 levels of 0.2 for CPS, 0.1 for CAS and NSS, and 0.35 for DAS.

Trends: Except for percentage yield of bolts and pins, all other six trends for yield are favorable. Quality from operations and as warranty returns had all favorable trends. The eight productivity trends are split equally between favorable and sustained (NSS product and all nonproduct except CPS). Cycle time trends are all favorable and/or sustained. Scrap/ waste trends are all favorable and/or sustained.

CHAPTER 6

Exercise 6.1

1. [5.3a] The word "good" makes this comment prescriptive. The examiner cannot judge whether the system is "good" or "bad." If Category 7 asks for results on this system, then the data will determine whether the system is "good" or "bad." Even then, the examiner

need not use the word ''good'' but only comment on the Results scoring dimensions. By repeating the purpose of the Item using the words in the Area to Address, the comment is nonprescriptive.

2. [5.3c] This comment is prescriptive and non-value-adding. This Item and Area to Address do not specifically ask for employees' views of management and leadership. While such views may be asked for in a survey, these views are not required for surveys, and surveys are only one possible source of data for this Area to Address [see Note (3)]. The comment would be more value added by identifying the specific subArea to Address to which it applies—it is unclear whether this refers to 5.3c(1) or 5.3c(2)—and by using the words in the Criteria.

3. [5.1b] This is prescriptive and non-value-added. Words implying a requirement should be worded by using the words of the Criteria. Rather than ''needs to include,'' a better approach might be ''The response does not include cash bonuses. . . . '' However, even with this wording, the comment is prescriptive because the phrase ''cash bonuses'' does not occur in this Area to Address. The phrase ''union worker'' may also be questioned, unless the applicant has identified this as an employee category. Thus, a better comment might be ''The company's compensation and recognition approaches do not appear to extend to all employees, such as union workers.''

4. [5.2a] This is a nonprescriptive comment. It is also a value-added comment, although it could be improved by making reference to the specific subArea to Address, especially since there are five. For example, the comment could state that ''[5.2a(1)] The company's key performance plans and needs are met through TESS by identifying potential.''

5. [5.2a(5)] This is a nonprescriptive and value-added comment. The phrase ''it is unclear'' is perfectly acceptable when followed with the specific criteria wording of the Area to Address. In this case, three things were required to be considered and, apparently, one was not—the one stated in the comment.

Exercise 6.2

<u>Purposes</u> senior leaders guide to set direction, develop and sustain leadership system
<u>Work Units/~~Key Areas~~</u> 11 senior executives in leadership system; leadership system to entire organization

1.1 Leadership System *(80 pts)*

Score Dim.	Area to Address	STRENGTHS
SY	a	CFI's credo, "To All Customers, We Promise Service, Satisfaction, and Value," translates to meeting the needs of its three stakeholders: shareholders, customers, and employees.
SY	a(1)	The senior staff holds itself responsible for world-class goals, benchmarks, customer inputs, and third-party quality standards. The senior management team uses various approaches (including active customer relationships through monthly and weekly meetings and quarterly meetings with stakeholders) to set levels on customer satisfaction, operational, financial, and market results.
SY	a(2)	CFI leadership system consists of their Management By Planning process coupled with a cascade review process to set direction and performance expectations, from which they developed five key business strategies. The strategies are based on their six values, which include customer-orientation and continuous learning. Companywide performance goals are set that aim for benchmark levels.
SY	a(3)	Senior executives communicate values, directions, expectations, customer focus, and continuous learning through various methods, e.g., new-hire orientation, management training, CFI culture workshop, BUMs, one-on-one meetings, informal communication sessions, and printed media. These are reinforced through feedback from employees, operations reviews, performance reviews, internal assessment processes, customer feedback, third-party surveys and assessments, independent external surveys, and ongoing training.
SY	a(4)	Overall company and work unit performance to plans and goals are reviewed in a variety of ways, daily, monthly, quarterly, and annually. The senior leadership heads the cross-functional support organization, which handles weakening or inadequate performance as a result of their reviews.
SY	a(4)	The leadership system is improved through the continuous learning (e.g., an annual 360° review of all senior managers, system effectiveness assessments, and the use of several personality and behavior assessment tools) of its senior leaders.
Score Dim.	Area to Address	AREAS FOR IMPROVEMENT
DE	a(1), a(3), a(4)	It is unclear the extent each senior executive is involved to [a(1)] set direction and seek opportunities; [a(3)] communicate and reinforce values, directions, expectations, customer focus, and continuous learning; and [a(4)] review overall performance, reinforce company direction, and improve the leadership system.
SY	a(1)	There is no description of a system for how senior leaders seek future opportunities.
CI	a(4)	There is no clear evidence of leadership system refinement and improved integration from cycles and analyses, e.g., number of improvement cycles the MBP process has gone through.

Purposes public responsibilities, practices good citizenship
Work Units/Key Areas locations - international (8) and national (7-8 major)
1.2 Public Responsibility and Citizenship *(30 pts)*

Score Dim.	Area to Address	STRENGTHS
SY	a(1)	CFI's key practices include publishing a code of conduct, which is reviewed annually with each employee, and giving legal training on ethical behavior — all new employees receive 4 hours and senior management, procurement personnel, customer contact employees, and project managers receive 40 hours. Each sector holds an annual environmental planning session to make 2, 5, and 10 years projections of its regulatory, legal, and ethical requirements on process costs, throughput, efficiency, and impact on surrounding communities. Site-committee reviews give specific consideration to process by-products.
CI	a(2)	CFI addresses its risks and regulatory, legal, and ethical requirements by including formalized product and process risk assessment, new business financial ROI analysis, product market assessment, environmental risk evaluations and planning sessions, regulatory scenario simulations, business simulations, and product level "business wargames" simulations.
SY	b	CFI promotes quality in partnerships with public agencies and organizations in various ways including cosponsorship of the 45th Annual Fastener Reliability Testing Institute Conference, funding employee-presented papers worldwide, donations, and sponsorship of Pennsylvania's Quality Award.
Score Dim.	Area to Address	AREAS FOR IMPROVEMENT
SY	a(1)	Except for regulatory requirements of by-products included in the strategic plan, there are no measures and targets for legal and ethical requirements and for risks.
CI	a(2)	There are no descriptions of systems for anticipating public concerns and for addressing these issues in a proactive manner.
DE	b	It is unclear whether the company and employee support extends to all major sites and all locations, especially in non-US communities.

Purposes strategic planning process: setting strategic direction, development of action plan (deployment)

Work Units/~~Key Areas~~ to entire organization, suppliers (major)

2.1 Strategy Development Process *(40 pts)*

Score Dim.	Area to Address	STRENGTHS
SY	a	CFI develops strategy through an annual planning cycle that goes from an analysis of the current situation to next year's operating plan. This cycle yields a product line business plan, a strategic long-range plan (SLRP), and annual plans that derive from the MBP process. The resulting strategic plan with five strategies includes measurable objectives and key results that define how objectives will be accomplished.
SY	a(1)-a(5)	In the analysis, the executive staff includes customer input to define world-class targets, Current Situation Analysis and benchmarking information to address the competitive environment, risk assessments, and the capabilities of suppliers and/or partners (through SCQI), and their own capabilities (through $C_{pk}s$).
DE/CI	b	The senior staff uses the MBP to translate the strategies into action plans through a breakdown analysis that yields tactics and projects from the corporate and strategic objectives. First line management and team leaders are included through a "catchball" process. The SLRP and annual plans that include supplier requirements are communicated and deployed through meetings (BUMs) and internal newspaper to the organization and through partnerships to suppliers and partners. Cascade reviews ensure alignment and tracking of performance.

Score Dim.	Area to Address	AREAS FOR IMPROVEMENT
SY	a(2)	It is not clear — especially since most measures reported in Category 7 do not have competitive comparisons — how CFI analyzes the competitive environment.
SY	a(3)	CFI's strategic planning process does not appear to systematically address financial, market, and societal risks.
SY	a(4)	It is not clear that the approach to addressing company capabilities includes human resource, technology, and business processes to seek new opportunities.
DE	b	The extent of deployment, alignment, and clear communication of the strategic plan is not clear because (1) some objectives do not have deadlines, (2) it is not clear how the human resource plan is derived from the strategic plan [see comments to Item 2.2], and (3) it is not clear that the seven major suppliers are partners.
CI	b	There is no evidence of refinement of strategic planning from tracking performance relative to plans.

Purposes key performance requirements and measures, HR plans, future projections
Work Units/~~Key Areas~~ entire organization, suppliers (major)

2.2 Company Strategy *(40 pts)*

Score Dim.	Area to Address	STRENGTHS
SY	a	CFI has specific action plans for all five key business drivers for each sector that are developed and deployed through a cascading "catchball" process so that corporate objectives (Table 2.2-1) eventually get translated into specific tactics at the line management level and specific projects at the team level. These action plans include key performance requirements and associated performance measures at different levels of the organization. Projects are funded annually using ZBB methodology, which allocates resources.
SY	b(1)	Changes in work design to improve flexibility, innovation, and rapid response include self-directed teams, self-audits, flexible manufacturing, reduction of management layers, increase of core competency skill teams, and a virtual work force buffer.
SY	b(2)	CFI's plans for employee development, education, and training include achieving a multi-skilled core work force, training a specialist cadre on advanced technologies, developing long-term skill needs, and developing a "buy" category of skill needs.
SY	b(3)	To compensate and recognize employees, CFI uses Employee Cash Bonus Program (levels will change from 15% to 25%), Executive Bonus Program, Stock Option Program (matching corporate contributions starting in 1997), achievement and recognition awards, and in 1997, it will revise career planning guidance to increase emphasis on employee growth and multi-skilled capabilities.
SY	b(4)	Recruitment goals include doubling the number of key external experienced hires from their External Sourcing Program, decreasing the cost per hire, increase offer and accept rates, increase the number of entry- to mid-level professionals filled by new college graduates, increase the number of non-Asian minority and technical female hires, and evaluate employee wellness programs.
CI	c	Table 2.2-1 has objectives and measures for the years 1997 to 2000 that address all five key business drivers. These goals reflect both world-class and best-in-class benchmarks for a three-year period and have targets to meet or exceed all competitive benchmarks in this time frame.

Score Dim.	Area to Address	AREAS FOR IMPROVEMENT
SY	a	Table 2.2-1 does not have information on resources committed to each year's plan.
SY	a	There is no clear distinction between short- and longer-term plans, since only CO4 objectives have dates and they are for the current year.
SY	b(1)-b(4)	The connection of the human resource plans to the strategies (Table 2.2-1) is not clear because they do not specify the strategy(ies) from which they are derived.
SY	c	There are no specific projections for any year beyond the current year.
CI	c	There are no specific comparisons nor explanation for the targets being "world-class" when current performance does not often meet its goals or bic comparison.
DE	a	It is unclear whether the cascade process extends to the individual/work level at all sites, US or non-US.

Purposes determine requirements/expectations/preferences; understand/anticipate needs; develop opportunities

Work Units/~~Key Areas~~ Big 5 auto and all major airframe manufacturers; top defense contractors

3.1 Customer and Market Knowledge *(40 pts)*

Score Dim.	Area to Address	STRENGTHS
SY	a(1)	CFI uses a Customer Expectation Determination process to gain knowledge about customers and markets and identify business opportunities that begins by identifying customer/market segments by sector and includes customer and competitor data. Information stored and analyzed in the MDS includes market share, competitor comparisons, product performance and comparisons, and customer comments. The entire set of data is validated through focus groups and various contact personnel.
SY	a(1)	The listening post is part of the Customer Expectation Determination process. Sales representatives attend an enhanced course on customer listening. CFI also analyzes new technologies and loss of significant orders, and searches for potential customers. Engineering stays current by reading technical journals and attending trade shows.
SY	a(2)	An Engineering, Sales, Production, Administration team assembles focus groups to determine specific features and their importance. The approaches to collecting information and their frequency vary by sector but include accessing professional societies, CFI and outside representatives, field service representatives, and customer surveys. CFI analyzes the data stored in the MDS to ensure objectivity and reliability by cross comparisons of inputs.
CI	a(3)	The Customer Expectation Determination process is a closed loop with the listening post evaluating and improving the adequacy, timeliness, and reliability of the information. As a result, CFI has improved its surveys and training.

Score Dim.	Area to Address	AREAS FOR IMPROVEMENT
SY	a(1)	It is not apparent that key competitor data are considered in determining or selecting customer groups and markets.
DE	a(1)	It is unclear how the listening approaches vary for CFI's different customer groups, which have different customer types, needs, and environment.
SY	a(2)	It is not apparent that information on customer retention and complaints is used to determine key product and service features and their relative importance.
CI	a(3)	It is unclear how often the Customer Expectation Determination process is evaluated and improved since it may be changed only when significant changes in customer attitude and opinion occur.

<u>Purposes</u> determine, enhance customer satisfaction: strengthen relations, improve offerings, support planning

<u>Work Units/~~Key Areas~~</u> Big 5 auto and all major airframe manufacturers; top defense contractors; four major competitors

3.2 Customer Satisfaction and Relationship Enhancement *(40 pts)*

Score Dim.	Area to Address	STRENGTHS
SY	a	Customers can access CFI through toll-free telephone and fax numbers 24 hours/day, 365 days, extensive voice and e-mail, home phone numbers of facility managers, postage-paid self-addressed cards attached to shipments, and 24-hour availability of staff at Service Centers.
SY/ CI	a(1)	Contact personnel meet weekly to establish service standards, e.g. response time to answer the phone, time to respond to problems, time to resolve urgent and critical problems, and problem escalation to manager. These staff use a three-step process for improving service standards: multiple inputs, an action focus group, and follow-up results. Follow-up often means additional training.
SY	a(2)	All formal and informal complaints are logged into the MDS, standardized, and classified as critical (resolve in 2 hours) or urgent (resolve in 24 hours). Critical complaints are assigned to field sales engineers and urgent complaints are assigned to field sales representatives. Assignees report each morning at product meetings. The MDS and ODS, which are available to everyone, automatically generate reports every four hours on complaint distribution and accumulate data on all complaints received anywhere in the world.
SY	b(1)	CFI follows up on customers by special surveys, monthly private visits to customers with past complaints, mail-back cards, and call-backs made by Service Center managers. Products with three or more complaints in a three-month period are addressed at monthly department meetings.
SY	b(2)	CFI uses a variety of surveys with different purposes and frequencies to determine customer satisfaction. The surveys ask questions related to satisfaction about their present supplier, intention or reason to change suppliers, expectation to continue with same supplier, and recommendation of current supplier. These surveys, with additional correlations, indicate which customers are likely to reorder.
SY	b(3)	Contracted universities and colleges, IFI surveys, and sector supplier information provide information about competitors. These are viewed as completely objective and reliable since the sponsor or provider are unidentified. CFI also does competitive product analyses.
Score Dim.	Area to Address	AREAS FOR IMPROVEMENT
CI	a(1)	The extent of refinement, integration, and maturity of personnel contact performance through cycles and analyses is not clear.
SY	a(2)	It is unclear how the complaint management process ensures that complaints are resolved effectively.
SY	b(1)	It is not clear that products receive prompt and actionable feedback with a potential three-month delay.
DE	b(2)	There is no difference noted in methods and/or measurement scales for different customer groups.
DE	b(3)	It is unclear what data are collected on all four major competitors, since some measures in Item 7.1 lack competitive data.

<u>Purposes</u> selection, management, use of information and data to support processes, improve performance
<u>Work Units</u>/~~Key Areas~~ key performance areas to all internal (sectors, sites) and external (suppliers, partners, customers) users;
4.1 Selection and Use of Information and Data *(25 pts)*

Score Dim.	Area to Address	STRENGTHS
SY	a(1)	Sector teams select data to be collected in five key areas: customer related, financial and market performance, human resources, supplier/partner performance, and product and service performance (including support functions). Comparisons and benchmarking data are also included. CFI uses a data system model that incorporates data from the CSS to each product sector in a way that addresses all five key business strategies. Senior management determines which top-level data should be common.
DE	a(2)	CFI relies on a worldwide data and information system with five major databases that are accessible through LANs, WANs, and PCs to deploy to users including PTP suppliers.
SY	a(3)	Sector teams hold weekly meetings with users, developers, customers, and suppliers to address whether the data are appropriate, needed, current, reliable, and accurate. Local PC terminals and at-home PCs ensure rapid access. Automation, flags, IS management (e.g., backups and diagnostics), and combinations of passwords and authorized entry lists, help maintain reliability.
CI	a(4)	The Data Management Team uses semiannual reviews (asking three critical questions) to improve successfully (see Figure 7.5-16) the data system uptime and responsiveness.
Score Dim.	Area to Address	AREAS FOR IMPROVEMENT
SY	a(1)	CFI views its shareholders as groups to satisfy, yet no data address ROI for investors. The application does not mention whether it collects data on pricing (one of five key customer requirements).
SY/ DE	a(2)	There is no description of how alignment with key company goals is ensured nor how appropriate information and data are deployed to external users, e.g. key customers and non-PTP suppliers.
SY	a(3)	It is not clear how internal software reliability is met.
CI	a(4)	There is no clear evidence of refinement and improved integration of information and data and its effective use (as it is with deployment in Figure 7.5-16) through cycles and analyses.

<u>Purposes</u> selection, management, use of comparative information and data to improve overall performance
<u>Work Units/~~Key Areas~~</u> key measures and processes
4.2 Selection and Use of Comparative Information and Data *(15 pts)*

Score Dim.	Area to Address	STRENGTHS
SY	a(1)	CFI determines its needs and priorities through the strategic planning process by identifying areas where competition is great and market share is low, there are gaps in knowledge of competitive performance, and others do better on CFI's critical competencies. Relevant critical processes are benchmarked by sectors, with each sector responsible for benchmarking two to three specific functions and Corporate adds up to five more areas annually.
SY	a(2)	The criteria for seeking sources of comparative information and data include identifying benchmark partners that will have the most immediate affect or provide longer term capability, determining competitor performance, and identifying companies outside the industry with better performance than CFI and its competitors.
SY	a(3)	Stretch targets are set by considering the benchmark team's data and costs, process, disruption, criticality of processes, and impact on other processes, with many goals set through the PTP process.
CI	a(4)	Comparative information and data's effectiveness are evaluated at the annual strategic plan update. Their effectiveness are improved by selecting benchmarking partners on the basis of their potential contribution and by doing public domain searches before formal benchmarking visits.
Score Dim.	Area to Address	AREAS FOR IMPROVEMENT
SY	a(1)	It is unclear how the criteria of great competition and low market share ensure improvement of overall company performance on the five key strategies since each sector is market leader with a constant lead over the past five years.
SY	a(3)	The response states *what* information and data are used to set stretch targets but not *how*, especially since most goals are below the benchmark and bic levels shown in Category 7 and CFI claims to set world-class targets (Item 1.1).
CI	a(4)	There does not appear to be a fact-based process for evaluating and improving comparative information and data and their deployment.
DE	a(1)-a(3)	While every key performance area (see Items 7.1-7.5) has at least one measurement and/or indicator with comparison results, most do not, making it unclear the extent of deployment of the use of comparision information and data.

<u>Purposes</u> analysis and review of overall performance to assess progress and identify key improvement areas

<u>Work Units/~~Key Areas~~</u> organizational units; suppliers/partners

4.3 Analysis and Review of Company Performance *(40 pts)*

Score Dim.	Area to Address	STRENGTHS
SY	a	Data from the five information systems are available and updated on demand through an extensive LAN, WAN, and PC network. Each system has basic information and analytical tools.
SY	a(1)	The MDS contains customer data from various sources, which are accessible through the LAN and PCS. The data include market share analyses by sector, customer complaints, customer survey results and other issues, e.g. product delivery promises, new product design and production status, delivery dates.
SY	a(2)	CFI monitors operational performance and capabilities (which are correlated), e.g. production status, C_{pk} data, on-dock deliveries, employee data, and technical specifications, through the ODS, HRDS, and TDS.
SY	a(3)	The MDS contains competitive performance information, e.g. market share, prices, and product compatibility, which are analyzed to project costs and performance gaps.
SY	a(4)	The FDS provides management with sales, inventories, profits, and cash flow, in addition to analyses showing correlations between profit margins and lower costs from improved process performance.
CI	b	CFI uses several reviews at different levels of the organization to assess progress relative to goals, plans, and changing business needs (Table 4.3-1). Review findings are translated into priorities through MBP process, which includes deployment of new plans throughout the organization and to suppliers.

Score Dim.	Area to Address	AREAS FOR IMPROVEMENT
SY	a(1)-a(4)	There is no description of *how* the performance data are integrated in each subArea 4.3a(1)-4.3a(4).
CI	b	The response does not include *how* review findings are translated into improvement priorities.
CI	b	There is no evidence (see Items 7.2-7.5) of refinement and improved integration from the analyses and reviews.
DE	b	It is not clear how non-PTP suppliers get review information appropriate to them.

Purposes how work/job design and compensation/recognition lead to employee contribution to company performance

Work Units/~~Key Areas~~ all categories of employees; all sectors and locations

5.1 Work Systems *(40 pts)*

Score Dim.	Area to Address	STRENGTHS
SY	a(1)	Employees can take the initiative and assume responsibility through various teams: self-audit, manufacturing self-sustained, PDTs, project, NWTs, problem-solving, task forces, review boards, and decentralized suggestion programs, resulting in improved performance, e.g., $17.4 million savings, reduced product introduction time, and reduced throughput time. Over 550 active teams existed in January 1997.
SY	a(2)	Flexibility, cooperation, rapid response, and learning is fostered through education and training to develop multi-skilled employees and reduction of management layers. For example, through HR SLRP, CFI deployed 91% of its Macon operation, with a variety of financial and supportive actions. In Los Angeles, CFI partnered with Technical-Vocational Institute of LA to create an associate's degree program in metallurgical technology. Over 95% of all decisions are made through team processes.
SY	a(3)	Employees communicate at BUMs, written publications, e-mail, and voice mail.
CI	b	Employees are evaluated on both individual and team involvement through the CFIAA, with 223 successful PITs between 1995 and 1996. Based on survey results, CFI altered its employee performance rating scale and introduced a "trending" component.
Score Dim.	Area to Address	AREAS FOR IMPROVEMENT
SY	a(1)	It is not clear to what extent teams are used at all sites, especially nondomestic since the 1995-6 sample of PIT abstracts was only for domestic sites and results in Item 7.3 do not separate US from non-US employees.
SY	a(2)	It is unclear how the approaches used to foster flexibility, cooperation, rapid response, and learning address current and changing customer requirements.
SY	a(3)	It is unclear how these forms of communication lead to better meeting customer and/or operational requirements.
DE	b	It is unclear whether the compensation and recognition approaches apply to all categories of employees, e.g., management and nonmanufacturing personnel.
CI	b	It is unclear how the compensation and recognition approaches reinforce overall work systems, performance, and learning objectives.

<u>Purposes</u> education/training address plans, build knowledge/capability, improve employee performance/development

<u>Work Units/~~Key Areas~~</u> all categories of employees; all sectors and locations

5.2 Employee Education, Training, and Development *(30 pts)*

Score Dim.	Area to Address	STRENGTHS
SY	a(1)	CFI uses four methods to meet education and training needs that range in duration of deployment and maturity of organizational deployment: functional area training departments, CFI University, Corporate Education and Development, and external training consultants.
SY	a(2)	Training and education design starts with employees annually updating their career enhancement forms, resulting in recommendations regarding education, training, and work assignments.
SY	a(3)	CFI has an extensive system for delivering training called TESS, which includes developing partnerships, various delivery modes, and training effectiveness evaluation, and also relies on the CFI University Deployment system with its functional "colleges" and expert training consultants. Corporate Education and Development provides numerous courses on CFI's values and practices to support them, some specifically for new hires.
SY	a(4)	TESS tracks employee education and training progress with employee evaluations on skills, knowledge, capabilities. A three-step process is used to reinforce on-the-job training, which includes post-tests and simulation practices.
CI	a(5)	CFI evaluates and improves its education and training through measures of their effectiveness and has increased its spending on education and training 24% since 1989 — this is three times the national average.

Score Dim.	Area to Address	AREAS FOR IMPROVEMENT
SY	a(1)	It is unclear *how* these education and training methods address key performance plans and needs.
SY	a(2)	There does not appear to be a system for designing education and training and the CFI University Deployment System just recently started. It is unclear whether the designs support the company's approach to work and jobs since employees may reject recommended courses.
DE	a(3)	It is unclear whether the extensive delivery system extends to non-US locations.
CI	a(5)	It is unclear how the evaluation and improvement of education and training take into account company performance and employee objectives and, without results, how many cycles of refinement have occurred.

Purposes how work environment/climate supports employee well-being, satisfaction, motivation
Work Units/~~Key Areas~~ all categories of employees; all sectors and locations
5.3 Employee Well-Being and Satisfaction *(30 pts)*

Score Dim.	Area to Address	STRENGTHS
SY/ DE	a	To proactively prevent accidents or incidents, Safety Awareness Teams regularly audit each plant and improvement teams are assigned to find root causes. All hazardous materials are identified, "red flagged," and their reduction measured and tracked, aiming for 45% reduction in solvent-based incidents by 1998, elimination of ozone-depletion compounds by 1999, 50% hazardous waste reduction by 1998, and 60% reduction of cumulative trauma injuries by 1997.
SY	a	The Safety Improvement Team fosters and directs the quality of environment, health, and safety (EHS), including championing improvements through equipment vendors and publication of performance standards. EHS issues include illness, injury, and ergonomics.
SY/ DE	b	CFI has implemented various programs worldwide to improve employee well-being and satisfaction, e.g., an extensive EAP that includes mental health, chemical dependency, child-care, 100% tuition reimbursements, financial support; recreational facilities; nine-week sabbaticals. These vary by location following local laws and customs.
SY	c(1)	Employee satisfaction is determined through regular surveys, focus groups, one-to-one interviews, BUMs, and other assessment and feedback tools.
CI	c(2)	The HRET, a multi-sector team, assesses how human resource strategies and practices contribute to business performance. They have shown involvement reduced turnover by 14% and increased employee satisfaction by 43%, contributed 67% of cycle time improvements, and 83% of quality improvements.
Score Dim.	Area to Address	AREAS FOR IMPROVEMENT
DE/ SY	a	It is not clear that the EHS efforts are applied to all locations since data in Figure 6.2-13 (Lost Work Day Cases) refer only to U.S. locations and the ergonomic improvements may be only in Boston. The responses do not address potential differences among employee groups, e.g., locations, jobs. There are no goals for illness and ergonomics.
SY/ DE	c(1)	There is no description of the key factors that affect employee well-being, satisfaction, and motivation nor how CFI assesses its work climate. There is no mention of how well-being and motivation are determined.
CI	c(2)	There does not appear to be any correlation between employee well-being and motivation and business results. It is not clear how these relations lead to identifying improvement activities.

<u>Purposes</u> product/service designed; production/delivery processes designed, implemented, improved
<u>Work Units/~~Key Areas~~</u> all key products (4 types - sector dependent) and customers (auto, airframe, defense)

6.1 Management of Product and Service Processes *(60 pts)*

Score Dim.	Area to Address	STRENGTHS
SY	a(1)	The listening post activities yield understanding of customer requirements for new products and services. FSEs contribute through their knowledge of customer requirements and needs. Customers provide detailed designs, which are reviewed, evaluated, and approved by customers and a CFI sector product team. CPS uses industry standards, CAS uses standards and user specifications, and DAS uses military specifications.
SY	a(2)	The Product Design Cycle includes four phases — Concept/Feasibility, Engineering and Validation Test, Production Validation Test, and Product Maturity Acceptance — with reviews after the first three phases to ensure quality and operational requirements are met through DOE analysis. Sectors modify the design review steps to meet their needs. Process goal is C_p's $\geq$ 2.0.
SY	a(3)	Inclusion of engineering, manufacturing, quality, logistics, marketing, field service, purchasing, suppliers, and customers in the design review, and EVTs and PMAs ensure trouble-free introduction and delivery. A PDR ensures that dimensions, materials, and suppliers are screened for capabilities, design margins, and safety allowances, and that PTP relationships are established. A FDR ensures that capabilities are achieved in early production. A PAR ensures that they meet all requirements in full production. Finally, the DFQR process ensures that production processes have been fully considered before launch.
SY	b(1)	Receiving material check, drawing and upsetting, machining and threading, heat treating, chemical, product review, shipping and distribution are the key processes that must have C_{pk}'s $\geq$ 1.5 to maintain appropriate quality, cycle time, and cost requirements.
SY	b(2)	Periodic audits, performance sampling, and complete audits (e.g., chemical and physical) are used to manage processes and process steps, with specific actions for out-of-control situations.
CI	b(3)	CFI relies on departmental teams using process analysis and research, benchmarking, alternative technologies, and information from customers to evaluate and improve its product and service processes. Changes in processes from one sector are passed on to other sectors.

Score Dim.	Area to Address	AREAS FOR IMPROVEMENT
SY	a(1)	There is no description of how changing technology is incorporated into product and service designs.
DE	a(2)	It is unclear how production/delivery process designs differ by sectors because of different products.
SY	a(3)	There is no mention of how delivery processes are coordinated with design and production processes to ensure trouble-free introduction and delivery.
DE	b(1)	It is unclear how each sector's key processes and principal requirements differ because of different products and customers.
CI	b(3)	The evaluation and improvement process description does not include evidence of refinement and improved integration as a result of cycles and analyses.

<u>Purposes</u> support service design, management, and improvement
<u>Work Units/~~Key Areas~~</u> all support functions' key processes; all sectors

6.2 Management of Support Process *(20 pts)*

Score Dim.	Area to Address	STRENGTHS
SY	a(1)	Each support service department determines its key processes and principal requirements from information supplied by the strategic planning process to set priorities. Process teams work with internal customers to set limits for each process step, which must have C_{pk}'s $\geq$ 1.5.
SY	a(2)	Support processes are designed by process teams, who flowchart processes, compare them to similar processes, fully document them, and structure them using the continuous improvement methodology, including necessary measurements and sampling plans.
SY/ DE	a(3)	The key support areas are Corporate R&D, Site Services, Human Resources, Organizational Learning, Sales & Marketing, Product Distribution, IS, and Administration, which must have C_p's $\geq$ 2 to maintain cycle time, accuracy, and costs requirements, e.g., FDS requirements include accuracy, time to generate reports, containment of costs and revenues, and timely reports (see Item 7.5).
SY	a(4)	Support processes are managed through process control applications, heavily weighted in paper handling and administration, and through specific plans for the frequency of sampling and the parameters to be measured.
CI	a(5)	Support processes are evaluated and improved through process analysis and research for new techniques and equipment, benchmarking in the goal-setting mode, alternative technology for personal computers and communications, and information from customers at regular meetings. This approach has significantly improved time to pay invoices and days to close the books.
Score Dim.	Area to Address	AREAS FOR IMPROVEMENT
SY	a(1)	The response does not provide specific details on how key requirements are determined.
SY	a(2)	The response does not provide details on the sampling plan and specific parameters.
SY/ DE	a(3)	There are no key support processes nor their specific requirements listed other than FDS.
SY	a(4)	The response does not describe *how* processes are managed.
DE/ CI	a(5)	It is unclear whether the evaluation and improvement process is applied to all support areas since there are no examples from Site Services, Organizational Learning, Sales & Marketing, and Product Distribution. Thus, it appears that the use of process analysis, benchmarking, alternative technology, and customer information is reactive and not specifically designed to achieve better performance proactively.

Purposes supplier/partnering processes, relationships, performance management and improvement
Work Units/~~Key Areas~~ all key suppliers (7 major and top 155 by dollar volume) for all sectors
6.3 Management of Supplier and Partner Processes *(20 pts)*

Score Dim.	Area to Address	STRENGTHS
SY	a(1)	CFI established the PTP process to better meet performance requirements through lessons learned. CFI views suppliers at its top two levels (PTP and certified) of five as preferred suppliers. Certified suppliers must meet requirements on quality, delivery, and price with processes attaining $C_{pk} \geq 1.5$.
SY	a(2)	CFI ensures requirements are met through process capability and control requirements. Noncertified suppliers meet requirements through incoming inspection on product quality while purchasing reviews price and delivery. When lot rejection rates exceed 250 ppm, a SCAR is sent to the supplier who is then visited to develop a Corrective Action Plan. CFI uses a Cost of Doing Business factor to make subsequent procurements with all suppliers. PTP suppliers are linked to the EDI while others receive Supplier Rating System information through the mail.
CI	a(3)	CFI provides supplier training and recognition to improve suppliers' abilities to meet requirements. Suppliers are encouraged to become certified ($C_{pk} \geq 1.5$) so that inspection is eliminated and the CODB factor also encourages suppliers to maintain high quality, so fewer inspections result in lower costs. CFI meets annually with top 40 suppliers to develop improvement plans. Its Preferred Customer Certification Program determines whether they were customer of choice based on timeliness, quality, clarity of communication, supplier satisfaction.
Score Dim.	Area to Address	AREAS FOR IMPROVEMENT
SY	a(1)	It is unclear what the delivery and price requirements are to be qualified, PTP partner, or certified supplier.
SY	a(2)	It is unclear how supplier C_{pk}'s and whether they can maintain them are determined. There is no description of how purchasing ensures that pricing and delivery requirements are met.
SY	a(2)	There appears to be a discrepancy between when a SCAR is issued (250 ppm) and the quality requirement of $C_{pk} = 1.5$ (3.4 ppm): a 75-fold difference in number of defects.
CI	a(3)	There may not be an improvement process for addressing pricing and delivery requirements.
CI	a(3)	The PCCP, introduced last year, has not completed a cycle yet.
DE	a(1)-a(4)	It is unclear whether PCCP extends to all seven major suppliers.

Purposes summary of customer satisfaction and dissatisfaction
~~Work Units~~/Key Areas satisfaction with quality, delivery, price, responsiveness, ease of doing business; value & patents; customer retention and complaints

7.1 Customer Satisfaction Results *(130 pts)*

Score Dim.	Area to Address	STRENGTHS
LE	a	Current level for all-sector customer satisfaction is above "B" for NSS and DAS and for customer retention is 100% for NSS. Current level for customer complaint calls for NSS and CAS is below 0.1/$000 sales.
TR	a	The long-term trends for customer retention and customer complaint calls are favorable for all four sectors.
TR	a	The long-term trends for customer dissatisfaction as measured by customer complaint calls show decreasing dissatisfaction for all four sectors.
CO	a	CFI measures each sector's customer satisfaction in five areas: delivery, price, quality, responsiveness, and ease of business (eob). Current levels by sector are good in several areas relative to competitors. CFI is far superior to its best competitor on number of patents issued.
Score Dim.	Area to Address	AREAS FOR IMPROVEMENT
LE	a	Current levels are poor for CPS's customer retention and for DAS's and CPS's customer complaint calls.
TR	a	There are no trends for the second business strategy (Figure 7.1-8): "To be recognized as the producer of the highest value fasteners," measured by perceived value. There are no trend data for customer satisfaction with delivery, price, quality, responsiveness, ease of business for CPS, DAS, and NSS.
CO	a	There are no comparisons for 13 of 33 indicators shown: all-sector customer satisfaction for CPS, DAS, and NSS; customer retention for any sector; value for any sector; and complaints for any sector. CAS composite performance is worse than the competitor shown, who may not be the best competitor. For 9 of the 20 indicators shown in Figures 7.1-4 and 7.1-7, the current levels are no better than the best competitor.

<u>Purposes</u> summary of key financial and marketplace results
~~Work Units/~~Key Areas financial: ROI (shareholders), profit margins (CFI); marketplace: market share, sales

7.2 Financial and Market Results *(130 pts)*

Score Dim.	Area to Address	STRENGTHS
LE	a	Profit margins for CPS are above '97 goal.
TR/ CO	a	All four sectors have excellent, sustained current levels and trends for %TAM compared to best competitors. Profit margins show improving trends for CAS and CPS.

Score Dim.	Area to Address	AREAS FOR IMPROVEMENT
KA	a	There are no data for shareholders' ROI, a critical stakeholder requirement.
LE	a	Current profit margins are below '97 goal for NSS and substantially below '97 goal for CAS and DAS.
TR	a	Profit margin trends are unfavorable for DAS (due to increased pressures from government and competitors) and flat for NSS during past five years.
CO	a	There are no comparisons of profit margins to competitors or benchmarks.

<u>Purposes</u> summary of human resource results: employee well-being, satisfaction, development, work performance
~~Work Units/~~Key Areas survey measures; team/individual awards & involvement; training; turnover, safety, worker's compensation

7.3 Human Resource Results *(35 pts)*

Score Dim.	Area to Address	STRENGTHS
LE	a	Current performance is equal to or better than '97 goals for Training Hours for HRL, SE, and SNE; Turnover for SE and SNE; Lost Work Days; and GPTW.
TR	a	Trends for 18 of 24 measures shown are favorable: Lost Work Days, Worker's Compensation, employee ratings of customer orientation and quality, Turnover, SE service, Training, individual and team awards, Team Growth, Team Involvement, and Suggestions.
CO	a	SE Turnover is better than benchmark (in the industry).

Score Dim.	Area to Address	AREAS FOR IMPROVEMENT
KA/ LE	a	Lost Work Days, Worker's Compensation, and the Survey Results were not separated by sector. Results for Worker's Compensation, employee ratings, HRL Turnover, Team Growth, HRL and SE Team Involvement, and Suggestions were worse or substantially worse than their '97 goals.
TR	a	Trends in employee surveys for three of the six values (Results, Risk Taking, Discipline) are unfavorable.
CO	a	There are no goals or comparisons for Service years, employee survey ratings, and team awards. Of the six indicators that had bic or benchmark comparisons, only SE Turnover was better.

Purposes summary of supplier and partner performance
~~Work Units~~/Key Areas supplier level; delivery, price, and quality (C_{pk}s and corrective action); Cost of Doing Business

7.4 Supplier and Partner Results *(25 pts)*

Score Dim.	Area to Address	STRENGTHS
LE	a	Of the 155 suppliers that deliver 80% of supplies by dollar volume, 148 were certified in 1994.
TR	a	The trends for all measures shown (PTP, Receiving History, certified and noncertified supplier quality, SCARs, and CAR closures) are favorable.
CO	a	G&A and materials delivery levels are near the bic level.

Score Dim.	Area to Address	AREAS FOR IMPROVEMENT
KA	a	No results are shown for price and Cost of Doing Business, two of the four principal requirements for key suppliers. Data are not shown specifically for the seven major suppliers: Southern States Steelmill, Tilken Steel Supply, Alacon Aluminum Foundry, Nippon National Mill, Precise Explosive Corporation, Wilmont Wire, Inc., and Northern Rod & Bar Distributor.
LE	a	The graph's scale for certified supplier quality was too gross to tell whether the 3.4 ppm, which is required by $C_{pk} = 1.5$, is attained: it does not appear to be met.
CO	a	Only Supplier Receiving History and SCARs had bic's and, along with non-Certified Supplier Quality, had '97 goals. No results met goals or bic.

Purposes summary of product and service results
Work Units/Key Areas C_{pk}s, cycle time, productivity, quality, delivery; accuracy, speed, access - support processes

7.5 Company-Specific Results *(130 pts)*

Score Dim.	Area to Address	STRENGTHS
LE	a	Levels are excellent for percent critical processes with C_{pk}'s $\geq$ 1.5 (CPS, CAS, and DAS); cycle time indicators (CPS and CAS); yield for screws (CAS and CPS); percent calls resolved (CAS); percent shipment on time (CAS). IS availability is also excellent in uptime and system requirements; and % Reclaimed Material exceed '97 goal, Time to Resolve Critical Problems and System Response equal '97 goal.
TR	a	The trends for almost all indicators shown are favorable and sustained.
CO	a	Results for Scrap Material exceed bic, % Reclaimed Material exceed '97 goal, Time to Resolve Critical Problems and System Response equal '97 goal.

Score Dim.	Area to Address	AREAS FOR IMPROVEMENT
KA	a	Results are not shown by sector for IS indicators, Self-Assessment, and all HR indicators.
LE	a	It is not clear whether the goals cited are for all sectors/products or for some sectors/products. If for all, some sectors/products have poor levels: rivets (process yield), DAS and NSS (operations yield and lead time to order fulfillment), and DAS (problem call resolved within 24 hours). Current levels are substantially below '97 goal for 15 of the 47 indicators shown.
LE	a	The strategic objectives for 100% of critical processes (Table 2.2-1) is C_{pk} > 2.0 (CPS), 1.8 (CAS), and 1.7 (DAS) but data are not shown relative to these levels.
CO	a	Only Warranty Returns, Operations Productivity for both Products and Non-products, Scrap Material and % Reclaimed Material have bics and performance for the first four is substantially poorer than the bic.

CHAPTER 7

Exercise 7.1

SUMMARY SCORESHEET

	CRITERIA			AWARD SCORES		
	APPROACH-DEPLOYMENT					
Item	SY	DE	CI	Score	Pts	Total
1.1	90	50	50	60	80	48.0
1.2	50	30	40	40	30	12.0
2.1	60	70	40	60	40	24.0
2.2	40	90	50	60	40	24.0
3.1	60	60	60	60	40	24.0
3.2	70	90	60	70	40	28.0
4.1	60	70	70	70	25	17.5
4.2	40	40	40	40	15	6.0
4.3	30	70	50	50	40	20.0
5.1	50	40	20	40	40	16.0
5.2	30	30	50	30	30	9.0
5.3	40	50	80	60	30	18.0
6.1	60	40	60	60	60	36.0
6.2	20	20	30	20	20	4.0
6.3	50	50	40	50	20	10.0
	RESULTS					
Item	LE	TR	CO			
7.1	30	20	30	30	130	39.0
7.2	40	50	80	60	130	78.0
7.3	30	30	20	30	35	10.5
7.4	60	50	40	50	25	12.5
7.5	30	70	30	50	130	65.0
TOTALS				1000		501.5

SCORING DIMENSIONS

SY = Systematic DE = Deployment CI = Continuous Improvement
LE = Levels TR = Trends CO = Comparisons

CHAPTER 8

Exercise 8.1

Table B.22   Answer to Exercise 8.1: Preparation for Consensus

<u>Purposes</u> summary of supplier and partner performance

<u>Key Areas</u> supplier level; delivery, price, and quality (C_{pk}s and corrective action); Cost of Doing Business

7.4 Supplier and Partner Results *(25 pts)*

Score Dim.	Area to Address	STRENGTHS
LE	a	Of the top 155 suppliers by dollar volume, 148 were certified in 1994. While the number of suppliers has decreased, the number of certified suppliers, and the percent of business they represent, has increased from 1992 to 1996 in all four product sectors (Table 7.4-1).
LE/ TR	a	Supplier performance data (e.g. on-time delivberies) shown have excellent levels and positive trends. Both certified and noncertified Supplier Quality Results show dramatically improving performance trends.
CO	a	G&A and materials delivery levels are excellent compared to bic.
Score Dim.	Area to Address	AREAS FOR IMPROVEMENT
KA	a	No results are shown for price, one of the three principal requirements for key suppliers and for Cost of Doing Business, a key measure of supplier performance (both identified in Item 6.3).
CO	a	Of the six graphs showing key measurements of supplier performance, only two have comparable data to best-in-class and none have benchmarks. In both comparisons to bic, CFI lags behind its competitors and no explanation is given.

Exercise 8.2

Table B.23   Answer to Exercise 8.2: Conflict Resolution—Corrective and Preventive Actions

Issue	CORRECTIVE ACTION	PREVENTIVE ACTION
A	• Do as a group • Assign to individual at the meeting • Reschedule meeting	(For A only) • Leader provides form and instructions to all and requires copies *before* meeting
B	• Review comment definitions • Have two comments: Strength and Area For Improvement • Use an "unclear" comment	(For all issues, A through E) • Agree before meeting on how each type of conflict will be resolved
C	• Ask both sides to identify what is missing or included • Add a comment that satisfies both • Modify an existing comment	• Develop an evaluation sheet on the skills needed for consensus: show the evaluation sheet to each member and have self- and other-evaluations
D	• Identify the specific word or phrase that is nonvalue-added/prescriptive: choose another word	• Before consensus, ask for suggestions from each member on how to resolve each type of conflict
E	• Identify from the scores on the scoring dimensions the minimum and maximum range possible and discuss at that level • Identify where scores on the scoring dimensions differ and discuss at that level • Identify where comments associated with the different scores on the scoring dimensions may be the cause and discuss at that level	• Ask each member before consensus, how they would rate themselves in being able to avoid each type of conflict

CHAPTER 9

Exercise 9.1

Table B.24 Answer to Exercise 9.1: Site Visit Issues Worksheet for Item 3.1

Site Visit Issues Worksheet

Examiner Initials *KCM* Applicant Number *CS*

Item No. *3.1*   Issues:

A. [a(1)] Are key competitor data considered in selecting/determining customer groups and markets?

[SY}

B. [a(1)] How do listening approaches differ by customer groups? [DE]

C. [a(2)] How are customer retention data and complaints used to determine key product service

features and relative importance? [SY]

D. [a(3)] How is CED process evaluated and improved? [CI]

Strategy (Person to Interview, Evidence)

A. Who to ask: IS/MDS representative

What to ask: Who are your key competitors? Describe how data on competitors enter the MDS and the

CED process? How are the data used to select customer groups and markets? Can you show me an

example?

B. Who to ask: sales representatives from different sectors, e.g. CAS and NSS

What to ask: Describe the CED process for your sector. How does it vary according to different

customer groups within your sector?

C. Who to ask: Engineering/Sales/Production/Administration team members

What to ask: Describe the focus group process. What are the inputs to the process? Do they include

customer retention and complaint data? How were these data used? Can we see some minutes from

your last finished focus group? What did you achieve?

D. Who to ask: manager/director of responsible for CED (by sector?)

What to ask: When was the last time the CED changed? Why?

Table B.25   Answer to Exercise 9.1: Site Visit Issues Worksheet for Item 3.2

Site Visit Issues Worksheet
Examiner Initials <u>*KCM*</u>   Applicant Number <u>*CS*</u>

Item No. *3.2*   Issues:

A. [a(1)] Determine the extent of refinement of personnel contact person through cycles and analyses. [CI]

B. [a(2)] Determine how the complain management process ensures complaints are resolved effectively. [SY]

C. [b(1)] Determine how products receive prompt and actionable feedback with a potential three-day feedback. [SY]

D. [b(2)] Determine if different survey methods and/or scales are used for different customer groups. [RE/DE]

E. Determine what data are collected on the four major competitors. [DE]

Strategy (Person to Interview, Evidence)

A. <u>Who to ask:</u> contact personnel, Service Center manager

<u>What to ask:</u> Describe the current service standards. How do contact personnel learn them? How are they revised? When are they revised? When was the last time they were revised? Do you have records documenting these revisions?

B. <u>Who to ask:</u> FSE, FSR

<u>What to ask:</u> Describe the complaint management process and your role. What is the standard for resolving complaints. How often are problems not resolved within this standard? Show me documents indicating how and when complaints are resolved and whether satisfactorily.

C. <u>Who to ask:</u> service center manager/central engineering group representative

<u>What to ask:</u> Describe the process for addressing product complaints and your role in the process. What happened the last time a product received three complaints? What evidence do you have that the customer was satisfied with the resolution and its timeliness?

D. <u>Who to ask:</u> CFI contact person with universities doing surveys

<u>What to ask:</u> Do you use the same methods for surveying different customers from different CFI sectors? If so, why? If not, describe the differences.

E. <u>Who to ask:</u> IS representative

<u>What to ask:</u> Tell me what data are collected on your four major competitors. How are these data used?

CHAPTER 10

Exercise 10.1   CFI scored in band 4, as a result of an individual scorebook. See Table 10.1 for an explanation of the scoring bands. There is evidence of effective approaches to many Areas To Address, with deployment varying among work units.

The comprehensive leadership system, while improved through individual learning of its leaders, does not appear to involve them all. CFI's approach to its public responsibilities and citizenship do not appear well deployed to non-U.S. communities. In addition, there is little evidence of a proactive systematic approach addressing public concerns.

The strong leadership system depends on its extensively deployed Management By Planning process. One major weakness is the lack of goals for any year beyond the current. Another is that its human resource component does not appear to be derived from the strategic plan. However, the deployment of CFI's efforts to develop and manage its employees is almost complete.

CFI has a strong customer focus, relying on a Customer Expectation Determination process, surveys and other listening approaches to understand customers and markets and make improvements in its processes. Further refinement may depend on clearer differentiation among customers when segmenting, listening, and surveying.

While there is a strong description of a benchmarking process and some examples of its benefits, many measures do not have goals, comparisons, or benchmarks. So, it is unclear how benchmarking is actually used to set stretch targets. Analysis of companywide performance is weak, which may be due to the lack of goals in the strategic plan.

CFI relies on an extensive set of teams to effectively address work system needs as shown by team performance and process results. It appears that a major reason for the successful employee contributions is the multifaceted education, training, and development system. However, without the identification of key factors affecting employee well-being, satisfaction, and motivation, it is not clear that the work environment addresses all employees' needs.

Compared to CFI's sound, systematic approaches in addressing its core and supplier processes, its approach toward support process management is weak. There are beginnings of systematic approaches without much evidence of a fact-based improvement process in place.

Results vary from poor to excellent. Some areas (e.g., market share, sales, and some process measures) show excellent levels and sustained improvements. Other areas (e.g., human resource performance and customer satisfaction) show mediocre or poor performance against goals and best competitors. While market share is excellent, financial results are poor to mediocre, and no results are shown for measures of interest to shareholders, a critical stakeholder.

CHAPTER 12

Exercise 12.1   1.

Table B.26   Answer to Exercise 12.1: Summary Scoresheet for Case Study (Award Levels I and II)

SUMMARY SCORESHEET

CRITERIA				AWARD LEVELS								
APPROACH-DEPLOYMENT				LEVEL I			LEVEL II			LEVEL III		
Item	SY	DE	CI	Score	Pts	Total	Score	Pts	Total	Score	Pts	Total
1.1	90	50	50	90	80	72.0	70	80	56.0	60	80	48.0
1.2	50	30	40	50	30	15.0	40	30	12.0	40	30	12.0
2.1	60	70	40	60	40	24.0	60	40	24.0	60	40	24.0
2.2	40	90	50	40	40	16.0	60	40	24.0	60	40	24.0
3.1	60	60	60	60	40	24.0	60	40	24.0	60	40	24.0
3.2	70	90	60	70	40	28.0	80	40	32.0	70	40	28.0
4.1	60	70	70	60	25	15.0	70	25	17.5	70	25	17.5
4.2	40	40	40	40	15	6.0	40	15	6.0	40	15	6.0
4.3	30	70	50	30	40	12.0	50	40	20.0	50	40	20.0
5.1	50	40	20	50	40	20.0	40	40	16.0	40	40	16.0
5.2	30	30	50	30	30	9.0	30	30	9.0	30	30	9.0
5.3	40	50	80	40	30	12.0	40	30	12.0	60	30	18.0
6.1	60	40	60	60	60	36.0	50	60	30.0	60	60	36.0
6.2	20	20	30	20	20	4.0	20	20	4.0	20	20	4.0
6.3	50	50	40	50	20	10.0	50	20	10.0	50	20	10.0
RESULTS												
Item	LE	TR	CO									
7.1	30	20	30	NA	130	NA	30	130	39.0	30	130	39.0
7.2	40	50	80	NA	130	NA	40	130	52.0	60	130	78.0
7.3	30	30	20	NA	35	NA	30	35	10.5	30	35	10.5
7.4	60	50	40	NA	25	NA	60	25	15.0	50	25	12.5
7.5	30	70	30	NA	130	NA	70	130	91.0	50	130	65.0
TOTALS				550		303.0	1000		504.0	1000		501.5

SCORING DIMENSIONS

SY = Systematic   DE = Deployment   CI = Continuous Improvement
LE = Levels   TR = Trends   CO = Comparisons

2. Write an Executive Summary for the case study at award level I.

CFI scored in band 5, as a result of an individual scorebook. See Table 11.1 for an explanation of the scoring bands. There is evidence of effective approaches to many Areas To Address and identification of key measures for many areas of importance to the organization.

The comprehensive leadership system improves through individual learning of its leaders. CFI has several approaches to its public responsibilities and citizenship. However, there is little evidence of a proactive systematic approach addressing public concerns.

The strong leadership system depends on its Management By Planning process. One major weakness is the lack of goals for any year beyond the current. The other is that its human resource component does not appear to be derived from the strategic plan.

CFI has a strong customer focus, relying on a Customer Expectation Determination process, surveys and other listening approaches to understand customers and markets and make improvements in its processes.

While there is a strong description of a benchmarking process and some examples of its benefits, it is unclear how benchmarking is actually used to set stretch targets. Analysis of companywide performance is weak, which may depend on the lack of goals in the strategic plan.

CFI relies on an extensive set of teams to effectively address work system needs. These teams and individuals are educated, trained, and developed through a multi-faceted system. However, without the identification of key factors affecting employee well-being, satisfaction, and motivation, it is not clear that the work environment addresses all employees' needs.

CFI has sound, systematic approaches in addressing its core and supplier processes that include key process measures. However, it has only the beginnings of systematic approaches toward support process management.

Appendix C—Case Study

BUSINESS OVERVIEW

1. Basic Description of Company

Nature of Business
Colony Fasteners, Incorporated (CFI), is the world leader in the design and manufacture of fasteners. It has a distinguished history as the oldest fastener manufacturer in the United States, steeped in tradition dating back to 1877. The company started as a supplier of bolts, screws, rivets, and staples to the U.S. Army in the decade after the Civil War ended. Its original founders were two brothers, James and Thomas Pote, who served in the war as armorers. During their service, they were constantly frustrated with the quality and durability of the fasteners used for the artillery and undercarriages. They saw the need to supply a higher quality product to the Army and mobilized around the opportunity. With their background, experience, and service connections, they founded Colony Fasteners in Philadelphia, Pennsylvania.

Originally, the product lines were limited to the types of fasteners used by the Army. Quickly, they expanded their products as new markets and customers were identified. Significant opportunities occurred in supplying the U.S. Navy's shipyards in Philadelphia and the surrounding areas. The company saw rapid growth with the defense building booms during wars and conflicts.

Significant growth occurred after World War II and during the Korean War. Off-shore expansion began utilizing the tremendous leverage of inexpensive labor and facilities. Product lines grew when business segmentation began in the mid-1950s. CFI reorganized, establishing three significant business sectors: Consumer Products, Commercial and Automotive, and Defense and Aerospace. Each

sector served a distinct market. Customer segmentation occurred, with new approaches to customer satisfaction emerging. Strong partnerships were forged with the defense establishment; ties to the automotive industry were deeply rooted; and CFI was leading the commercial market. Figure 0-1 shows how CFI is segmented according to business markets. Included in the business segments is the Corporate Support Sector (CSS), which is the organizational unit responsible for all corporate functions, such as Information System (IS) and Human Resources (HR).

The Nuclear and Specialty Sector (NSS) was established in the late 1950s with the advancement of the nuclear power industry and requirements for exotic materials and manufacturing processes. It was also the expansion of the aerospace environment that drove the requirement for special types of fastener devices that included explosive components and special processing. CFI introduced fasteners with strain gauges embedded in the products.

Size, Location, Ownership
CFI is a worldwide manufacturer with nearly $1 billion in sales and 21 sites in the Americas, Europe, and Asia.

The world headquarters is in Philadelphia. Manufacturing locations by sector are Consumer Products (Juarez, Mexico; Sao Paulo, Brazil; Xiang, China; El Paso, TX); Commercial and Automotive (Dearborn, MI; Milwaukee, WI; Macon, GA; Jacksonville, FL; Oyama, Japan; Nagoya, Japan); Defense and Aerospace (Philadelphia, PA; Santa Ana, CA; Los Angeles, CA; Boston, MA); and Nuclear and Specialty (Los Angeles, CA; Philadelphia, PA; Salt Lake City, UT [specializing only in explosive fasteners]; and Berlin, Germany). Other locations include sales offices in most major U.S. cities and significant cities around the world, a regulatory office in Washington, DC, and regional sales hubs (East Coast office is Philadelphia, PA; West Coast office is Los Angeles, CA; Great Lakes office is Detroit, MI; Southeast office is Dallas, TX; Asia/Pacific office is Tokyo, Japan; European office is Calais, France). Note that the majority of employees assigned to a sales hub are located out of small offices and their homes to more conveniently locate them with their customers.

The Colony Fasteners Case Study was prepared for use in the 1995 Malcolm Baldrige National Quality Award Examiner (MBNQA) Preparation Course. It has been modified to correspond to the 1997 MBNQA Criteria.

The Colony Fasteners Case Study describes a fictitious company. There are no connections between the Colony Fasteners Case Study and any company, either named Colony Fasteners or otherwise. Other companies cited in the Case (customers, suppliers, etc.) are also fictitious.

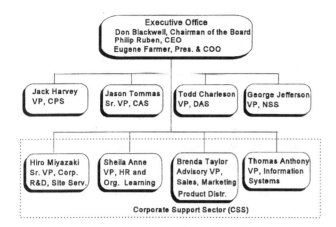

Figure 0-1 Senior management organization.

Nearly 56% of employees and 70% of sales are in the U.S. sites, with Philadelphia (8.2% employees, 11.4% sales), Los Angeles (17.7% employees, 12.1% sales), Dearborn, MI (9.2% employees, 13.6% sales), Santa Ana (7.8% employees, 5.2% sales), Milwaukee (2.1% employees, 11.1% sales), Jacksonville, FL (2.9% employees, 5.0% sales), and Macon, GA (4.1% employees, 4.2% sales) being the major U.S. sites.

In 1972, with growth and expansion driving the corporate direction, CFI went public on the New York Stock Exchange (NYSE symbol: CFI).

Major Markets
Today, CFI is strong, reflecting a growth pattern that is unparalleled in its industry. The company is represented in all major industrialized countries in the world, with manufacturing locations spanning from Asia to South, Central, and North America and to European Economic Community (EEC) countries.

Products range from exotic to ordinary. CFI has products sitting on the moon, embedded in spacecraft heading out of this solar system, and holding together deep sea mining equipment 20,000 feet below the ocean's surface. Explosive products are included in most aircraft life-critical pilot ejection systems and in 85% of all automotive passive airbag restraint systems. Each and every nuclear reactor in the United States and most in the free world have CFI fasteners at critical locations in their systems. The defense sector provides fasteners to all branches of the U.S. military and most armies of the free world. CFI fasteners are used in critical locations, from the compressor turbines of jet engines to the wheel studs supporting most of the rolling armament around the world. The ordinary products include pins, bolts,

rivets, and screws used to assemble a wide variety of household products, from refrigerators and lawn mowers to cabinet hinges.

CFI's markets are segmented into four distinct sectors. Each sector serves a worldwide customer base that is serviced by a network of distributors, wholesalers, jobbers, and retail sales outlets. The four sectors are as follows.

1. *The Consumer Products Sector* ($250 MM) designs and manufactures simple screws, rivets, pins, and bolts of inexpensive materials, which are sold at low cost for all types of uses. Major customers include a large base of distributors, wholesalers, jobbers, and retail outlet chains.

2. *The Commercial and Automotive Sector* ($400 MM) designs and manufactures fasteners used in industrial products and by all major automotive manufacturers around the world. The largest users of CFI products include the "Big 3" in the US and the "Big 2" in Japan. Most smaller manufacturers in the US, Europe, South America, and Japan are also consumers of the same products supplied to the major automotive manufacturers.

3. *The Defense and Aerospace Sector* ($200 MM) designs and manufactures high-quality, high-performance fasteners for special products used in airframe, spacecraft, and defense products. Customers include manufacturers of airframe, spacecraft, and defense products, which purchase or contract CFI-fabricated fasteners. Because the products are so specialized in construction and require extensive testing and qualification, CFI dominates this market.

4. *The Nuclear and Specialty Sector* ($50 MM) designs and manufactures fasteners for nuclear reactors, fusion devices, and radiation-hardened products and fasteners of extremely complicated design, materials, and applications like explosive bolts for ejection systems on fighter aircraft. Few manufacturers in this market contest CFI's presence. Most manufacturers of defense-related aircraft use CFI products from this sector (e.g., explosive bolts for ejection systems). The nuclear power market is well served by the products from CFI. They are in almost all nuclear installations around the world.

Employee Profile
CFI has a unique culture, one that is recognized throughout the world by its customers and

competitors alike. It is open, communicative, and constructively challenging. Employees openly talk and challenge each other. Managers and executives seek to ensure the highest quality products, in the least amount of time, and with the highest value for the customer. It is the highest embodiment of an "open door policy" seen in our benchmarking efforts on human resources and organizational development. Teams are actively involved throughout the world, driving CFI to excellence with a minimum of organizational barriers.

Figure 0-2 shows employee growth to 9941 since the company's formation in the late 1870s. The shift to off-shore labor is responsible for the transition between the U.S. and non-U.S. workers. The employee base at CFI contains hourly, nonexempt, and salaried contributors (approximately 61%, 18%, and 21%, respectively). Most hourly workers have completed high school or its equivalent (92%). A large percentage (56%) of the salary nonexempt have some college education, a two-year degree, or technical school credentials. Salaried employees have an expectation of being college graduates. While the majority of them have bachelors (83%), masters (32%), and doctorates (14%), a small number (17%) are actively pursuing their academic goals using CFI's education support package.

The corporation started a profit-sharing program with its employees in 1988. The approach annually splits corporate profits over a specified profitability value, pending a Board of Directors review: 50% for the corporation, 50% for employees (which is shared equally among all worldwide employees).

Today's employees live a common vision while striving for higher levels of performance.

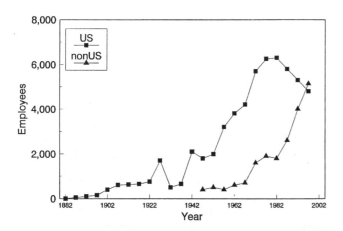

Figure 0-2   Employee growth history.

2.   Customer Requirements

During the 1960s and 1970s, some customer focus was lost. The demands of new technology, growth, and new marketing development and the rapid expansion of the defense and aerospace business put a veil in front of customer awareness. CFI lost ground relative to its customer satisfaction levels.

In the mid-1980s, it became apparent that something had happened. Customers were no longer first on the list of critical business priorities. Senior management reflected on the company's roots and determined that if this course continued, it would lose entirely its eroding market position. Ultimately, the company could suffer irreparable damage.

Senior management defined the elements of change in how the company would operate. Customers would again be placed first and foremost in everything employees do. Some old approaches to customer satisfaction were reinstalled. The notion of "Back to Basics" began to drive the company the way it was originally founded. These changes occurred in the mid-1980s. CFI's customers noticed the change in how they were being serviced and how their needs were again a driving force in the business relationships. As a result, CFI established five key requirements by which they ask customers to measure them:

- Delivery
- Quality
- Price
- Responsiveness
- Ease of doing business

The two brothers began the business with a credo founded in quality:

To All Customers We Promise Service,
Satisfaction, and Value.

To this day, this credo hangs in every CFI location worldwide. They instilled this spirit in employees, customers, and suppliers from the very beginning, believing that if they, and all their employees, lived true to these words, a successful enterprise would emerge. Today's business success is living testament that their vision was clear.

CFI's visibility occurred before the extensive scandal erupted concerning counterfeit bolts and fasteners illicitly distributed throughout the industry. It helped to prevent serious tainting of CFI's reputation. The scandal was a wake-up call to the industry and its customer base. CFI used this opportunity to further its already established reemergence of customer orientation. The scandal drove Congressional passage of the Fastener Quality Act (FQA) of 1990 for new regulations in the industry and placed a pall over all suppliers in varying degrees.

Four years ago, a major customer initiated the need for suppliers to be oriented to the Malcolm Baldrige National Quality Award (MBNQA) Criteria, and CFI began proliferating the six-sigma approach to its supplier base. This reinforced and placed further emphasis on CFI's process controls, which had already begun in the 1950s. Six sigma is now used in mainstream product production, support services, business services, and outreach to CFI's supplier base.

3. Supplier and Partnering Relationships

CFI uses a worldwide network of distributors, wholesalers, jobbers, and retail sales outlets to move its products. Of the 788 suppliers, 420 are raw material suppliers and distributors; major suppliers include Southern States Steelmill, Tilken Steel Supply, Alacon Aluminum Foundry, Nippon National Mill, Precise Explosive Corporation, Wilmont Wire, Incorporated, and Northern Rod & Bar Distributor. They supply materials such as wire, rod and bar stock, explosive components, and lubricants. Many suppliers additionally provide the materials and equipment needed to turn the raw materials into sellable products. These include cutting tools and small and large manufacturing equipment used to test and evaluate the quality of the finished products. Some services are contracted by CFI, such as maintenance, cafeteria, health services, and temporary workforce employees.

Suppliers are included in product design, verification, qualification, and analysis of field failures. Each supplier is expected to perform according to contract. They are measured and managed using these contract expectations. Through several forums and types of communication vehicles, their inputs are used to improve the delivery cycle, increase customer satisfaction, and improve profitability for every link in the delivery chain.

4. Competitive Factors

Position
CFI is the leader in our industry. Because it has been in existence since the late 1800s, many strong bonds have been established between it and its customers. These bonds and partnerships contribute to its position in the industry.

Competitors
CFI has four major competitors: Special Performance Products (SPP), Critical Life Components, Incorporated (CLC), Worldwide Pins Corporation (WP), and Top Flight Hardware, Incorporated (TFH). In many areas, however, CFI has hundreds of competitors, such as the Consumer Products Sector. Most competitors are small and have a limited life span of 5 to 10 years. In the Commercial and Automotive areas, CFI is a leader, but has strong competition from off-shore manufacturers supplying competitive products at very low prices. Some competitors have been in business for a very long time and have demonstrated their staying power. They are the ones offering the greatest challenge to maintaining and growing our current market share position. CFI has been supplying the defense industry for over 100 years and has clearly demonstrated in this market its willingness to meet ever-changing and very demanding requirements. While there are many competitors, most are short lived and are driven through contract awards. CFI is the largest U.S. supplier of products to this market segment. Nuclear and Specialty Sector products are driven, almost exclusively, by contracted specifications and requirements. CFI has few competitors in this market segment. It has the leadership position in a small field of specialty fastener manufacturers. Often, the small manufacturer accepts a contract for specialty products then subcontracts the work to CFI because of our manufacturing capabilities and demonstrated design knowledge.

5. Other Factors

Regulatory Environment
CFI is in a highly regulated industry in some market segments. Because it supplies products to the defense, aerospace, and nuclear market, it is bound by a wide variety of requirements and regulations associated with each one. Additional regulations and requirements are imposed on CFI for the products it manufactures and markets outside the United States.

Environmental regulations and requirements are similar to most manufacturing operations. CFI is regulated on the amount and type of effluents and waste discharge, safety considerations for its workers, and community safety activities.

There are some unique regulations and requirements imposed on the Salt Lake City facility due to its processing of explosive materials. These include employee and community safety, testing and evaluation operations, and registration of some devices with bureaus of the U.S. and foreign governments.

Changes in Strategy
In today's daily operations, CFI is always focused on the future, especially in terms of customer needs and expectations and operational results. This is evident in the graphs, tables, and figures. Many show 1997 values; these represent the best foresight of the 1997 expected results.

The 1960s and 1970s were business heydays. Growth was dramatic, with the defense and automotive sectors leading the contributions. Technology advancements were happening at blinding speed.

During the 1980s, CFI took a hard look at how it addressed its customers' needs. Many staff members had seen the successes of process control and began exploring new methods of process improvement and control. They were early converts of the teachings emerging from the universities and technology-based companies. During these years, many engineers and managers versed in quality principles, who are today's quality leaders and visionaries, were brought in to teach and share process improvement methodologies.

The original credo of the two brothers forms the basis for all actions, internally and externally.

TERMS AND ABBREVIATIONS

A & B

Benchmarking. Process of identifying the best practices in a specific area and the levels for their resulting output; also, b'mark.

bic. Best in class

BUM. Business update meeting; a method used to periodically communicate key corporate messages.

C & D

CAR. Corrective action request.

CAS. Commercial and Automotive Sector.

Certification. Supplier qualification process.

C/F. Concept/feasibility; a phase of the new product development process.

CFI. Colony Fasteners, Incorporated.

CFIAA. CFI Achievement Award; CFI's "Nobel Prize."

CFIUS. CFI University system.

CFC. Chlorofluorocarbons.

CIS. Corporate information system.

CO. Corporate objective.

CODB. Cost of doing business.

C_p. Ratio between the full distribution of a process and its allowable specification limits.

C_{pk}. The single-sided ratio (worst case) between the one-sided distribution of a process and its allowable specification limits.

CPS. Consumer Products Sector.

CSA. Current situation analysis; an approach to data and information aggregation and analysis.

CSS. Customer Support Sector.

Customer Window. An analytical tool that quantifies subjective data using two crossed axes and related scoring.

Cycle time. Time it takes to complete a process.

DAS. Defense and Aerospace Sector.

Design rules. The detailed design requirements used during the new product design process for CFI fastener products.

DFM. Design for manufacturability.

DFQR. Design for quality and reliability.

DMR. Discrepant material report.

DOC. Department of Commerce.

DOD. Department of Defense.

DPM. Defects per million (opportunities).

E & F

EAP. Employee Assistance Program.

EBP. Executive Bonus Program.

EDI. Electronic data interchange.

EHS. Environmental, health, and safety.

EIA. Engineering Information Architecture.

E-mail. Electronic mail.

Empowerment.   Chartering employees to make important decisions and participate in key business decisions; based on the principle that employees know their job best and that decisions should be made at the lowest possible levels.

EPA.   Environmental Protection Agency.

EVT.   Engineering and validation test; a phase of the new product development process.

Fastened Together.   CFI company newspaper.

FDR.   Final design review.

FQA.   Fastener Quality Act (1990).

FDS.   Financial Data System.

FSE.   Field sales engineer.

G & H

G&A.   General and administrative.

GPTW.   Great Place To Work; a CFI core value.

GRP.   Graduate Rotation Program.

GSS.   General Site Services.

HRDS.   Human Resource Data System.

HRET.   Human Resources Evaluation Team.

I, J, K, & L

IFI.   Industrial Fastener Institute.

IS.   Information System.

ISO 9000.   International Organization for Standardization 9000; an international set of standards for quality system elements.

JIT.   Just in time; usually reserved for supplier-customer delivery processes.

LAN.   Local-area network.

M & N

MBNQA.   Malcolm Baldrige National Quality Award.

MBP.   Management by Planning.

MDS.   Marketing Data System.

MRB.   Material Review Board.

MRC.   Management Review Committee.

NASA.   National Aeronautics and Space Administration.

NRC.   Nuclear Regulatory Commission.

NSS.   Nuclear and Specialty Sector.

NWT.   Natural Work Team.

O, P, Q, & R

ODS.   Operations Data System.

OSHA.   Occupational Safety and Health Administration.

PAR.   Product acceptance review.

Partners.   (1) customers; (2) suppliers; (3) internal customers/suppliers; (4) business engagements, domestic and foreign; and (5) government and regulatory agencies.

PAS.   Performance against schedule.

PCCP.   Preferred Customer Certification Program.

PC.   Personal computer; often a node on a LAN.

PDCA.   Plan, Do, Check, Act; a process used to analyze a process methodically and improve it.

PDR.   Preliminary Design Review.

PDT.   Product (or Process) Development Team.

PIT.   Performance Improvement Team.

Plan.   The strategic, tactical, and operating plan that results from semiannual execution of the MBP process.

PLBP.   Product line business plan.

PM.   Preventive maintenance.

PMA.   Process maturity acceptance; a phase of the new product development process.

POR.   Plan of record; annual financial operating plan.

PTP.   Pass Through Partnerships; an approach used to communicate lessons learned upstream and downstream.

PVT.   Process validation testing.

QAT.   Quality Action Team.

QIT.   Quality Improvement Team.

Q'Link.   An electronic vehicle used to communicate quality messages and plans around the world.

QST.   Quality Steering Team.

RCA.   Root cause analysis.

ROI.   Return on investment.

S & T

SAT.   Safety Awareness Team.

SCAR.   Supplier Corrective Action Request.

SCQI. Supplier Continuous Quality Improvement.

Sectors. CFI business units; product sectors.

SFE. Society of Fasteners Engineers.

SIT. Safety Improvement Team.

Six sigma (6σ). A statistical measurement and analysis process used to determine process capability.

SLRP. Strategic long-range plan.

SMDE. Single-minute die exchange.

SNE. Salaried nonexempt employees.

SO. Strategic objective.

SPC. Statistical process control.

Tactic. A level of the strategic plan defined by MBP.

TAM. Total available market.

TDS. Technical Data System.

TESS. Training and Education Support System.

Top Hat Award. Recognition program at the local level within a sector.

Total quality. Performance in response to CFI corporate values.

360° review. An employee's annual review process that uses data and information from management, peers, and subordinates.

U, V, & W

Upset. A process used to minimize material loss during fastener heading.

Values. Six key concepts on which CFI behaviors are based.

WAN. Wide-area network.

X, Y, & Z

ZBB. Zero-based budget; a process that determines which strategic plan elements are going to receive funding for the coming period.

1 LEADERSHIP

1.1 Leadership System

CFI's unwavering credo has always been

> To All Customers, We Promise Service,
> Satisfaction, and Value.

This translates into CFI's mission to do an outstanding job for shareholders, customers, and employees. The leadership system balances each group's distinct set of expectations and needs. Shareholders expect a fair return on their investment. Customers expect advanced performance solutions with superior quality and service, competitive pricing, on-time delivery, and organizational responsiveness. Employees expect challenging jobs, the means to be successful, and recognition for their contributions and achievements.

1.1a(1) Set Directions, Seek Opportunities

The senior management team drives CFI's strategic directions to new levels of customer satisfaction, operational results (including product quality and human resources), and financial and market success. The approaches used include

- active customer relationships used to derive the next set of expectations and insights into where the marketplace is heading,

- quarterly visits with customers, suppliers, and partners around the world to gather data about CFI and world-class competition,

- monthly and weekly meetings with customers to collect information about customer satisfaction levels and to stay current on customer-recognized world-class standards,

- sponsorship of critical benchmark studies to bring into the business unique approaches that contribute to improvements at the sector and corporate levels,

- review of competitive intelligence assembled using a formal data and information gathering methodology that strives to reinforce the company's belief in ethical behavior, and

- evaluation of government directions acquired via the dedicated office in Washington, DC, and at other key Department of Defense (DOD) and National Aeronautics and Space Administration (NASA) locations.

1.1a(2) Leadership System Description

Values
The senior executives ensure CFI achieves its mission and serves its unique interests through a dynamic foundation of corporate values and key business strategies.

CFI's values are slightly adjusted periodically to maintain behavioral balance as the company matures. Today, CFI has six values that represent its corporate culture and define how its employees behave and what customers can expect from its employees' performance (Table 1.1-1).

Company Direction
Management by Planning (MBP) is the CFI approach for policy deployment (see Item 2.1). It is a top-down, cascaded, and validated approach that identifies the critical strategic objectives, strategies, tactics, and projects required to secure continued corporate success. Inputs about CFI's current situation integrate with key organizational management structures into short- and long-range plans. The strategic and tactical plans, including owners, leading or lagging indicators, and goals for success, are transferred to all layers of the organization.

High-Performance Expectations
The leadership team developed five key business strategies to address its customers' expectations of world-class high performance:

1. Deliver products to customers on time and defect free (six sigma levels).

2. Be recognized as the producer of highest value fasteners.

3. Be the technology leader in the introduction of revolutionary fastener products.

4. Protect the environment at all worldwide locations and set benchmark levels of compliance.

5. Be recognized as number one in employee satisfaction at all worldwide locations.

The implementation of our strategies starts with setting challenging and competitive goals. Active comparisons and benchmarking have shown all levels in the organization how we compare and are used as the basis for setting targets that will result in CFI "being the benchmark" in all key areas. In the process of cascading our goals throughout the organization, a key element in achieving the

Table 1.1-1 CFI Values and Behaviors

Value (It means to us ...)	Behaviors (We strive to ...)
Results - We are results oriented.	Set challenging goals; Execute flawlessly; Focus on output; Assume responsibility; Confront and solve problems.
Risk Taking - To succeed we must maintain our innovative environment.	Embrace change; Challenge the status quo; Listen to all ideas and viewpoints; Encourage and reward informed risk taking; Learn from our successes and mistakes.
Customer Orientation - Partnerships with our customers and suppliers are essential to our mutual success.	Listen to our customers; Communicate mutual intentions and expectations; Deliver innovative and competitive products and services; Make it easier to work with us; Serve our customers through partnerships with our suppliers.
Quality - Our business requires the continuous improvement of our performance to our Mission and Values.	Set challenging and competitive goals; Do the right things right; Continuously learn; Develop and improve; Take pride in our work.
Great Place To Work - A productive and challenging work environment is key to our success.	Respect and trust each other; Be open and direct; Work as a team; Maintain a safe workplace; Recognize and reward accomplishments; Be an asset to the community; Have fun!
Discipline - The complexity of our work and tough business environment demands a high degree of self-discipline and cooperation.	Properly plan, fund, and staff projects; Pay attention to detail; Clearly communicate intentions and expectations; Make and meet commitments; Conduct business with uncompromising integrity and professionalism.

performance objectives is for each layer of the organization to take pieces of appropriate objectives. People from each organizational layer decide how much each can contribute to the objectives so that the end results, when aggregated, will meet or exceed the objective.

Customer Focus
The entire management system, from planning and execution to individual performance review, includes key elements of internal and external customer needs and expectations. Our four major product sector structure enables us to focus these entire organizations on the unique requirements and expectations of their customers. Within each sector's organization, a mirroring of major customer organizations occurs whenever possible, with dialog occurring at several levels between CFI and its counterpart customers.

Continuous Learning
Continuous learning is a way of life at CFI. The leadership team actively reviews how it leads, plans, and provides strategic guidance:

- Annual 360° review of all senior managers. At the executive office level, this includes semiannual review by designated members of the Board of Directors. Annual reviews of the entire senior management teams are conducted by the board in conjunction with the annual corporate financial review.

- Employee surveys are performed biannually, with 100% of the corporation participating. Contained in the survey are cross-referenced questions targeted at determining the effectiveness of company leadership.

- System effectiveness assessments using various models are conducted on all sectors of the corporation. Contained in the instruments are areas that address the effectiveness of management approaches and the styles used by the leadership team.

- Many personality and behavior assessment tools are used to aid personal development of the senior management team and its individual members. Examples include the Myers-Briggs type indicator, Survey of Management Practices assessment, and Quality Leadership surveys.

1.1a(3) Communication and Reinforcement

Communication
A wide range of communication activities is used to continually project quality values, objectives, goals,

and expectations throughout the CFI organization. Among these are the following:

- New-hire orientation is frequently taught by senior management, providing all employees with a detailed presentation of the CFI values and what they mean to the senior leadership.

- Management training courses and curricula offer extensive information and experiential learning on applying and role modeling the CFI values. These courses are designed for each management level.

- The CFI culture workshop is propagated throughout the organization and taught monthly for all new employees. It provides an in-depth presentation of the corporation's values, behaviors, and culture.

- Business update meetings (BUMs) are quarterly meetings presented to all employees worldwide. The agenda is to communicate openly the changes and the status of the corporation. Typical topics include the resurrection of Back-to-Basics, competitive threats, new product developments, and interpretations of CFI values in relation to recent business course changes.

- One-on-one meetings are core to CFI's culture, providing an opportunity for employees to raise issues important to them with their managers and supervisors. The schedule and agenda are set by the employees, with a guideline that these one-on-one meetings should occur at least monthly to maintain an open communication line.

- We disseminate our values through informal communication sessions such as open meetings by factory managers to communicate how they perceive and deploy our values. Business sector managers lead "open door days" for individual employees to discuss their concerns and issues with the senior managers of their businesses.

- Printed media provide a formal method of communicating values, objectives, and goals. These include newsletters, posters, brochures, and a magazine, all helping to promote better understanding of CFI values. Examples include *Fastened Together*, which is the company's core magazine containing all types of messages; *Voice of the Customer*, which describes the customers' perspective of our products and services; and *Q'Link*, which is the company's quality communication vehicle. Voice and electronic mail (E-mail) are used by the senior executive team to communicate real-time messages to all locations around the world using global broadcast capabilities.

Reinforcement

Senior executives continuously monitor and reinforce performance in response to company values through feedback from employees, operations reviews, performance reviews, internal assessment processes, customer feedback, third-party surveys and assessments, independent external surveys, and ongoing training. Examples of these include the following:

- In 1996, CFI conducted its biannual worldwide employee survey to measure performance in response to corporatewide values. Several changes were made by the leadership team due to the feedback of survey respondents, including simplifying the description of company values, modifying CFI's performance appraisal system, changing some of the basic employee training, improving the strategic planning system.

- All levels of management are retrained every year in developing and delivering annual performance reviews. This training includes guidelines for measuring employee performance in response to the six values.

- CFI actively seeks customer information on how well it is performing to its values. Focus teams use a common instrument to regularly conduct self-audits.

- Independent external surveys also provide key data used in monitoring CFI's performance in response to customer requirements. In a recent *Industry Age* survey released in January 1995, commercial and automotive customers rated CFI as number one among all suppliers in quality, reliability, product line coverage, and company reputation.

- Third-party assessments are typified in the use and interpretation of the MBNQA Criteria as they relate to CFI's business. As seen in Figure 1.1-1, CFI adopted the MBNQA model and realigned the elements to better match its culture, behaviors, and business operations. CFI actively uses local, state, and national award programs as a forum to invite experts into its organizations to assess and respond to its systems.

- Performance is monitored through extensive surveys on company values. This ongoing focus provides feedback on how well the values are role modeled and the extent to which they drive day-to-day activities.

1.1a(4) Review Company's Overall Performance

Senior executives are intimately involved in measurement, assessment, and review of all facets

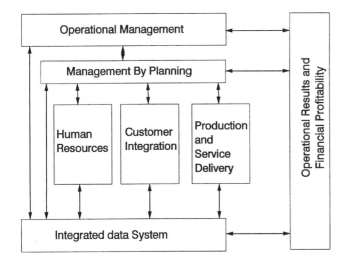

Figure 1.1-1 Colony Fasteners, Incorporated business model.

of CFI operations. They actively participate in periodic reviews at the corporate and sector level. They drive reviews of new proprietary product development programs for high-profile customers. All information is used to manage the business sectors for higher yields and increased contributions to market share growth.

If a business sector or geographic area shows a decline in performance, the senior manager teams with key leaders of that unit to ensure that adequate steps are taken to accelerate continuous improvement and reverse the worsening conditions. Often, they use specialists from other parts of the operation. Figure 0-2 shows a high-level mapping of cross-functional support from the Corporate Support Sector to the business sector organizations. Organizational barriers are minimized using philosophies centered on the six values. Issues are always driven to closure using the lowest possible levels of employees. Since employees embedded in the affected operation often know more about the root cause than outsiders, CFI utilizes this to assemble corrective action teams. When problems cut across sector boundaries, or have an impact on the entire corporation, members of the executive office actively participate in problem resolution.

1.2 Company Responsibility and Citizenship

1.2a Societal Responsibilities

1.2a(1) Practices, Measures, Targets
CFI strives to lead all competitors in each country in which it operates and, wherever possible, drives

business sectors to achieve and exceed the most stringent requirements. CFI regularly reviews its processes to reduce costs, improve throughput, increase efficiency, and minimize the negative impact on its surrounding communities. Annually, each sector holds an environmental planning session in which projections are made of emerging requirements for the 2-, 5-, and 10-year horizon (see Table 2.2-1).

Specific considerations are given to the by-products of CFI's processes, including solid waste, scrap material, effluents, airborne contaminants, and ancillary waste products. Each site has a committee dedicated to reviewing their outputs and results of environmental planning sessions and look for ways to minimize the impacts. Examples include the Los Angeles, California, site's reduction in the effluents it releases to the surrounding communities and the Philadelphia, Pennsylvania, site's over 300% reduction of the amount of solid waste delivered to the local landfill.

CFI expects all employees to conduct themselves with uncompromising integrity. The Code of Conduct Handbook is reviewed with all employees annually at their performance reviews. CFI requires 4 hours of legal training on ethical behavior for all new employees and over 40 hours for senior management, procurement personnel, customer contact employees, and project managers. Evidence of the training's effectiveness is the lack of any inquiries, challenges, or sanctions over the actions and conduct of any employee.

1.2a(2) Anticipate, Assess, Address
The fastener industry is overseen by regulatory agencies, defense system accountabilities, and product liability considerations. In anticipating the FQA, CFI's planning process started with an analysis of the proposed regulations issued by the U.S. Department of Commerce (DOC) to implement the requirements of the final regulations. CFI has taken key actions to align our practices with the regulations.

Regulatory agencies include the U.S. DOC, DOD, Occupational Safety and Health Administration (OSHA), Environmental Protection Agency (EPA), Nuclear Regulatory Commission (NRC), state and local nuclear regulatory agencies, and foreign governmental agencies. A large part of CFI's revenue base comes from defense-related fastener production. Regulations address purchasing and overview infrastructures of all major defense contractors, other non-U.S. national defense departments, and industry regulations for defense products. Product liability considerations come from all product sector customers. The magnitude ranges from minimal financial impact to life-critical liability.

CFI uses several approaches to assess the risks inherent in our business. These include the formalized product and process risk assessments (used during the design process), new business financial return-on-investment (ROI) analysis, product market assessment, environmental risk evaluations and planning sessions, regulatory scenario simulations, business simulations, and product level "business war game" simulations. These are integral to the new business acquisition and management process.

1.2b Community Involvement

We recognize that our responsibility for quality excellence extends to the communities in which CFI does business. To promote a greater awareness of quality in partnership with public agencies and organizations, employees from CFI participate in a variety of programs. Among these are the following:

- CFI cosponsored the Annual Fastener Reliability Testing Institute Conference at Bainmear University in California.

- Employees presented a wide variety of papers at conferences around the world. In 1996, they gave over 235 quality-oriented papers or significant presentations at conferences, symposiums, and retreats. All employee efforts to participate in these activities are funded by CFI.

- CFI donated more than $500,000 in grants to local schools to support advancements in science, engineering, and technical vocations.

- CFI is a principal sponsor of the Pennsylvania Quality Award. The chief executive officer (CEO) is on the award Foundation's board of directors and three executives are members of the Board of Examiners.

2 STRATEGIC PLANNING

2.1 Strategy Development Process

2.1a Strategy Development

CFI's executive staff is responsible for developing the corporation's overall strategic direction, resulting in the five key business strategies for meeting customer requirements. The strategic planning process (Figure

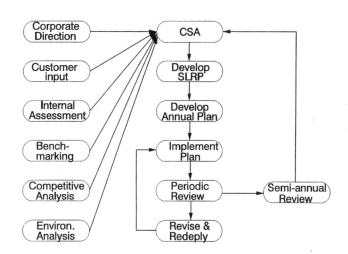

Figure 2.1-1 Management by Planning process.

2.1-1) is a closed-loop system that encourages continuous improvement in CFI's plans by including concise, measurable objectives that describe what will be done and an accompanying set of key results that defines how objectives will be accomplished. CFI integrates the corporate direction, customer surveys, internal assessments, benchmarking information, competitive analysis, supplier capability, and environmental factor to formulate both long- and short-range business–human resource–quality plans.

Figure 2.1-2 describes the annual planning cycle that provides CFI with its long- and short-term plans. It includes the following steps:

1. Accumulation of information about the business and competition (current situation analysis).

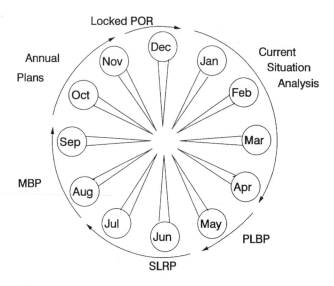

Figure 2.1-2 Annual planning cycle.

2. Integration of the information into product line business plans (PLBPs).

3. Use of this information to create the SLP.

4. This information feeds the development of the strategic and tactical management plans (MBP).

5. Building the annual operating plans and budgets (annual plans).

6. The culmination is the next year's operating plan and budget (locked plan of record [POR]).

The MBP process was developed in response to customer expectations and needs and business needs. CFI participates in Bueland's Total Quality Excellence assessment. Other tools and supporting approaches include benchmarking and internal assessment, which were piloted, refined, and maintained by CFI's Quality Technology Group. MBP integrates world-class features, such as policy deployment and planning, found through benchmarking U.S. and Japanese companies. To improve the annual planning process, data are collected through one-on-one discussions, surveys of training effectiveness, and polls of the network of CFI's total quality managers.

CFI's strategic objectives from the strategic long-range plan (SLRP) and annual plan are deployed to all sectors (Figure 2.1-3), with each department formulating its specific tactics and projects continually reviewed and revised as needed to ensure that goals are met. Figure 2.1-3 also shows the aggregated review process. CFI's president, Eugene Farmer, reviews strategic objective (SO) progress to plan during monthly operations reviews,

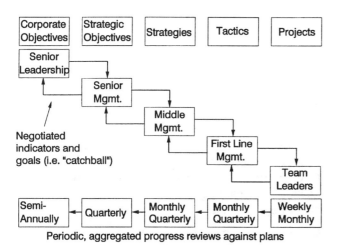

Figure 2.1-3 Cascaded MBP plan development and aggregated review process.

which enable the business units to optimize resource utilization and improve their plans.

2.1a(1) Customers, Markets

CFI's goal is to provide world-class fastening and assembly solutions to meet or exceed customer requirements for advanced products, superior quality, competitive pricing, on-time delivery, and responsive service and support. To accomplish this, CFI is committed to an ongoing process of defining world-class targets that best serve customers and developing plans to achieve them.

CFI relies on many sources for obtaining customer information on current and future requirements, which are product, service, and relationship oriented. Among these are CFI-directed customer surveys and focus groups, third-party-directed customer surveys, customer forums, customer visits, and customer partnership feedback (see Figure 2.1-1).

The SLRP is a three-to-five-year plan that outlines world-class goals for achieving customer requirements. This is consistent with the planning window of the majority of customers in the aerospace, automotive, nuclear, and explosives markets. These goals are expressed as CFI's strategic objectives. Using the SLRP as a framework, CFI's annual plan is formulated. In addition, all CFI business sectors develop annual plans, specific to their business needs, in support of CFI's corporate plan. The annual plan includes financial data, operating performance indicators, and the goals to be accomplished during the next year.

In preparation for the SLRP and the annual plan, individuals and teams are assigned by CFI staff to review current and projected customer needs to identify competitive gaps in CFI performance. Data are gathered through such means as internal and supplier assessments to compare current quality levels and capabilities with external benchmarks. Figures in Category 7 show examples of CFI's quality goals as compared to world-class benchmarks.

2.1a(2) Competitive Environment

A primary element in developing CFI's strategic plans and objectives is the current situation analysis, which collects and analyzes information to set the business direction. This analysis is the first step in the strategic quality planning process and is followed by the SLRP and annual plan. Information used in the analysis is continually reviewed for changes, and plans are adjusted accordingly. Figure 2.1-1 shows the Current Situation Analysis (CSA) phase of the MBP.

Competitive and benchmark data (see Item 4.2 for process details) are used to measure CFI's performance against world-class levels both within and outside their industry to ensure that customer expectations are met or exceeded. CFI routinely collects and analyzes information on competitors that produce comparable products and services. Product data on technical capabilities, product portfolios, manufacturing performance, and quality levels are analyzed. Also examined are service data in such categories as pricing, field support, guarantees, warranties, and shipment throughput time.

2.1a(3) Risks: Financial, Market, Technological, and Societal

Each proposed strategy for CFI's products and services is analyzed to determine key sensitivities of approach in influencing increases in market share, environmental impacts (both beneficial and adverse), complexity of production, and degree of new technology required, with an eye to near- and long-term financial impacts. Each factor is weighted based on company strategic objectives and integrated to provide a summary score of the risk of each approach. This risk factor is combined with other factors in establishing company strategies.

2.1a(4) Company Capabilities

Process capabilities, which are based on periodic annual internal assessments, are used to review CFI capabilities, provide data on performance, and identify priorities for improving the competitive position. This information may take the form of performance indicators, C_{pk} metrics, or anecdotal information. Data are gathered from employee feedback, as well as from evaluation of the previous year's plan results.

2.1a(5) Supplier and/or Partner Capabilities

CFI reviews supplier capabilities, which are key elements of the strategic quality planning process, and incorporates supplier quality initiatives such as CFI's Supplier Continuous Quality Improvement (SCQI) approach. In addition, the SCQI approach is key to the Corporate Materials Group's annual plan.

2.1b Strategy Deployment

The MBP is a planning process that generates a strategic and tactical plan. Corporate objectives spawn strategic objectives, which spawn strategies, which spawn tactics, which spawn projects, which is where all work is done. Anybody at CFI can look at the work he or she is doing and be able to recognize how it connects and supports the attainment of one or more corporate objectives and ultimately the company's profitability.

Figure 2.1-3 shows the methodology used to develop the cascaded corporate objectives. It notes the "catchball" process used to start at the top and develop a tentative set of next-level objectives or plans, and those members of CFI who are the targeted owners respond and negotiate what the action, metrics, and goals will be. When this step is complete, the results are locked in. Then, the process repeats itself on the next lower level until it has been negotiated all the way to the project level.

CFI's SLRP and annual plans are communicated and deployed in several ways throughout each CFI sector. Special meetings are held each year to provide the information contained in these plans to all levels of employees across each business sector. At least once a year, the internal publication *Fastened Together* publishes the corporate values and strategic objectives from each major business sector within CFI. BUMs are held for all employees on a quarterly basis to outline corporate and sector goals, as well as the performance to achieve those goals and corresponding indicators. Quarterly MBPs are also formulated at all exempt levels to ensure the support of annual CFI objectives. CFI's open communication style promotes the deployment of the plans and goals within the corporation through such means as posters, bulletin boards, communication kiosks, and frequent one-on-one discussions.

CFI's plans and goals are communicated to suppliers primarily through supplier partnerships. Plans outlining supplier requirements are transmitted from CFI's Corporate Materials Group, which also monitors suppliers to ensure that they continuously meet overall quality plans.

2.2 Company Strategy

2.2a Strategy and Action Plans

Table 2.2-1 summarizes CFI's customer requirements and key business strategies. Previously, MBPs included "stretch goals" with an acceptable achievement rate of 70%. Today, our MBPs target 100% achievement of objectives and key results, ensuring that commitments to our customers are met.

CFI drives alignment between its suppliers, partners, and sectors by actively integrating them into the SLRP cycles that happen throughout the year. For the suppliers, the Pass Through Partnerships (PTP)

Table 2.2-1 CFI Corporate Objectives, Strategic Objectives, and Strategies

	Corporate Objectives	Strategic Objective Goals				
		CPS	CAS	DAS	NSS	CSS
CO1	Deliver 6 sigma products to customers on time	➤ Drive 100% of critical process to C_{pk} > 2.0	➤ Drive 100% of critical process to C_{pk} > 1.8	➤ Drive 100% of critical process to C_{pk} > 1.7	➤ Drive 100% of critical process to C_{pk} > 1.5	➤ Identify critical process, 80% to C_{pk} > 1.8
CO2	Be recognized as the highest value producer of fasteners	➤ Customer value matrix of > 9/7 (†)	➤ Customer value matrix of > 8/8	➤ Customer value matrix of > 8/9	➤ Customer value matrix of > 8/9.4	➤ Customer value matrix of > 8/9 (‡)
CO3	Be the technology leaders in the introduction of revolutionary fasteners	➤ Introduce 3 major product lines in 1997 ➤ > 3 patent awards	➤ Drive > 11 design wins in automotive ➤ Introduce 6 new product lines ➤ > 11 patent awards	➤ Drive 8 major subcontractor design wins ➤ > 7 patent awards	➤ Win all nuclear bids ➤ > 5 patent awards ➤ Introduce 1 new product line	➤ Engage > 6 process benchmark activities ➤Develop best-in-class IS ➤ Implement HR transition plan
CO4	Protect the environment at all worldwide locations with benchmark-level results	➤ Eliminate CFCs by 1997 ➤ Reduce effluents by 50% in 1997 ➤ Reduce solid waste by 30%	➤ Eliminate CFCs by 1997 ➤ Reduce effluents by 60% in 1997 ➤ Reduce solid waste by 20%	➤ Reduce CFCs by 60% in 1997 ➤ Reduce effluents by 50% in 1997 ➤ Reduce solid waste by 30%	➤ Reduce CFCs by 50% in 1997 ➤ Reduce effluents by 50% in 1997 ➤ Reduce solid waste by 45%	➤ Reduce solid waste by 60% ➤ Increase electronic information usage by 100%
CO5	Be recognized by our employees as number one in employee relationships at all worldwide locations	➤ Score > B on employee survey in all six values	➤ Score > B on employee survey in all six values	➤ Score > B on employee survey in all six values	➤ Score > B on employee survey in all six values	➤ Score > B on employee survey in all six values

† The customer value matrix is shown in Figure 7.1.8. The first number represents the "satisfaction with product cost" axis and the second number represents the "product fitness for use" axis.
‡ For the Corporate Support Sector, customers include both internal and external customers and partners. The first number (horizontal axis) represents "service and support availability," while the second number (vertical axis) represents "service and support quality."

approach is used to link all key suppliers (e.g., either technology based or primary source) into the design and manufacturing cycles.

Table 2.2-1 illustrates the linkage between CFI objectives as they translate into partner expectations, activities, and projects. The linkage is through the periodic MBP plans. CFI has pushed its MBP process into the operating systems in the more advanced and mature suppliers and partners to strengthen further its linkages and gain greater leverage.

Projects are given priorities and funded on an annual basis using zero-based budget (ZBB) methodology. Projects are given priorities based on their importance in meeting the overall plan. Resources, including staffing and budget requirements, are allocated accordingly. This process ensures that adequate resources are allocated to provide a high level of quality to all projects. Projects are initiated and terminated on the basis of the current situation analysis. In addition, a yearly developmental budget is formulated to allocate direct spending (e.g., training, employee recreation, materials, and capital) and indirect spending (e.g., facilities allocation) dollars, which are reviewed against the plan on a monthly basis.

2.2b   Human Resource Plan

CFI's total quality leadership is driven by "our employees, who are our fundamental strength; by our commitment to their development and well-being; and by the shared goals of customer support, productivity, and continuous improvement." The Human Resources Strategic Long Range Plan (HR SLRP) embodies these principles. The plan was developed through analysis of the company SLRP, projection of the future environment, and consideration of various CFI human resource data and survey results.

2.2b(1)   Changes in Work Design

Key strategies in the plan addressing changes in the work design include

- increasing self-directed work teams to enhance flexibility and innovation,

- increasing self-audits to reduce cycle time,

- implementing flexible manufacturing to enhance flexibility and utilization,

- reducing an additional management layer within one year to enable rapid response to changes,

- increasing use of core competency skill teams across sectors to deploy resources rapidly in response to changes, and

- achieving a 20% virtual work force buffer through part-time and contract employees to achieve flexibility in meeting work demands without having an impact on the core work force.

2.2b(2)   Employee Development

Key plan strategies addressing employee development include the following:

- Expanding the breadth of skills of all employees to achieve a multiskilled core work force.

- Training a specialist cadre on advanced product and process technologies to lead change.

- Developing and publishing long-term projections of skill needs by each year of the planning horizon. These skill projections will be integrated with individual employee development plans to retrain personnel with declining skills.

- Developing a "buy" category of skill needs to be filled through part-time and contract hires when long-term needs for the skill set are not cost effective for full-time core employees.

- CFI will increase the number of managers attending its core management development program by approximately 210 per year. Since 1994, over 730 managers have participated in this program. CFI also enhances and strengthens dual-career ladders for managers and individual contributors.

2.2b(3)   Changes in Compensation and Recognition

Leadership at CFI means committed performance in response to values, business strategies, and customer requirements. These goals are incorporated into annual, quarterly, and monthly objectives. Key results are developed by managers and employees in support of their business groups' direction. Objectives, along with goals for enhancing and developing capabilities required to improve performance continuously, also form the basis of individual performance assessment.

Performance in response to objectives is measured using a performance appraisal system that rewards quality over quantity. This is accomplished through a compensation system that is based on merit. For example, all salary exempt (SE) and salary nonexempt (SNE) personnel are evaluated on quality and quantity, but weighting assigned to quality is 50% greater than for quantity. Competitively increased pay raises for employees acquiring greater skills and accepting responsibilities on a team are critical changes to how CFI addressed compensation in prior years.

We share our financial success with employees and provide them with incentives to achieve quality results through an Employee Cash Bonus Program based on company profitability. Historically, this amounts to approximately 10-days pay and is distributed after the closing of the second and fourth fiscal quarters. In addition, 15% of our employees are identified for exceptional contribution to the group's success. This designation earns them a bonus payout that is 60% greater than the standard payout. Plans are to increase the level from 15% to 25% in the next two years. CFI also has another bonus plan that has 44% of our exempt employees, managers, and individual contributors involved. It is called the Executive Bonus Plan (EBP), with targets developed to support sector business performance. Traditionally, the EBP offers bonus amounts equivalent to 20% to 45% of an executive's base annual salary.

Of all exempt employees, 65% participate in CFI's Stock Option Program (SOP). These data compare to 51% participation in competitive companies and not more than 10% participation in many other industries. Starting in 1997, CFI will contribute one-half of every dollar an employee contributes to the SOP. A stock participation plan is open to all employees, providing a sense of ownership and commitment to CFI's success.

In addition to performance-based increases, between 10% and 20% of our employees are promoted annually, being recognized for increased performance and enhanced capabilities. In 1997, career planning guidance will be revised to increase emphasis on employee growth and gaining multiskill capabilities and an expanding variety in work assignment.

CFI rewards individual and team achievements in corporate, sector, and department programs through the CFI Achievement Award (CFIAA). Each sector also conducts its own Sector Recognition Award (SRA) program, including cash awards and a public ceremony within the sector, to acknowledge accomplishments that deserve sectorwide recognition. Managers also extend less formal, more spontaneous recognition, such as movie tickets, dinner for two, and gift certificates, to reward quality efforts.

Many awards are peer generated, such as the monthly Peer Recognition program in the Dearborn, Michigan, facility; the Employee of the Month program in the Milwaukee, Wisconsin, location; the Quarterly Top Hat Award in Human Resources; and those given at monthly shift meetings such as the Profuse Thanks program in Salt Lake City, Utah.

Although teams are a way of life at CFI, recognition of individual performance was the rule in the past. Starting in 1987, a significant shift occurred, reflecting the desire on the part of employees and managers to recognize total team performance. Team awards are often cross-functional, cross-organizational, and multilevel in composition.

CFI will implement skill-based pay that will enhance career development and empowerment of multiskilled nonexempt employees. We will also

identify and deploy the best-known methods for reward and recognition of teams and individuals.

2.2b(4) Recruitment

Supporting human resource's strategic objectives is a focused set of improvement strategies, tactics, and projects with quarterly goals. For example, CFI will increase the number of entry- to midlevel professional positions filled by new college graduates from 45% to 75% by 1997. In addition, CFI will double the number of those hired by its Graduate Rotation Program (GRP) and increase to 6% and 15%, respectively, its non-Asian minority and technical female hirings.

Other strategic goals include

- doubling the number of key external experienced people hired from our External Sourcing program,

- decreasing the cost per hire, and

- increasing both offer and accept rates by more than 10% to 70% and 80%, respectively.

Improvement tactics and goals targeting the Great Place to Work (GPTW) value include

- evaluation of expanding employee wellness programs,

- strategies in the areas of postretirement benefits, child-care, and elder care, and

- implementation of alternate starting times to provide greater flexibility for single parent and ''two-working-parent'' families.

Other items on the improvement agenda that will increase quality hires in the future are

- partnerships with local schools and universities including involvement in education, and the kindergarten through 12th grade (K–12) level through employee tutoring,

- assistance to outside institutions in math and science curricula development, and

- sponsorship of local and national math and science competitions.

2.2c Performance Projections

CFI uses the customer requirements and business strategies noted in Item 1.1 to build the long-term strategic objectives outlined in Table 2.2-1. These strategic objectives, which in turn support customer requirements and key business strategies, have primary owners responsible for ensuring that they are met. CFI senior staff measures success in achieving objectives through a set of indicators and goals.

CFI's managers and support organizations also develop a set of strategies for their organizations to support overall CFI strategic objectives. Figure 2.1-3 illustrates how the corporate quality, operational, and customer goals cascade down to the organizations using some review processes noted in Section 4.3b.

For example, using Corporate Objective CO3 from the corporate MBP (Table 2.2-1) outlines are made of the major goals and indicators required for each sector to meet the overall objective. Not seen in this high-level summary of goals are the strategic objectives, strategies, and tactics that have identified owners and are measured by indicators and goals derived from benchmark data, customer input, competitive information, and organizational requirements.

CFI must respond to its customers' demand for an ever-increasing level of performance from their suppliers. Table 2.2-1 outlines the high-level operational goals necessary to meet customer requirements for the 1997 to 2000 time frame. These goals reflect both world-class and best-in-class benchmarks for a three-year period and have targets to meet or exceed all competitive benchmarks in this time.

3 CUSTOMER AND MARKET FOCUS

3.1 Customer and Market Knowledge

CFI uses a closed communications loop to collect, analyze, and utilize data from and about customers. In the center is the Marketing Data System (MDS), which is described in Category 4. This worldwide system provides the focal point for all marketing actions. The system contains listening posts to gather information continually about customers and potential customers and their needs and expectations.

The Customer Expectation Determination process (Figure 3.1-1) is continually improved by evaluating and feeding back modifications and improvements to make the process more accurate and responsive with greater focus on the customer.

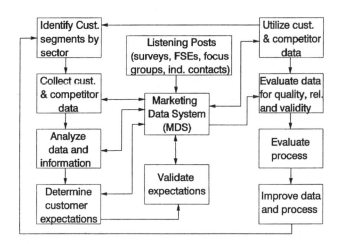

Figure 3.1-1 Customer Expectation Determination process.

3.1a(1) How Customer Groups are Determined

Consumer Products Sector—Consumer products are marketed primarily through distributors and sold through wholesale and retail stores to individuals who make the final satisfaction determination.

New competitors emerge daily. In spite of intense competition, with some suppliers entering the market with very low priced products, the market has been growing steadily. Many customers of higher end, more profitable products were influenced to buy through their outstanding experience with our consumer products. So, CFI continually pursues excellence in products and complete satisfaction of the end customer, as well as the distributors, wholesalers, jobbers, and retailers of the products.

Commercial and Automotive Sector—This sector has two major segments of customers, the commercial consumers using CFI products in everyday industrial use and the automotive customers with high-volume, short lead time, and special design needs.

The first segment is commercial users that procure through distributors, sales representative, and commercial supply houses. The second segment is the automotive customers: the Big 3 in the United States and the Big 2 in Japan, as well as most of the European automakers. These customers are most concerned about consistency of products and responsiveness in delivery. They traditionally practice just-in-time manufacturing with little inventory and rapidly changing delivery requirements.

Although using the same quality level of products, these two segments have differing needs, and competitors approach each in a different manner. CFI has to be aware of these needs and respond to both segments accordingly. Price, delivery, and quality are all important in varying degrees with these customers.

It takes more than CFI's present customers to expand markets and increase market share—CFI must gain customers from competitors. Automotive customers are a good source of competitor information as they usually use competitor facts to leverage CFI actions. This information is recorded in the MDS, which directly feeds the competitive intelligence efforts, product designs, and strategic planning efforts.

Defense and Aerospace Sector—The customers in this sector are also divided into two segments, defense and aerospace. They are similar in nature as they primarily buy to military specifications and usually at the lowest price.

This sector had a severe problem with counterfeit parts in the 1980s when distributors delivered substandard bolts with insufficient strength. This resulted in many of our defense and aerospace customers refusing to buy through distributors, and they now require certifications and firm proof of the quality of the product. CFI has responded, and the episode ended to CFI's advantage. The number of competitors has decreased, and the cost of extra proof of compliance has helped the competitive situation. As a result of the formalized bidding process in this sector, competitors are easier to identify, and the differences are exposed in the bidding process.

Nuclear and Specialty Sector—The Nuclear and Specialty Sector has two major customer segments. The first, nuclear, are those customers procuring products to meet the strict nuclear regulations, with required inspections, audits, and proof of materials and certified processes. Competitors are fewer in this segment, and the total market continues to shrink as a result of environmental difficulties and global pressures concerning industry safety.

The second customer segment in this sector, specialty, buys very special products made according to unique requirements and unusual specifications. We find that there is less competition for these customers. Most competitors do not have the technical capabilities in equipment and people to respond adequately to the requirements. This sector has few competitors, and we meet on limited competitive occasions and know the representatives well. However, it is still important to pursue vigorously the few customers of these competitors to determine their expectations now and in the future.

Some of our specialty products are unique (e.g., underwater explosive bolts for deep submersible vehicles), and competitors have difficulty copying our product. CFI takes advantage of this situation with our unique products by selling purchase agreements with a competitive total price for all fasteners.

Listening and Learning
The individuals collecting the information on customers are trained to listen carefully and pass on essential information without distortions and personal biases. Sales representatives receive an enhanced course in customer listening. This training is built on the standard course that all CFI employees have attended. To learn to listen is essential in discussions with outsiders to understand what they are trying to say. In the case of future products, the statements may be somewhat vague as customers are talking about something that does not exist, although there is a real issue.

CFI continually monitors the business and physical environments. The company has business strategies in each area. The company is the world benchmark for environmental protection. To remain in this leading position, CFI must be continually aware of regulatory changes and requirements around the world. This requires the listening posts to be proactive in searching new laws and regulations whatever the geographic location or particular situation.

CFI maintains its innovative technology leadership by having the technical organizations of engineering follow the latest technical writings and patent filings and attend the major trade shows. This includes reading the *Fastener Technology International Journal* and attending the International Trade Show.

When new, innovative products are ready for launch, customers who are leaders in the field are provided early production parts to evaluate and stress in real-life applications. This is one method used to ensure adequate value for the uses intended and to look for improvement opportunities.

When significant orders are lost, a "won/lost" analysis is performed to determine the cause and establish process changes to ensure that future losses will not occur. As part of this process, focus groups of lost customers are formed.

With the market becoming smaller in some areas, as noted in the Defense and Aerospace Sector, and the company planning to expand market share, each and every lost customer is very important. The reason for loss or defection must be determined, and corrective processes must be established.

Another task of the listening posts is to determine potential customers who may not be aware of CFI's technical capabilities. Each sector's listening post representative is always on the lookout for business for other sectors. Employee profit sharing covers the total company. It is to the advantage of each individual to improve the company's profitability and be a part of the strategic growth process.

3.1a(2) Specific Features and Importance Determination

With the diverse customer base in each sector, approaches are different yet similar. CAS is used to represent how information is collected and analyzed in all sectors.

CAS has many methods to determine customer needs and requirements. A few examples are described to show how the type and depth of information are assembled for analysis.

Professional societies have groups collecting and assembling information about products that are important to CFI. For instance, the American Society for Mechanical Fastening maintains a large number of standards for widely varied fastener applications. CFI is very active in the subcommittees that survey the industry for new applications and develop more demanding requirements.

CFI sales representatives are continually visiting and exchanging information with major automotive companies around the world to determine what is occurring with present products and what changes are going to be necessary in the future.

Outside sales representatives who handle CFI products for commercial customers provide weekly reports to CFI of their observations of their customers, especially showing how the present products perform and what changes are needed.

Another important input from customers comes from field service representatives. These individuals have constant contact with industrial and automotive customers and usually are involved with situations that show the best or the worst of the company. Customer opinions are captured into the MDS from regular weekly reports and informal discussion inputs.

Customer surveys are contracted to universities and colleges across the country. These surveys, directed and financed by CFI, go to all users of the products of CFI. This includes customers, as well as noncustomers. Included are some competitors, who also happen to be customers.

Data from all inputs are collected in the MDS. Accumulated data are aggregated and compared with each input to determine objectivity and validity. From these data, which are available to all employees, customer requirements and expectations are accurately determined and trends become apparent. Engineers and marketing representatives note them for indication of necessary changes, future modifications, or new products.

A team representing engineering, sales, production, and administration assemble focus groups for the areas in which the data indicate changes are occurring. Focus groups are formed by various customers who provide information to define requirements for product modifications and additions. These focus groups are utilized to generate priorities, which are reviewed and modified by CFI employees using the other data.

3.1a(3) Evaluation and Improvement

The listening post function continually evaluates the adequacy, timeliness, and reliability of the information being received and utilized for decision making. The output of the focus groups has resulted in several improvements in the process (see Figure 3.1-1).

The focus groups have directly faced the issue of the best methods for the listening post to use and have recommended specific training sessions that have been included in the training program for customer contact personnel.

The network of inputs does a good job of determining customer expectations. It also accomplishes the purpose of indicating areas in which the process can be improved. The MDS has been a help in assembling data on a real-time basis, with analysis indicating where data are missing or do not appear to track so adjustments can be made.

For example, the surveys contracted to universities and colleges are continually improved by soliciting comments from those who do not respond. The surveying institution must personally contact any person or organization that does not answer; the question, Why did you not answer? is posed to these people. Responses that indicate problems with the structure or method of questioning are used in the reengineering of the survey to make it more effective.

In the annual strategic planning process, opportunities for comparing projected changes are exposed. When significant changes of customer attitudes and opinions occur, the total customer satisfaction determination process is reviewed for changes and improvements.

3.2 Customer Satisfaction and Relationship Enhancement

3.2a Access and Complaint Management

Customers have several means to contact the company on critical or noncritical situations. During the initial customer contact, the salesperson gives information on how to reach a responsive individual at CFI.

Toll-free 800 numbers are provided for both telephone and FAX to access a group of service contact personnel on duty 24 hours per day, every day. Each facility also has computers that receive electronic mail and electronic data interchange (EDI) communications.

Facility managers around the world have given their home phone numbers to major customers to call if they feel they have not received a proper response or escalation of an issue requires their intervention. The on-duty service person has been instructed to give the appropriate manager's number so the customer has an opportunity to bring a question or issue to a higher level if they feel it is necessary.

All large shipments have a tag affixed with a postage-paid card self-addressed to the originating location. The cards have a series of boxes to be checked indicating possible problems and a space for written comments if desired. All distributors, wholesalers, and jobbers have a supply of these cards and insert one in each CFI customer shipment. This approach is an important way to ensure that customers can provide questions and feedback to the company.

Customers and PTP suppliers are listed in the company phone book and have access to the CFI telephone system. EDI is used by many customers interconnected with appropriate data systems.

3.2a(1) Requirements, Deployment, Improvement

The people who staff the service posts 24 hours a day are on teams that meet weekly to establish the service standards to meet the criteria of totally satisfying the caller. Service standards include

- response time to answer the phone,

- time to respond to the problem,

- time to resolve critical and urgent problems, and

- problem escalation to the manager.

Standards are improved in a three-step process:

- *Inputs.* Inputs include (1) feedback gathered from customers that have been contacted by supervisors; (2) comments gathered by managers talking to customers; and (3) information gathered by field sales engineers (FSEs) from customers and employees;

- *Action.* Focus groups are formed with the Service Center employees, who meet weekly to receive inputs. The groups determine actions to be taken.

- *Results.* The results of the focus groups can take several forms. They may determine to modify standards or establish new standards. Often, the decisions are that additional training on customer interfacing or problem solving is necessary. The results can lead to additional training concerning products.

Customer contact personnel are aware that customers have been given the appropriate home phone number of the facility manager. Their responses must reduce and eliminate the need for any customer to bring an issue to the manager.

If it is necessary to escalate the call by transferring it to another number for additional information, the first receiver does not get off the line until the second person has responded and is also on the line. This is a warm transfer. The service standard is that no more than two transfers will be made and three individuals maximum can handle a single call. Training is continually added to provide the customer contact personnel additional skills to handle more calls themselves and to reduce transfers and escalations.

3.2a(2) Complaint Management

The MDS is an essential part of the complaint resolution process. All formal or informal complaints are logged into the system. The responsiveness and accuracy of problem resolution are the result of rapid, accurate inputs. All formal comments go to the Service Center at each facility, and the customer contact personnel on duty log the information in a format that is standardized throughout the company. All complaints or comments received in the field are input into the MDS on portable computers using cellular phones and logged using an identical format.

Once in the data system, comments are automatically aggregated with all other comments. The analysis program in the system presents the data in Pareto distribution charts and by correlation analysis. These data are retained for future comparisons.

Complaints are categorized into critical and urgent. Critical issues are immediately assigned to a field sales engineer for immediate answers. These critical issues are to be resolved within two hours. Urgent issues are assigned to field sales representatives in a revolving manner so that each input has an individual immediately assigned. Urgent issues are to be resolved within 24 hours.

Each morning at the product meeting, the individual assigned to handle the comment or complaint that was received reports on its status. The assigned individual is expected to understand the situation fully and offer the progress, or status, at that time.

The date for complete resolution is placed in the MDS. Any date beyond the two days to resolve gets flagged. At each day's meeting, all open issues are reviewed. If an instance misses the assigned date, a double flag is applied, the issue is escalated, and an expert is immediately assigned to help with the solution. The issue is not completely resolved until the solution is filed in the MDS, making the information immediately available throughout the world.

The information about customers comes from many people in different organizations in different parts of the world. Surveys taken by third parties from the Industrial Fastener Institute (IFI) and contracted universities and colleges form the basic information. This aggregated data and information include the following:

- Information is collected from customer contact representatives with direct constant contact. These are the sales representatives who are assigned to, and should know, that customer best. The field sales engineers are also very close to the customer as they spend considerable time at the customer's facilities working with the people at all levels in the customer's organization.

- Service Center contacts have knowledge as a result of discussions concerning problems or answering requests for information. Although the information is not as direct, it becomes more useful when combined with the other data collected and aggregated in the data system.

- Customer contact reports are reserved from all levels of management when managers perform site visits or customer calls.

- Design engineers get involved with customers when developing a new product or working on an ongoing problem, and their knowledge is added.

- Suppliers are another good source of information as they are often also a supplier to the customer and usually a supplier to competitors of CFI.

- Benchmarking investigations often involve customers in examining various processes for analysis and incorporation.

3.2b Customer Satisfaction Determination

3.2b(1) Follow-Up with Customers
CFI utilizes several techniques to follow up with customers. To better ensure customer satisfaction, additional surveys are performed. On a random basis, one of the universities is contacted to perform a special survey of selected customers who are selected because of past specific problems with delivery, cost, or loss of an order.

To ensure that problem resolutions are prompt and complete, five customers from the Service Center comment list are selected monthly. The facility manager arranges a private visit, by which problem resolution is ensured, customer satisfaction is investigated, and a relationship is further established.

Feedback comes from these visits and from the mail-back cards. Sample cards are selected each month, and the manager places a call to the person who filled out the card. This person might be a receiving clerk or a manager. Feedback is recorded in the MDS.

Management also handles the telephones in the Service Center. The individuals are expected to meet the established service standards and handle any situation that arises day or night. This provides the manager a good evaluation of how customers rate the company and how to foster improved relationships with that specific customer. Each manager is expected to take on this assignment for two hours every two weeks.

Field sales engineers are assigned specific products and facilities. Sales representatives are assigned specific customers. Both groups take action if the reports involve their products, facilities, or customers.

Any time a product appears on a report three times in a three-month period, the central engineering group is involved. The monthly meetings of each department within each sector include in their agendas the status of the customer complaints and the corrective actions accomplished to solve the problem permanently.

3.2b(2) Process Description
The primary process for determining customer satisfaction is through surveys. IFI surveys the total

fastener industry twice a year. Individual companies participating are not directly identified.

CFI contracts with nine universities and three colleges to conduct 12 surveys a year, one each month, each by a different institution. The CFI-sponsored surveys are sent to both customers and noncustomers. From a competitive information view, the questions are structured so that distinctions are possible to decode the IFI survey to identify the major participants.

In addition, CFI directly conducts one or two surveys each year. These surveys are specialized and conducted to obtain specific information about future customer behavior. Survey questions include the following:

- Are you satisfied with your present supplier?
- Do you have any reason to change suppliers?
- Do you know of any supplier that can furnish the same value as your present supplier?
- Do you expect to continue using your present supplier?
- Would you recommend your present supplier to others looking for a fastener provider?

This information and that from sales representatives on upcoming orders from purchasing functions and manufacturing organizations provides us clues on how customers are likely to behave in the future.

The mail-back cards are another source of input to the process. They have limited reliability as not all customers fill them out and return them. Although these data may be limited, they are used with caution concerning the statistical validity of aggregated information they present.

The measurement scales for the two primary surveys are different. IFI uses a 1-to-10 scale, with 10 being the best for the various questions. CFI uses "A," "B," "C," "D," and "F," with a 9 or 10 considered an A, 8 or 7 a B, 6 or 5 a C, 4 or 3 a D, and 2 or 1 an F. All sections use the same designations.

3.2b(3)   Satisfaction Relative to Competitors
CFI utilizes several methods to determine customer satisfaction relative to competitors. The best, most objective, and most valid are the surveys performed by the contracted universities and colleges.

These surveys are sent to a long list of major fastener users, some of whom are known to be good customers of competitors. The information returned provides insight into how satisfied the customers are with the competitor suppliers. This information is completely objective and valid as the surveys are not identified as to the sponsor or provider. The information gathered is shared with all participants so the competitors receive the same information, although not coded to specific companies.

Some other methods utilized by CFI to determine competitor results are through field sales engineers. These employees have good contacts with customers and also with competitor representatives.

CFI purchases competitors' products on the open market and performs analytical tests. The information is valuable; however, caution is applied because it is not void of CFI bias that might compromise its objectivity. The information is added to the survey results for validation. If it reinforces and correlates with other information, it is accepted.

Customer satisfaction must be earned and retained while competitors are constants trying to gain customers from CFI. The information flow concerning how well competitors are doing is actively pursued. Information about competitor success with customer satisfaction comes from third-party surveys, customers of CFI, and suppliers.

CFI performs semiannual surveys of the total fastener industry. The survey covers a wide range of customers and is totally objective and valid as far as any supplier to the fastener industry is concerned. In the survey, several questions are asked about the satisfaction levels and how the various fastener suppliers react to customer needs.

The outputs of the surveys provide direct comparison information about relative customer satisfaction. CFI utilizes this information and reports to the employees the successes and issues in the pursuit of total customer satisfaction.

The automotive industry has strong ties to suppliers and maintains extensive records concerning the quality of parts and delivery and cost information. These reports compare suppliers of industries such as fasteners and provide comparison information. CAS customers provide these reports to CFI, and the information is compiled in the MDS databank.

The nuclear industry has fewer suppliers and limited customers. The industry publishes reports from product users that compare sources in the area of customer satisfaction. This source of information gives input that can be compared to other data.

Suppliers are another source of information concerning customer satisfaction as they provide materials and supplies to the fastener industry and their customers are the competitors of CFI.

4 INFORMATION AND ANALYSIS

4.1 Selection and Use of Information and Data

4.1a(1) Types of Data

Data are collected on the four product sectors and the one corporate support sector and are structured to lead to excellence in the five key business strategies of the company. Senior management determines which top-level data should be common to uniformly drive the excellence in the five key business strategies across the corporation and which should be unique to ensure excellence in the sectors. Data are collected in five areas (see Items 7.1–7.5).

4.1a(2) Deployment

At the core of the CFI data system model (Figure 4.1-1) is the worldwide data and information system and its five major database structures, which are set up according to the sectors they support. Sectors draw data and information from the information system, utilizing the data and information to create unique applications and data structures. These are accessible using various local-area network (LAN) and wide-area network (WAN) technologies. The architecture and measurement of the effectiveness of this data system are the responsibility of the CSS Information System Group.

Top-level data are decomposed to successively lower levels throughout the sectors down to the team level. Since employee involvement through teams is a key corporate strength, collection, analysis, and use of

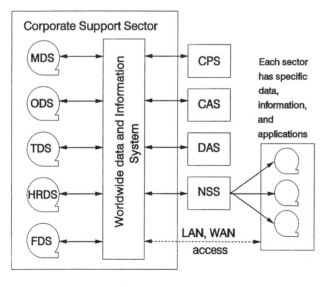

Figure 4.1-1 Colony Fasteners, Incorporated, data system model.

data at this level are the cornerstones to manage effectively by fact. The strong linkage of data through all organizational levels enables appropriate action to be taken at the lowest possible level and identification at all levels of the connectivity and impacts to the five business strategies. At all levels, internal and external customers and suppliers are linked into the data stream to achieve the strong customer focus.

4.1a(3) Requirements, Access, Reliability

Requirements
Each sector utilizes teams of concerned employees who are responsible for the selection of the data to be collected. These teams consist of users, developers, customers, suppliers, and Information System (IS) experts. They formally meet every Friday afternoon at 1:00 P.M. and hold informal meetings when special circumstances occur. The formal meetings are documented and ensure that each data task is reviewed for continual improvement.

In the data management team's formal analysis, as well as team activities within continuous improvement, one item addressed is whether the right data are reaching the right people. The teams analyze whether the data from results show process outputs of importance to customers and whether in-process data enable prediction of output to gauge the performance of the process. In addition, teams assess whether the recipients of the data are the appropriate persons for taking action on the data. As a means of canceling collection of data that is no longer of value, an additional consideration is: Is this data being used?

At the weekly meetings of the teams responsible for the data to be collected, users not assigned to the team are invited on a random basis, and anyone interested has an open invitation. These non-team members are solicited to express concerns and make suggestions as to methods to make the data more available and useful to them. The data are collected for the convenience of the users.

All process operators, and this includes those from support functions, utilize their PC terminals to communicate with the other team members by electronic mail, with addresses preloaded by name and function. All employees can submit comments on data timeliness, accuracy, and clarity via E-mail. These comments often result in actions by the teams to request training sessions either on the job or in the classroom if the situation appears to be widespread. Often, teams will design the training and sometimes do the training.

Access
Data are managed on a companywide Information System's network using PC terminals for local use and a centralized mainframe in Philadelphia connected by satellite links. The local PC terminals are linked in local-area networks so that all employees have access to real-time data anywhere in the world. In all locations, a minimum of 90% of the employees has a PC terminal readily at hand. Thus, data are accurate, reliable, from real-time situations, and readily accessible.

Many employees have PCs at home, networked to the company data systems. The company pays one-half the purchase cost and arranges for the purchase, which reduces the cost another 15%. CFI pays for a dedicated telephone line to the employee's home to enable unencumbered communications service.

Reliability
Data reliability is ensured by several means. Most data are collected automatically and directly filed in the data system to ensure reliability.

Software utilized within the data system is designed to analyze the data as it is collected and immediately flag a large or significant variation or erroneous entrees. The flag alerts the operators to review the situation immediately. The data teams regularly review the number of flags that occur for each data item, reflecting on both data collection and actual process performance.

IS personnel back up daily all data to ensure that loss does not occur if power outages or other disruptions occur. Weekly, IS personnel also verify data accuracy through automatic diagnostic routines.

4.1a(4)   Evaluation and Improvement
Semiannually, a formal top-down data review occurs. Starting at senior management and cascading through all levels of the organization, including customers and suppliers, the following questions are asked:

- Have the current data enabled us to make decisions and set priorities?

- Are the data actionable?

- Do the data enable us to determine the performance of the process?

Recommended changes from these reviews are fed to a Data Management Team for analysis. This multifunctional team, composed of management, process teams, IS, customers, and key supplier personnel, using the five business strategies as a guide to ensure data continuity, makes appropriate changes in the data management system.

The formal data review process is supplemented with informal data updates by IS management teams (with representatives from all sectors); these updates result from benchmarks and continuous improvement. Figure 7.5-16 shows ten years of improvements.

4.2   Selection and Use of Competitive Information and Data

4.2a(1)   Needs and Priority Determination
The strategic planning process identifies business areas in which competition is great and market share is low. The planning process causes the businesses to review capabilities relative to competitors by collecting data primarily from public domain information. This information is analyzed to establish goals and stretch targets and set benchmark priorities.

The initial step in determining benchmark partnership needs is to identify areas that will have the most immediate effect on the business or to provide a longer term capability that is necessary for continual growth. The initial priority is to determine if the "best practice" is within a CFI sector. If not, then outside benchmarking partners are found.

In the rapidly growing automotive market, the strategic plan indicated that CAS was not adequately responding to customer delivery demands of short-term increases in product quantities with little or no lead time. A mutual customer revealed that Hubler Electric was delivering electrical connectors overnight.

Hubler allowed a benchmarking team to review their process in detail. CFI modified the process for storing and handling raw materials and the area layout and the paperwork processes. Now, CFI can respond to doubling the delivery quantity on the next shift after a request, compared to what had been 14 days (see Figure 7.5-6). This is one example of the PTP process.

Each business sector sets its own priorities for functions to benchmark. A master priority list is formulated from the individual sector priorities. Each sector takes lead responsibility for two to three specific functions. The 10 or more functions are typically both product and nonproduct related. This list is reviewed annually, reestablishing the top 10 functions. Additional issues are added, usually about five more for each sector each year, on an emergency basis if business conditions dictate.

4.2a(2) Criteria for Information and Data

Gaps in knowledge of competitor performance are the highest targets for gathering information. The second highest priority targets are processes that are critical competencies for our businesses. Within those critical competencies, our top priority is to determine our competitors' performance and then find those companies outside our industry with a process performance that is better than ours and our competitors'. Once found, CFI establishes a new partnering relationship to learn and understand how their processes are designed and performed.

After the benchmark partnership is established, a team familiar with the process being examined and trained in the benchmark process is sent to observe in detail the process and the metrics being utilized. The team often represents Engineering, Operations, and Information Systems from interested sections and Headquarters Administration to help ensure consistency and alignment with corporate directions.

4.2a(3) Stretch Targets

When conducting benchmark comparison analysis, both current and future gaps are set considering costs, process disruption, process criticality, and impact on other processes when setting stretch targets.

Benchmarking teams return to their home facility and modify applicable processes, making changes and modifications to result in a simplified process with less variability, better quality, and reduced cycle time. The new process is given to other CFI sectors via the corporate coordinator and data system.

Team members must often to travel to another plant in another sector in order to ensure optimum application of the specific process steps. The process steps for the investigation and adaptation of processes from other companies have been well established from many repeat actions and are well documented. There is no longer a not-invented-here attitude at CFI.

Process changes that have resulted from learning from other organizations in the PTP process have resulted in significantly improved results within CFI, including some support services. Often, the review of an individual process has resulted in modifying only a small part of an established process. Only a few individual steps are improved, and yet the overall results are substantially better. Process changes have significantly reduced variability and simplified processes throughout the company.

In a heat-treating process for fasteners for the Nuclear and Specialty Sector, the PTP suppller being examined was treating the bolts in a manner that resulted in significantly better performance. Detailed examination showed that the improvement was primarily in the device that loaded and unloaded the bolts, although the heating and quenching were not as good as what CFI was using. By changing only the handling device, we were able to achieve an overall 10-fold improvement, five times better than the total process that was reviewed for benchmarking.

Besides the process improvements noted, identified metrics are used for setting goals. Many stretch goals have been selected through the PTP process. Measures for competitive and benchmark metrics of best-in-class comparisons are continually plotted.

4.2a(4) Evaluation and Improvement

The benchmarking process' success is seen during the annual strategic plan update. Competitive comparisons reviewed at that time show increased market share, sales, and profits as the result of the improved processes throughout the organization due to the benchmarking activities.

Measurements for competitive comparisons and benchmark metrics of best-in-class companies are continuously plotted for many activities. As actual results move toward the established stretch goals and best-in-class measures, satisfaction with results and methodology is determined. If the range of change in the indicators is not aggressive enough to close the defined gap, we start activities to change the process.

Since 1991 when the benchmarking activities started, the process has matured and grown. Initial benchmark partners were often selected on the basis of convenience of location or personal knowledge of some influential person in the potential partner's organization. Today, partners are selected on the objective basis of having the potential to significantly help the sectors in their processes. Best-in-class goals are utilized in the assessment and comparison of process results.

Similarly, experience has shown the importance of public domain searches before beginning formal benchmarking visits. This has been of significant help in the selection of the right benchmarking partners.

4.3 Analysis and Review of Company Performance

4.3a Analysis of Data

With a centralized mainframe at the Philadelphia headquarters, data are beamed through a satellite to all facilities, which in turn network the PC terminals, real time, to make accurate data available to whomever needs it and is entitled to the specific information, including those employees that have home PCs linked to the company.

The company's five business strategies are constantly updated on the mainframe with the latest information with weighted values derived from various data inputs. The information is printed out at each facility on Monday morning for posting on a prominent bulletin board, giving all employees worldwide the latest status toward the business strategies.

The mainframe's five basic data systems (see Figure 4.1-1) are integrated for cross-communications, calculations, and analysis. The systems are separately available, through a password, for the specific functions with the need for the data. In addition, each facility has local-area networks with PC terminals for local monitoring and control. Data are constantly down- and uploaded from the mainframe.

Each system has

- databases for the basic information required for that function of that business,

- specific analytical tools required to manipulate the data for the required purposes, and

- matrices for each of the four sectors, with each sector using an access code for identification of the ownership of the data.

4.3a(1) Customer-Related Performance
The MDS has inputs drawn from customer surveys, individual customer inputs, and customer complaints fed through from quality reports, product replacement data, marketing, Service Centers, FSEs, and other organizational contacts.

Product delivery promises, new product design status, production status, and delivery dates are readily available from the system. Sales personnel at remote locations can interrogate a satellite channel for product delivery status. Inventory status of completed products is also available for delivery information for sales representatives (see Item 3.1).

Customer inputs are continually collected by various contacts and continuously fed into the MDS. Built into the MDS software is an analysis of markets that gives competitor's names with their respective market shares in each sector. Market share changes are maintained in the MDS for five years for projections.

CFI is a company that is process oriented and customer focused. The attention to process improves responsiveness and quality, reduces costs, and builds customer respect and loyalty. The data systems furnish the information needed by all functions to improve continuously.

Customer attitudes are important and of great concern and are always factored into management decisions concerning new products, new markets, and new and upgraded facilities. Balancing customer attitudes with ongoing required investments in new products and operational facilities is a major management task. The extensive data system provides the information to make these decisions.

Any open customer complaint or issue is flagged so anyone using the system is aware that some issue requires action. The database stores the problem resolution information and maintains the time required for resolution for two years.

4.3a(2) Operational Performance
The Operations Data System (ODS) has all production information, including purchased material status and inventories. Production status (e.g., productivity easements, cycle times, and quality issues such as scrap) is determined through software programs performing statistical analysis on various data groups. Data on on-dock-deliveries-completed compared to promise are retained for three years.

Because of the importance of process control to the company, individual processed have calculated C_{pk}'s on the basis of information fed into the database. This information is retained at the local facility with only summary information, such as the percentage of processes that have a C_{pk} of at least 1.5, being sent back to the mainframe. However, if detailed information is desired, it is possible to call up the details. The continuous improvement of C_{pk}'s across all functions, product, and support services is an indicator of the success of the process being utilized.

Local control is primarily utilized for the Human Resource Data System (HRDS), which monitors employee characteristics such as retention, time off for specific reasons such as accidents, and accumulated training courses scheduled, in process, or completed. Data concerning team participation and recognition for outstanding accomplishments are some types of information accumulated. Various software programs provide specific analysis of the data to show trends and variations. Periodic employee survey results are maintained for four years. Summary data are transferred back to the mainframe for overall company statistics.

The Technical Data System (TDS) is primarily for the use of engineering, with technical specifications and the capacity to provide mathematical calculations required in new process control initiations. Design of experiments (DOE) is widely used. The data system contains the information structure to facilitate the task.

The five systems' data are continually correlated to improve the overall accuracy and reliability of the information. This is especially critical because, as seen in Figure 4.1-1, sectors create many individual, or unique, data applications using information derived for the worldwide data and information system. For instance, as customer comments and product quality information integrate, discrepancies may occur. If this happens, the IS function immediately investigates to determine of there really are discrepancies and, if so, why and what corrective actions can be put in place to prevent future occurrences.

4.3a(3) Competitive Performance
Competitive performance information and data are primarily contained in the MDS. As pointed out above, market share and competitor accomplishments are available. Competitor prices and product compatibility are compared with CFI prices and product capability, and projected costs and performance gaps are estimated from marketing inputs.

4.3a(4) Financial and Market-Related Performance
The Financial Data System (FDS) provides management with real-time financial characteristics such as sales, inventories, profits, and cash flow. Headquarters and the sectors use the real-time and reliable data from facilities around the world to make timely decisions.

The company has been financially successful due to its ability to balance the priorities of customer needs, internal needs, and valuable resources. Sales increases are becoming more difficult with the downturn of the defense business and the low level of ongoing nuclear activities. The continually increasing profit margins are directly attributable to lower costs, primarily due to better performance of processes.

4.3b   Review of Company Performance

CFI's business and corporate support sectors have systematic and disciplined approaches for reviewing performance in response to plans and goals. These approaches include the following:

- Annual reviews that cover yearly performance and address long-range plans.

- Quarterly reviews that focus on cost review and performance relative to the annual plan.

- Monthly reviews that analyze CFI's performance relative to productivity, design, and annual plans and goals. These reviews ensure that corrective actions are taken for opportunities identified in the weekly and daily reviews.

- Daily and weekly reviews that target external customer input, internal quality results, and process corrective actions.

- Vendor of choice reviews that enable management to monitor CFI's performance relative to customer requirements and expectations.

- Sector operation reviews that focus on our performance relative to the annual plan and corporate plans at the business sector level.

Table 4.3-1 provides an insight into the types and frequencies of reviews, who typically participates, and who controls the agenda.

The annual strategic planning process establishes plans for the year for each sector. Basic information for this planning is established in the data systems and furnished as inputs to the planning process.

Within the company plans, each sector executive has contributing plans. With the policy deployment concept, sector managers have the authority to execute the plans and make modifications as market forces change during the year.

When the former Soviet Union collapsed and the Eastern markets opened, the company was one of the first fastener companies to establish contacts through the European office in Calais, France. Through the data systems, management was able to determine what investments in marketing personnel were necessary to penetrate the Eastern market initially, yet remain within established guidelines for the yearly plan. Although the magnitude of the opportunity was great enough that top management approval would have been required, this was not necessary since the information on the yearly plan was readily available in the data systems.

Table 4.3-1 Operational Reviews

Type	Leader	Freq.
POR	All Mangers	Monthly
PAS	Program and Project Leaders	Monthly
PLBP	Product Managers	Quarterly
SLRP	EO and Sector Managers	2x/year
MBP	All Managers	Monthly
Program	Program Managers	Monthly
Project	Project Managers	Per Plan
QST	EO	Quarterly
QIT	Sector Managers	Monthly
QAT	Team Leaders	Per Plan
MRC	Team Leaders	Per Plan
Cust. Focus Mtg.	Sector and Program Managers	Quarterly
Design Reviews	Programs Managers	Per Plan

Although yearly strategic plans are carefully set, the market dynamics dictate that modifications be made during the year. A strong extensive database utilizing up-to-date communications and data transfer techniques is essential. CFI has such a system, which has served the company well.

5 HUMAN RESOURCE DEVELOPMENT AND MANAGEMENT

5.1 Work Systems

5.1a Work and Job Designs

5.1a(1) Opportunities for Initiative
CFI's founding objective was to create a company culture that not only provided diverse opportunities for employee contributions, but that also actively involved employees in all aspects of their work. CFI's value of results orientation requires employees to identify, understand, and confront problems directly and constructively to achieve timely resolution. Implicit in these behaviors is ongoing communication and feedback at all levels. The company culture reflects a wide array of management practices and other processes that offer all levels of employees every possible opportunity to have ownership of projects and tasks, be accountable, and make a difference:

- Teams and task forces, which can be either long- or short-term teams, typically led by a "content expert," are formed ad hoc and are disbanded once an effective resolution is implemented and verified. Forums for improvement include task forces, material review boards, project teams, and problem-solving teams.

- A decentralized suggestion program fosters both "all-purpose" and functionally specific suggestion programs to expedite timely feedback and implementation of inputs. For example, the Defense and Aerospace Sector safety suggestion program features suggestion boxes and a "safe line" for confidential phone-in use. Inputs are reviewed weekly by a review committee for applicability and effectiveness. Feedback is provided immediately after the meeting to the employee who made the suggestion.

- Self-audit teams are employed across all CFI sectors. The teams are designed to evaluate internal operations and make necessary adjustments to support customer and internal audit requirements.

We believe that most tasks benefit from cross-functional and multilevel team efforts. Specific development plans differ by sector, but all focus on bringing together the necessary experts for solving problems and empowering them to take action. For example,

- Self-sustaining manufacturing vision at Sao Paulo, Brazil facility. In fall 1990, Sao Paulo announced a three-year plan to evolve its transitionally managed structure of hourly production operators into approximately 50 facilitated teams. These teams will assume many routine supervisory and technical tasks, such as basic troubleshooting and line inventory management. In 1994, all 700 + employees participated in an eight-hour empowerment workshop to kick off the process.

- "Three-Level Factory" vision. In 1993, the Juarez, Mexico, facility initiated a plan to evolve its total organization into a three-level structure. Level 1 is the Factory Steering Committee, made up of the plant manager and his staff. Level 2 has five peer support teams of middle managers and supervisors. Level 3 has approximately 40 Natural Work Teams (NWTs) of all operators, technician, and engineers who run each operation. Each NWT has an associated Performance Improvement Team (PIT) that focuses on continuous improvement for the operation. Over 200 PIT members received eight hours of orientation training that included extensive business information.

- Product (or Process) Development Teams (PDTs). PDTs are formed for developing and bringing new products into the market. Members are cross-functional and include product design and manufacturing engineers, marketing and planning personnel, and often customers and suppliers.

Expectations that employees should be involved and empowered are embedded in CFI culture. Employees perform their work as teams, and the company focuses on, acknowledges, and rewards the accomplishments of the team effort versus tracking the extent and effectiveness of involvement, such as

1. Between 1991 and 1995, employee involvement teams across the General Site Services and Customer Support Services groups reduced expenditures by $17.4 million through cost savings, reductions, and cost avoidance.

2. The Hybrid Rivet Product Development Team, which was cross-organizational and cross-site (including Oyama, Japan; Boston, MA; and Berlin, Germany). It introduced a product the fastest so far at CFI. The team used a modular design process to take the multimaterial rivet from initial product implementation to available samples in three weeks.

3. The Rivet-With-Mastic Task Force successfully reduced throughput times from eight weeks in 1991 to three weeks in early 1996. The team won a CFI Achievement Award in the fourth quarter of 1996.

5.1a(2) Flexibility, Cooperation, Response, Learning

Flexibility and mobility are critical to the success of CFI and its employees as they deploy personnel both to accommodate technological and business changes and to support employee career development goals. Areas of major focus since the mid-1980s and key components of the HR SLRP have formalized the CFI redeployment process and its integration with an enhanced internal staffing capability.

The redeployment process includes a comprehensive move package, formal career assessment, workshops on interviewing and resume development, retraining and funding for internal and external opportunities, and assimilation assistance for relocating employees. Through this process, the Macon, Georgia, operation successfully redeployed 324 employees, including 218 SNEs, for a total of 91% of those desiring placement.

CFI's culture values employees' skills, knowledge, and performance over formal position. CFI's principal goal is for decisions to be made at the level at which they are executed. To improve and speed the decision-making process, we have removed layers of management over the past five years. All CFI organizations are now at three to five levels from top to bottom, compared to seven to nine levels four years ago. A current review indicates that more than 95% of all decisions are now made through a team process.

To keep pace with increasing performance expectations and emerging skills, training needs are often addressed by training groups or functional content experts as described in Item 5.2. Strong relationships with community colleges and universities have resulted in customized training that enhances the skill set of current CFI employees while also ensuring a supply of externally qualified employees. Similar relationships are being established with high schools to help better equip them with fundamental skills before entering the workforce.

For example, in Los Angeles, CFI's ongoing relationship with the community college system produced a customized training program for computerized fastener designers that has continually evolved in response to changing technology demands. CFI's partnership with the Technical-Vocational Institute of Los Angeles resulted in the development of an associate's degree program in metallurgical technology. CFI employees also support such institutions by assisting with curriculum development and by teaching courses. In addition, CFI offers cooperative fellowships and part-time work opportunities to qualified students.

5.1a(3) Effective Communications

CFI believes that meaningful employee involvement must be supported by freely and openly sharing information about business operations with all employees. For example,

- BUMs are accomplished worldwide on a quarterly basis. CFI executives and senior managers update employees on performance relative to goals and plans through corporate overviews. The corporate information is enhanced with sector and factory specific information. The combined presentations cover the financial performance data, competitive analysis, and new product strategies. Employees are encouraged to raise concerns and make inputs during these meetings.

- Immediate information access through written publications distributed in all "information kiosks" located at key spots throughout all CFI buildings worldwide, the issuance of internal press releases before the news is available externally, and, through a wide range of sector-or function-specific magazines distributed monthly or quarterly. Information technology is driving CFI communication methods toward being electronically available 24 hours a day, all year, worldwide.

- Voice and E-mail are widely used to communicate between sites, as well as within sites.

5.1b Compensation and Recognition

Employee compensation, described extensively in Area 2.2b(3), includes Bonus and Stock Option Programs and quality-over-quantity-based pay increases and promotions. Team effectiveness through employee involvement is reflected in recognition awards. Employees are evaluated on both individual performance and support of group actions and goals. Individual development plans address the improvement needs of specific team members.

Several point-in-time "monitors" of team activity across organizations have supported our belief that employee involvement is continuously growing, such as

- Sample of quality improvement teams. Between June 1995 and March 1996, CFI's Quality Technology Group received abstracts documenting the success of 223 performance improvement teams across CFI's domestic sites.

- Surveys of current team activity. CFI surveyed its entire organization in January 1996 to estimate the number of active teams. Almost 400 multilevel and cross-functional teams were reported. A year later, more than 550 active teams were found, and results showed that "teams" are broadly defined to include any variety of problem-solving team, project team, improvement team, or natural work group.

CFI honors employees and teams worthy of corporatewide recognition. The CFIAA typically recognizes major accomplishments in customer support, quality, productivity improvements, and technical innovation and is considered CFI's "Nobel Prize." Winners receive CFI common stock and a plaque to commemorate the accomplishment. The award is presented at highly visible, sectorwide meetings and is widely publicized in a special edition of the corporate newspaper *Fastened Together*.

The most effective means of evaluating recognition and performance measurement systems is to survey CFI's internal customers—the managers who administer the systems and the employees who are reviewed and rewarded by the processes. Vehicles for soliciting this feedback include

- continuous surveys conducted on corporate, sector, and factory levels,

- management-hosted employee lunches, and

- one-on-one meetings conducted at the sector, factory, and department levels.

Changes were made to our exempt performance management system as a result of employee feedback from the 1995 culture survey. Employee performance ratings were reduced from five to three—outstanding, successful, and improvement required—reaffirming the efforts of the majority of our employees, who fall into the middle category.

We also introduced a component called "trending," which evaluates an employee's rate of change relative to his or her peers. It stresses the necessity of achieving a rating at least equal to one's peers by continuously improving one's performance. Managers were trained in the new system, and all exempt employees, including managers, were surveyed on the process. Results indicated that the concepts were good, but the content needed improvement. A task force was formed to refine the basic components, and revised training was delivered to all managers and exempt employees. Exempt employees will be resurveyed in the second quarter of 1997.

5.2 Employee Education, Training, and Development

5.2a(1) Key Performance Plans
CFI defines quality education and training as all training that provides employees with the skills and knowledge to support business strategies and

values. CFI presently uses four different methods to meet education and training needs: functional area training departments, CFI University, Corporate Education and Development, and external training consultants. Each approach for assessing training needs is specific to its target constituency and training type.

Functional area training departments, such as the manufacturing training departments or General Site Services (GSS) training, deliver specialized functional skills necessary for job performance. This training focuses on the skills required within the specific function. For example, the Corporate Information Services (CIS) training group offers skills training for its programmers, operators, and analysts. Training in Statistical Process Control (SPC) and Design of Experiments (DOE) is offered through functional training departments, which allows "how-to" application of the subject matter.

Training needs are driven by the operation's specific business needs and the assessment of proficiency against the required skill level. An example is Philadelphia's approach for just-in-time delivery of team orientation training to over 200 employees on PITs, described in Area 5.1a. Functional area training departments either assist and qualify employee content experts to develop and deliver the training or contract directly with external resources.

Figure 5.2-1 shows the deployment methodology used to embed skills and training throughout CFI. In the beginning, development experts provide training in selected "early adopter" organizations. At this time, the duration deployment is low and the organizational maturity is also low. Both conditions require intensive, highly competent training from the

content experts. In the next phase, the content expert develops additional content experts who are assigned to each business unit—in the same context as an internal consultant. These additional experts enable wider deployment throughout the organization. This cascaded deployment continues as the new content experts train additional inter-and intraorganizational experts (those employees assigned to a business area but capable of floating to other business areas).

5.2a(2) Education and Training Design
Employees are asked annually to update their career enhancement forms. This is done independently of the performance appraisal and merit pay review cycles to ensure that focus is on helping employees to plan how to increase their worth to the company. All employees are provided with "Careers at CFI," which describes potential career paths. All employees, after completion of their career enhancement forms, get an analysis called "My Career at CFI," with alternatives in training, education, and potential work assignments employees can follow to enhance their progression. Employees decide whether or not to accept the recommendations and enroll in training and education. The automated Training and Education Support System (TESS) Enrollment tracks training. TESS gives employees updates to their "My Career at CFI" analysis after they complete training, education classes, or changes in work assignment. TESS also notifies employees when changes are made to their profile following their annual performance review. The employee satisfaction survey, exit interview, and focus group discussions show that this methodology is viewed very favorably by employees as fully enabling them to plan their careers.

CFI University has defined committees of cross-organizational training employees to benchmark CFI training systems against companies both within and outside the fastener industry in five areas:

- curriculum development,
- training tracking systems,
- measurements and evaluation systems,
- professional development, and
- interactive technology.

Each committee's results and subsequent system improvements have been incorporated into the "common architecture" across every college in the

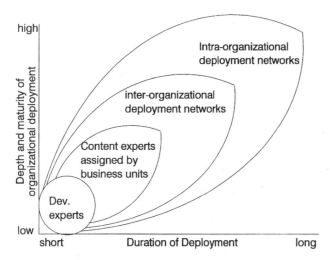

Figure 5.2-1 Training deployment approach.

CFI University system. Figure 5.2-2 shows the CFI University Deployment system, the development arm, various colleges, type of delivery mechanisms, and methods used to assess training effectiveness. This infrastructure is supported by TESS. The structural interaction of committees and colleges provides the building blocks for CFI to create a world-class training and development system over the next three years that will integrate all CFI training activity. The following improvements began in 1996–1997:

- CFI University's Curricula Development Committee has created a competency-based curricula development model that will be used to establish curricula for all functionally based colleges. When all colleges are operational, every discipline will have skill-based curricula, enabling all employees to identify the courses they need to make performance improvements.

- During CFI's 1995 Baldrige assessment effort, weaknesses were identified in CFI's system for measuring training effectiveness. To address these, cross-organizational teams have been dedicated as full-time resources for development of a CFI training evaluation system. This system requires that our training workshop students demonstrate learned behaviors on the job and will be deployed to six workshops in 1997. Line managers will verify that the system meets their need before implementation.

- CFI's deployment of TESS offers significant administrative improvements for the company's decentralized training environment as follows:

  - TESS tracks all training that employees take through any training resource.

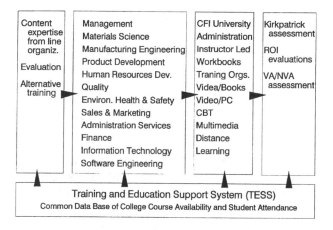

Figure 5.2-2 Colony Fasteners, Incorporated, University deployment.

- TESS provides information on any discipline's curriculum, as well as on training plans, career development, degree tracking, and certifications.

- All employees have access to TESS directly via on-line capabilities to learn about available training opportunities, understand their skill requirements, and register for courses.

5.2a(3) Education and Training Delivery
Components training focuses on the highly technical aspects of design, assembly, test, and production, including equipment engineering training for engineers and technicians, and process-flow training. Training needs are triggered by the introduction of new processes or technology, or by customer feedback. Components training employs a pool of technical content experts who develop and deliver training to all components' manufacturing organizations and who certify on-site content experts to deliver training programs.

Corporate Education and Development provides training on CFI's corporate culture and values, management development, and administrative service development. They provide employees with courses to help them understand performance to CFI values, beginning with a new-hire orientation on their first day titled, "What Makes CFI—CFI?" Other core orientation programs available to all employees include "CFI Culture," "All About CFI," and "CFI Operations, Philosophy, and Economics."

Employees are also encouraged to attend, and time is provided for them to take courses that teach specific practices to support CFI values, such as "Effective Meetings" and CFI's "Management by Planning." Management development programs, available to all levels of management, emphasize the importance of role modeling behaviors that support CFI values.

Corporate Education and Development recruits and trains personnel at each site to deliver its training programs. Organizations may arrange to have courses delivered to intact teams on a just-in-time basis, which facilitates immediate application of the subject matter to real workplace situations. Training needs are triggered by corporate surveys or through the CFI University system described below.

Extended education through external trade schools, colleges, and universities is encouraged to enhance employees' professional development. CFI provides on-site degree programs wherever resources are available, such as the program at Treadwall University in Philadelphia. If classes are offered on site, CFI pursues an active partnership with the school, such as the relationship between the Los Angeles facility and the Orange County Technical Vocational Institute.

External training consultants may be used when

- subject expertise is not available internally,
- it is more cost effective to train externally, or
- internal resources cannot respond to needs.

Employee training plans are jointly developed by the individual and the immediate supervisor and may utilize any of the above resources. To continuously improve our overall process of delivering appropriate training to all employees, CFI created the integrated CFI University system in 1991. An executive Management Review Committee (MRC) was established to ensure that CFI's total training investment supports business objectives and strategies. A rotating CFI executive staff member serves on the MRC for corporate leadership and guidance. Training managers identified for each business group or geographical area make up the CFI University Management Board. Quarterly meetings with the executive MRC ensure a closed-loop system that integrates total training activities with company business objectives and needs.

CFI University is composed of functional "colleges," which include training personnel from organizations across the company. Each college is chartered to identify the key skills and knowledge necessary for the quality execution of all jobs within its functional area, including total quality competencies identified by CFI's Quality Technology Group. They identified competencies from the bases of curricula for every discipline at CFI. The first of 12 planned colleges, Management Development, was formed in 1992. The colleges of Quality, Product Development, Finance, Information Technology, Materials, Manufacturing, Engineering, and Human Resources development have been established since then.

5.2a(4) Reinforcement

At the beginning of each training session, instructors are required to detail what skills, knowledge, and capabilities employees will possess at course completion. A copy is provided to each attendee's supervisor, who incorporates an evaluation of the employee's capability in using the new skill or knowledge into the employee's performance appraisal. After the year-end performance review, the training department analyzes the results to determine the effectiveness of the training and makes changes in the curricula, instruction, or delivery method.

CFI believes that effective on-the-job reinforcement of knowledge and skills involves

- designing performance objectives, based on what students need to know, into courses;
- evaluating whether courses have accomplished their performance objectives; and
- reinforcing the new performance on the job.

Examples of the process include operator skills training, multimedia training and information systems, and posttests and simulation practice.

Operator Skills Training— All manufacturing operator certifications are performance based. Behavioral checklists are used to ensure that operators demonstrate skill competency while running their equipment in the actual workplace before they are certified to operate the equipment.

Multimedia Training and Information Systems— CFI training increasingly incorporates multimedia instructional tools so that information can be reinforced after the learner leaves the classroom. For example, computer systems training offered by Planning System Training includes screen and report guides with field definitions for the user's workplace computer screen. In another example, components training interviews process flow students six months to one year after completing the course to determine its impact on their job performance and to evaluate gains in job competency.

Posttests and Simulation Practice—An example of posttests used in conjunction with effective training design is Los Angeles' Technician Training on CFI's ultrapure, high-carbon manufacturing process. Each complex task is broken down into a natural progression of skill requirements grouped into modules. Technicians must pass a posttest before progressing to the next module, thus reinforcing content and measuring knowledge for eventual task performance in the workplace.

Simulation Practice—Planning Systems Training uses simulation practice to introduce new features of CFI's central planning system. Teams of planners are trained at each site and practice skills in an on-line simulation of the actual system before the new system features are implemented in the workplace.

''Peer trainers'' are also trained at each site, with backup videos made of the training session for reinforcement of skills on the job.

5.2a(5)   Evaluation and Improvement

CFI considers various training activities to be quality focused, including customer-oriented training and courses on team effectiveness and interpersonal skills and CFI culture and values training. Several factors have influenced quality education at CFI. In the early 1980s, training in SPC was added to benchmark CFI's quality against that of leading Japanese companies and in response to the expectations of major customers. By the mid-1980s, structured problem-solving training and employee teamwork were deployed throughout CFI. To support CFI's current business objectives, training is increasingly focused on cycle-time reduction and benchmarking.

In addition, New-Employee Orientation Training has been systematically revised to reflect CFI's continuous improvement philosophy. Our current orientation program presents our corporate values and culture, total quality philosophy, business products, policies, and procedures. Training plans are then developed for new employees, who receive an average of 51 hours of functional and operations-specific orientation.

With almost 5% of CFI's annual payroll applied to professional training, the company spends more than three times the national average. Between 1988 and 1996, the number of training hours per CFI employee increased by 55%.

Total CFI dollars invested in training (which we consider to be a key trend reflecting total quality education and training) increased 24% between 1991 and 1996, to $26.3 million. CFI's training and development investment levels increased from 2.6% of total payroll in 1991 to 4.9% in 1996, compared to a major competitor's 3.4% investment of total payroll in 1996. Moreover, CFI's training and development investment per employee increased from $1725 per employee in 1991 to $2025 per employee in 1996. CFI's investment per domestic employee was $2460 in 1996. This compares to a 1996 U.S. average training expenditure of $471 per employee for companies with 10,000 to 20,000 employees.

To speed delivery and aid application and retention, both SPC and structural problem-solving training are delivered primarily just in time to intact teams encompassing virtually all employees.

5.3   Employee Well-Being and Satisfaction

5.3a   Work Environment

Several sectors, including DAS and NSS, are involved in using materials that could be dangerous to employee health. Therefore, inherent in the process improvement process are efforts to address both the reduction and elimination of materials hazardous to employees and the safe use of the material of elimination cannot be achieved. When any process requires the use of hazardous materials, metrics are established to track the reduction of those same materials. This gives continuing visibility and priority to the elimination of all hazardous materials. All accidents or incidents involving hazardous materials are given a ''red flag.'' Immediately, a team is created to eliminate the root cause of the problem, including reengineering the process to eliminate hazardous material usage. Benchmarking of processes of other companies is a high priority when it is determined that those companies have reduced or eliminated the use of hazardous materials and CFI has not.

To prevent accidents or incidents proactively, Safety Awareness Teams (SATs) in each plant conduct regular safety audits of the workspaces to ensure that they are maintained in a safe condition. Safety ''tickets'' are written for each violation. The supervisor of the area is responsible for correcting the discrepancies to the satisfaction of SAT. Quarterly, the SAT in each plant analyzes the data on violations to determine if there are systemic issues. Violation summaries from other sectors are also reviewed to determine if there are emerging or corporatewide issues. If systemic issues are noted, process improvement teams are formed to implement actions to prevent problems.

When accidents or incidents happen, an improvement team is formed with the responsibility to perform root cause analysis (RCA) for the accident or incident. The team is responsible for developing permanent improvements to prevent recurrence. When improvements are implemented, members from the safety organization validate that the improvement will eliminate the RCA-determined cause before the improvement team is disbanded.

Improvement in the quality of environmental, health, and safety (EHS) issues affecting employees is pursued at a number of levels within CFI. Integrated throughout CFI, from research and development (R&D) groups to manufacturing and beyond, EHS provides a "built-in" quality improvement process that assesses the impact of new process, product, and equipment introductions. CFI also champions EHS improvements across the industry through equipment vendors and has published extensive EHS performance standards in the *Fasteners Supplier Handbook*.

The Safety Improvement Team (SIT) fosters and directs EHS improvements and accident/incident reductions. The SIT established the Safety Bulletin Incident program to report and investigate accidents and incidents. This program ensures that incidents meeting predetermined criteria are formally investigated. It reviews findings, conducts RCA, and communicates corrective action among all CFI sites for purposes of elimination and prevention.

By analyzing trends and incidents, CFI safety committees make significant contributions to quality improvement. Safety suggestion systems and telephone hot lines support employee involvement.

CFI's EHS group responds to illness and injury and is proactive in promoting wellness through employee health fairs, cardiopulmonary resuscitation training, and publication of health-related newsletters. This group routinely conducts medical monitoring of employees and analyzes and acts on the aggregate test results. Each building also has an emergency response team with members that receive extensive emergency-preparedness training.

In 1996, CFI achieved a number of results based on ongoing ergonomic assessments. These include the implementation of a number of workcell improvements at the Boston site and a corporate strategy to provide improved ergonomic design for new CFI offices.

Key improvement goals for EHS are

- solvent-based incidents reduced 45% by 1998,

- eliminate ozone-depleting compounds by 1999,

- hazardous waste reduced 50% by 1998, and

- cumulative trauma injuries reduced 60% by 1997.

5.3b Employee Support Services

The corporate value of making CFI a "Great Place to Work," which states that employees are its fundamental strength, embodies the company's commitment to employee well-being. Employee feedback, the changing demographics of the workforce, industry trends, and recognition of the merging of work and personal lives continuously drive CFI to enhance its comprehensive program of employee benefits and services. Major goals and methods with an impact on employee satisfaction and well-being include the following:

- Enhancement of an internal staffing capability to facilitate redeployment and career planning, thorough training, and upgraded systems and capabilities.

- Continued focus on management development through training and assessment of management skill through culture surveys, management practice surveys, and demonstrated learning.

- Maintenance of a leadership position in benefits while maintaining costs and providing excellent customer service.

In the past few years, CFI introduced an employee assistance program, recreation center, a child care resource and referral network, and flexible start times.

CFI offers many special services to support employee health, satisfaction, and well-being. A key service is the Employee Assistance Program (EAP), which provides confidential, 24-hour treatments and referrals for mental health, chemical dependency, and general living problems to all CFI employees and dependents.

CFI opened recreational facilities and showers at all domestic sites in the late 1980s and sponsors on-site aerobic classes, employee sports teams, wellness programs, and stress management workshops.

A special program for domestic employees involves the granting of a nine-week sabbatical every seven years. This is in addition to their regular vacation accrual. The non-U.S. sites have comparable programs, but they are structured differently due to the local laws and customs of the country.

A child care resource and referral program, parental leave-of-absence policy, and preretirement counseling were introduced in 1991. CFI also provides 100% tuition reimbursement and a wide range of professional development support, including the Asian Network, Women in Technology Group, Black Student Network, New College Graduate Network, and Diversity Task Force, that specifically targets its diverse workforce.

To address the disproportionate rising cost of home ownership in California, CFI implemented a first-time home buyers' loan program, amounting to $30,000 of employee mortgage loans. This amount is loaded at the IRS minimum allowable interest rates over a five-year loan. Also, CFI initiated a broad-based effort to assist affected employees after the devastating earthquakes and riots in California, floods in Georgia, and natural calamities in Xiang, China. CFI immediately formed task forces after the events to meet employee needs, including housing arrangements, van or transportation pools for commuting from restricted areas, counseling sessions, and employee contributions, grants, and loans to address material damages.

5.3c Employee Satisfaction

5.3c(1) Methods
Employee satisfaction is determined most extensively through regularly conducted surveys, focus groups, and other communication forums. Examples include

- one-on-one interviews with the agendas controlled by the employees,
- employee participation in the periodic employee culture survey that is delivered to all employees,
- business update meetings for general communication and questions concerning business concerns, and
- various assessment methods and tools, including 360° input to managers, collective assessment of team dynamics, and individual learning and behavioral styles.

The employee perception survey process is biannual and typically includes questions regarding employee and department morale, job satisfaction, reward and recognition, management effectiveness, training effectiveness, quality of communication, and opportunities for career growth. Improvement plans are developed collaboratively between managers and employees and customized to meet the changing needs of employees and their organizations.

5.3c(2) Relation to Key Business Results
A multifunctional, multisector Human Resources Evaluation Team (HRET) meets on a quarterly basis to assess whether human resource strategies and practices are making a positive contribution to the performance of the business. In addition, the HRET determines if there are best practices occurring in individual sectors that should be expanded to other sectors. In this assessment, the HRET conducts a multivariable correlation of the business with human resource results. These correlations have, over time, established definitive correlations between company results and human resource initiatives and actions. For instance, technical and quality training have been shown to be responsible for approximately 60% of the contributions to reduction in cycle time and 73%

of the contributions to improvements in quality. Similarly, an increase in involvement has contributed 67% of the improvements in cycle time and 83% of the improvements in quality. Reverse correlations show that involvement has reduced turnover by 14% and increased employee satisfaction by 43%, which has cut employee overhead costs by 11%.

6 PROCESS MANAGEMENT

CFI utilizes process design, monitoring, and control as a basic strategy for the business, resulting in increased quality and productivity with minimized costs.

CFI uses the Motorola concept of six sigma (6σ), using the capability index $C_p = 2$ and $C_{pk} = 1.5$ considering a 1.5 sigma shift of the mean. A C_{pk} of 1.5 results in 3.4 parts per million (ppm) outside the specification limits. This concept is used throughout CFI in product and nonproduct service support functions and with suppliers.

To meet the process capability of $C_p = 2$, three-sigma limits for each process step are set. Figure 6.0-1 shows this relationship and the calculations of C_p and C_{pk}. This figure is from a Motorola publication, "The Nature of Six Sigma Quality," by Mikel Harry, Ph.D.

In Figure 6.0-1, the in-control process of $\pm 3\sigma$ is shown as B. The specification limits of $\pm 6\sigma$ are shown as A. The capability index $C_p = 2$ represents A/B = 6/3 = 2. If the mean of the process moves 1.5σ, the mean would be 4.5σ from a limit, shown as C. For an individual item, $C_{pk} = C/(B/2) = 4.5/3 = 1.5$.

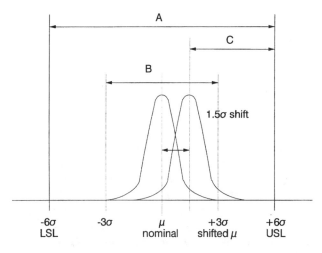

Figure 6.0-1 C_{pk} and C_p relationships.

If the mean of the in-control process shifts 1.5σ, 3.4 parts per million will be outside the specification limit. If the mean shifts only 1σ, the result would be 0.39 ppm, and with no shift, 0.002 ppm.

CFI has used this approach successfully, and the customers and suppliers understand the concept and participate in the fruits of the results.

6.1 Management of Product and Service Processes

6.1a Design Processes

6.1a(1) Customer Requirements
The design process is handled slightly differently for products in each sector due to different product requirements. Both internal, as well as external, customer satisfaction is always considered the prime driver for new or improved processes. Another driver is for manufacturability, which is processed in a program called Design for Manufacturability (DFM).

The listening post activities described in Area 3.1a are utilized to understand customer requirements better for the introduction of new products and services.

Inputs from the concerned functions convert customer requirements into product and service design requirements. This ensures customer needs are recognized as the basic reason for any changes, improvements, or new concepts.

A critical input to the design process is through the FSEs, who bring detailed customer knowledge to the design process. The FSE has spent a lot of time in the customer facilities, has talked to customer employees, and has first-hand information about the needs and expectations.

In the CPS, industry standards are utilized for configuration, and CFI processes are used. CAS parts are a combination of both standards and user specifications. DAS products are designed to military specifications with CFI processes.

6.1a(2) Production/Delivery Process Design
A high-level summary of the product design cycle at CFI is shown in Figure 6.1-1. The first activity in the cycle focuses on a new concept and its feasibility for design and production. Customers provide detailed designs that are reviewed, evaluated, and concurred by CFI sector product teams. After agreement by the customer and CFI, the order is accepted. The first review is a Preliminary Design Review (PDR) in which dimensions, materials, and suppliers are screened

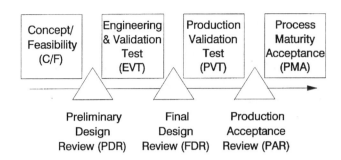

Figure 6.1-1 Product design process.

for capabilities, proper design margins, and safety allowances. At this PDR, preliminary processes are presented for customer concurrence, and PTP relationships are established among CFI, the customer, and associated suppliers.

During the engineering and validation test (EVT) activity phase, the new product is fully engineered and tested according to product specifications. Design capability margins and reliability are ensured. The results of the design and its testing are reviewed at the final design review (FDR). The initial production processes have been designed and checked for capability and verification that a process capability of $C_p = 2$ is attainable. The process itself and the limit specifications provided by knowledgeable customers are considered.

The production validation testing (PVT) activities follow the FDR. In this set of activities, the initial processes are put into place and early production begins. Processes are constantly reviewed, analyzed, and tuned to ensure that proper capabilities are attached. The results of these activities are reviewed during the product acceptance review (PAR). This is the final review before a new product is put into full-scale production. Once in full production, the product goes into the phase focused on process maturity acceptance (PMA), in which process capabilities are constantly reviewed, production output is ramped up, and product maturity begins.

In the TDS, statistical techniques are maintained in the Engineering Information Architecture (EIA). All designed products are subjected to a DOE analysis for assurance that the design is robust and that applied environmental conditions will not adversely affect the reliability or the performance of the product in the end-use conditions. The DOE is contained in the Design for Quality and Reliability (DFQR) section of the EIA.

Each sector maintains its own design capability, and all procedures and processes are documented and maintained. All sectors use the two-design review process steps noted in Figure 6.1-1, but they modify and adjust them according to the particular design program requirements.

With each sector, designs are documented in a single file, which ensures coordination of the many designs utilized when they are formalized and placed under configuration control. These files are summarized for the review of other sectors for the possibility of adaptation or overlap. The complete files are always available to other sectors if desired.

An important link between customers and CFI during new product design, as well as other times when close communication is required, is the EDI. Data are transferred between suppliers and customers of CFI. EDI is also utilized between the engineering organizations and the factories to facilitate transfer of information with a high degree of accuracy. Another important communication tool with outside customers and suppliers is the voice mail hookup by which outside organizations are treated as an arm of CFI.

Production process changes for new products are usually modifications used for similar products. Before FDRs can be approved, objective data must be presented demonstrating the distribution pattern of the material in the specific process steps. It must reference the measured sigma compared with the tolerance limits determined for that particular step. Usually, the variation is well within the capability index of 2 and often has a margin of 3 or more. The design review team determines which characteristics will be measured and when characteristics will be measured.

Each process step is documented with the sampling plan, which is used to ensure that process variability is monitored and maintained. The sample size, frequency of sampling, and parameters to be checked are listed. The sampling proves the distribution to be in control, and the sigma are automatically calculated by the ODS.

6.1a(3) Trouble-Free Introduction and Delivery
Typically, the functions represented in the design review are the Engineering, Manufacturing, Quality, Logistics, Marketing, Field Service, and Purchasing Departments, as well as supplier representatives and customers. At the PDR, all customer and CFI requirements are reviewed. All design reviews are documented and the results maintained in the TDS.

The computer-aided fastener design process embedded in the EIA is used for consistency and completeness. Suppliers are included in the early design phase since suppliers provide the basic raw materials (e.g., chemicals used for cleaning, plating, and other process steps) crucial to product and process consistency. Suppliers are often able to recommend better materials to meet such customer requirements as expected environments, the strength or other special needs, and the workability in the drawing, upsetting, and threading processes. The FSEs and marketing representatives make recommendations in conjunction with suppliers for the selection of appropriate materials that may result in reduction of waste material (see Figure 7.5-19).

The FDR provides data that show that the materials or services subjected to the specific processes meet the criteria of a distribution by attaining at least one-half the specification limit for the specific process step.

Many designs are modifications of existing products, and the established processes have been continuously improved over several years. The process teams have the experience and knowledge, along with the data systems described in Category 4, to understand fully where the processes might need possible additional modification. The DFQR process assures that production processes have been fully considered prior to a product's launching.

Design review inputs come from functional organizations and are used to determine the necessary actions by the design team. These inputs are furnished by the functional representative on the design team, who provides two-way communications to the functional organizations. This ensures that all levels of employees have reviewed the designs to ensure that any details have not been overlooked.

6.1b Production/Delivery Processes

6.1b(1) Key Processes and Requirements
There are seven key processes that must perform at a C_{pk} of 1.5 to maintain appropriate quality, cycle time, and cost requirements: receiving material check, drawing and upsetting, machining and threading, heat treating, chemical processing, product review for release, and shipping and distribution.

Receiving Material Check—The receiving material check varies with the material, end-customer requirements, and status of the supplier of that material. When the supplier is a key supplier that has been certified through the PTP process, the checking process only identifies the material and any certifications required by the end customers, as is usually required in the NSS. The PTP partner continually feeds statistical data through the EDI communication capabilities.

Other materials from noncertified suppliers will have chemical analyses or checks of physical properties. These checks are on a statistical sampling basis unless otherwise demanded by the individual customer. It is the primary goal of all sectors to reduce this effort as suppliers are certified through training and proven performance.

In handling incoming materials, bar codes are utilized to reduce cycle time and improve accuracy. Certified suppliers are provided with special bar code strips that identify the material lot number and required statistical process results information.

Drawing and Upsetting—The drawing process typically changes the materials that are received in spools, such as wire, to the proper diameter for the particular fastener. The controls on this process vary with the end requirements of size tolerance, strength, material coatings, or other special customer needs.

The upsetting process forms the heads on the end of the fastener, as with bolts or rivets. Some upsetting in the drawing process requires precise temperature and environmental controls. These processes are dependent on lubricants used during the metal-forming operations. Productivity gains have resulted from changes in lubricants as a result of supplier inputs and benchmarking visits.

Machining and Threading—Most fasteners require machining and thread cutting or rolling. Differences lie in the size, materials, and end use of the product.

The processes involved include the type of machine, usually with high levels of automation, and the type of cutting tools used, with the requirement of adequate sharpness, and required coolants. Threading is accomplished in a variety of ways depending on the physical characteristics and the customer end use. The operators use optical comparators on a regular basis. On a periodic basis, technicians from the labs select random samples for a complete analysis.

Heat Treating—Heat treating is considered a key process because of the critical nature of the end use, with the safety of people usually involved. This process includes chemicals, temperature controls, and various quenching techniques. It is highly automated with little intervention by operators, reducing process variability.

Chemical Processing—Chemical processing is vital to customers who use fasteners in environments hostile to the materials used. The amount and type of protection vary by sector and customer.

The process requirements may be plating, which includes the chemicals used, and the configuration of the baths with the times, temperatures, and agitation required. The process might be a dipped coating or a coating applied by an electrostatic process.

Product Review for Release—This key process is for assurance that all processes have been applied to the proper materials for the proper customers. With the facilities distributed around the world delivering to customers around the world, and with the large number of products, overall reviews are necessary.

Production control of all products is centrally controlled in the ODS. Bar codes are used extensively to result in rapid, accurate records. Problems are seldom discovered. However, to ensure customer satisfaction, this process is retained.

Shipping and Distribution—The distribution system is a key process for CFI due to the necessity of delivery to customers throughout the world from the 16 manufacturing facilities in various countries.

Customers have become increasingly demanding of just-in-time deliveries. CFI has learned to balance off-shore manufacturing to stage products in warehouse sites at strategic locations close enough to major customers to meet just-in-time requirements.

To accomplish these actions, a multilayer distribution system has been developed. This system provides bulk shipments from manufacturing facilities directly to large customers, as well as distributed warehouses. In turn, warehouses ship directly to customers, as well as secondary facilities where materials from all sectors are accumulated. This is particularly important for the Consumer Products Sector. As a result, accuracy of records and protection of parts are essential distribution system requirements. Automatic counting utilizes sensitive scales and bar codes. The automatic stocking process is computer controlled.

6.1b(2) *Process Management*
Every process is designed and proven before the design is released. The process certification consists of demonstrated success that the process has a capability of at least a C_{pk} of 1.5. As products are processed, distributions are automatically calculated via the ODS to ensure that the sigma is remaining as initially determined necessary. Periodic audits, performance sampling, and complete analyses (e.g., chemical and physical) are used to manage processes and process steps.

When it is discovered that the distribution is out of control or the variability has increased, the process is immediately stopped by the operator, who is empowered and expected to halt the process. The team responsible for the specific process is immediately convened, and it requests any technical capabilities that are needed to rectify the process problem. Design engineers, suppliers, quality engineers, data analysts, or whoever can contribute to the solution are utilized by the process team leader. The Plan, Do, Check, Act (PDCA) process is exercised at this time. After the root cause has been determined, the solution is installed, the process restarted, and the data are taken again.

The sample frequency is tripled, and no more deviations can be experienced for the next five shifts in order for the sampling frequency to go back to normal. The process team reviews the data records to determine any similar processes throughout the company. If any are found, the responsible teams are immediately notified in the other three sectors. FSEs liaison closely with customers, solving problems and providing a vital link back to the sectors.

6.1b(3)   Evaluation and Improvement
Within each department of each sector, processes are maintained by teams assigned the responsibility of designated processes. These teams continually review the status of processes to ensure that the relationship between the element being acted on and the limits assigned is within at least a C_{pk} of 1.5.

In the few cases when the C_p of 2 is not attainable initially, teams continue to work on improvements to the process steps in various ways, including benchmarking, R&D, reengineering, and examining similar processes within CFI. Customers are also contacted to relate to process capability indices. Special summary reports are structured for those processes with C_p's of less than 2 and reported in the departmental reviews.

Each sector's design process is reviewed quarterly. Representatives from the functional areas in the design process, as well as corporate representatives, review past data for results in quality and cycle time. To ensure continuous improvement, goals are set for improvement and reviewed for attainment at the next meeting. Assignments are established, with specific dates set for accomplishment (Figure 7.5-13).

At monthly departmental reviews for action teams, various characteristics are compared to goals set, and process teams report, on a rotating basis, the results of their activities. They report on how many processes have a C_{pk} of 1.5 and how many exceed that figure. Team recognition is awarded to the top five teams each month in each department.

Teams are continually examining processes in their areas of responsibility, looking for better ways to do things. Benchmark activities are extensively used for comparison with other organizations using alternative techniques that result in less variability, shorter cycle time, or lower cost.

Although each sector has different products, many processes are similar. During monthly reviews, teams have opportunities to compare process steps and results. In the case of support services, the difference in needs of the organizations are less, and usually the modified processes can be applied directly.

Process Analysis and Research
The assigned process teams are always on the alert to improve processes. For common processes, a section of the common R&D division researches processes for both improvements and totally new approaches. This information is available to the process teams in all sectors through the data system.

As a result of the data system providing information worldwide, any time a process shows improvement, the information is available to the other plants regardless of the sector affiliation. At the annual Recognition Celebrations, the process teams are recognized for the increases in capability indexes that they have accomplished.

Benchmarking
Benchmarking has been proved to be an excellent method for improving process characteristics, including simplification, reduced variation, and reduced cycle time.

When a benchmark partner in the PTP process is selected for a particular review, the process team members make the partners fully aware of their own process, including the specific measurements used to measure the process. During the visit, the partner's process is examined in detail with careful observance of incremental improvement data. Often, only a part of the process may be the superior part, and only that particular segment may be utilized.

Use of Alternate Technology
Technology has resulted in many improvements. Design engineers and process teams are always aware of opportunities to apply new techniques, equipment, and approaches to process control.

As an example of applying a new technique, a recent improvement in the DAS was the result of better temperature control of bolts that had a heat-treating requirement. One process team learned a new electronic method that used very high frequency radiation to heat bolts in a protective container. This new method reproduced the temperature variation to within ±0.3°C; the former equipment would only reproduce to ±1.0°C. This order of magnitude improvement resulted in a new C_p of 2.1 versus the earlier C_p of 1.8.

With the change, the process capability was improved to the point that heat-treating testing was eliminated. Only the regular sampling required to determine that the process is in control is used. The new technology was developed for a drug manufacturing process, but an alert process team member visualized the application to heating individual bolts.

Information from Customers
CFI maintains close customer relationships. Some customers also manufacture fasteners, although none has the broad range of products of CFI. These customers have provided benchmark partnerships, PTPs, that have resulted in many process improvements.

Other customers have helped in service areas such as stocking and delivery techniques. Customers want just-in-time deliveries, and CFI is dedicated to provide the service. In several instances, customers have suggested solutions and improvements to CFI's service deliveries by describing and demonstrating how cycle times could be reduced, and in many cases have provided better protection for the product. This has been most prevalent in the CAS, which has customers more experienced in ways of handling products and delivering just in time.

With many teams in action throughout the company in all sectors, internal customer feedback has been the source of many applications of improved processes and reduced cycle time. CPS stock handlers provided an idea to handle large skids of product by using air to lift the skid for better maneuverability. A base with air outlets on the bottom connecting to an air line permitted a lone stock handler to move skids weighing greater than 1 ton around the shipping floor.

6.2 Management of Support Service Processes

6.2a(1) How Key Requirements Are Determined
Each support service makes a determination of the key processes needed for support of its delivered products. The department determines the mission of its function as a result of the strategic planning process, deriving the departmental plans from the

strategic plan and discussions with its employees. The support functions are also connected to customers, both internal and external, as well as suppliers, with voice mail capabilities.

Planning teams are formed during the data gathering phase for the strategic plan, and priorities are established in order of importance to the business aims of the sector. The team lists all requirements for specific actions with the agreement of the team on the key requirements to establish priorities.

6.2a(2) Support Process Design
Process teams are also utilized in the support service functions. These teams are trained in process mapping, problem solving, and benchmarking. Processes are flow charted, compared to similar processes, and fully documented.

Support function processes are structured with specific limits for each step, and the process is measured to determine the sigma for the controlled process. These processes are expected to attain a capability of $C_p \leq 2$. Dialog with internal customers results in limits that are more easily defined. The process steps are documented, including the necessary measurements and the sampling plan with the specific parameters to be checked.

As an example, in the CAS, the Accounting Department designed an accounts payable process to be more responsive to small suppliers requiring regular cash flow to maintain their continuous improvement processes. An Accounting Department team met with suppliers and Purchasing to determine the best method for submitting invoices. It also met with the material receiving organization to determine the fastest, most accurate methods of verifying material acceptance (see Figure 7.5-26).

A new process was designed and installed that selected limits in cycle time for each step in the paying process. The resulting sigma was determined to ensure that the process operated at a $C_p \leq 2$. sampling plans were installed to ensure that the process would remain "in control."

Another process that has been significantly improved is the reduction in time to close the books at the end of each month. This required the efforts of a cross-functional team composed of members from Human Relations, Marketing, Accounting, Operations, and IS. The team met weekly and continues to meet to maintain the rate of improvement (Figure 7.5-27).

Most processes in support organizations are established and changed by assigned process teams using the continuous improvement methodology.

New processes usually evolve from new technology and new techniques to go with additional requirements. An example of this has been the upgrading of the IS process. As the company has grown and expanded around the world, significant additional demands were placed on the system. At the same time, both hardware and software with additional capabilities became available.

To take advantage of the new capabilities and to meet growing requirements, a significant amount of coordination with all sectors, suppliers, and customers was needed. Facilities around the world were consulted to ensure adequate inputs for requirements and agreement of acceptable internal data system cross-communications and available data outputs.

The new IS system was completely designed before going on line in 1991. The system was installed with measurements concerning response time and availability for data inputs. Limits were established, and the resulting sigma operated within the required process capability considerations.

6.2a(3) Key Processes and Requirements

Figure 0-2 shows the corporate functions and Item 7.5 lists some key support processes. Each key process has principal requirements that are determined by assigned teams in the areas of the process. The support functions now use measurements in parts per million (ppm) rather than percentage. They are tied to the production facilities with EDI, and they design and monitor their processes to the goals of $C_{pk} > 1.5$ to reduce cycle time, improve accuracy, and lower costs.

For example, the requirements of the FDS are concerned with accuracy, time to generate reports, containment of all costs and revenues, and timely output reports that are clear and understandable by those receiving the reports.

6.2a(4) Process Management

The measurement plan is similar to those in the product areas. All process steps are designed with a documented process. The steps are continually assessed to be in control with a calculated sigma to ensure a C_{pk} of 1.5 or better. Support process steps have specific plans for the frequency of sampling and the parameters to be measured, usually cycle time, accuracy, and costs.

Support functions require continual training of employees involved in statistical techniques to ensure their comfort and competence with these types of measurements. The process control

applications in support functions have normally been heavily weighted toward measuring and controlling paper-handling and administrative-type processes. This has proven to be a significant driver in increased organizational performance, resulting in less cycle time and lower operating costs.

6.2a(5) Evaluation and Improvement

The planning teams use an established methodology for the approach of reviewing processes. Each key process has established measurements with goals of continuous improvement assigned. Processes are reviewed through process mapping, using questions like: Is the process step needed? Is it meeting the requirement? or Can it be done better by modification of equipment or operator training? This same methodology is repeated in all functions, by all teams, to ensure continuous improvement.

Process Analysis and Research

Support processes are analyzed to define the steps for measurement improvement. Research is primarily done when new techniques or equipment are utilized, such as the data system redesign with new computer capabilities.

Similar techniques are used in the engineering areas, where new workstations have become available. Word processing techniques have completely superseded all typing duties. The application of bar coding techniques is a good example of improving data input cycle time and accuracy.

Process teams in all functions are continually investigating new capabilities that often require additional training. If required, the teams arrange, and sometimes perform, the training.

Benchmarking

Benchmarking activities have been mentioned in several areas. CFI has discovered the advantages of benchmarking the goal-setting mode and the more important advantage of process review capability and improvements.

Benchmarking has been utilized to a high degree in support areas. A real advantage is that new processes have applicability in most sector businesses. The major difference in support processes is that we generally go outside our industry to find high-performance processes. A new process, such as preventive maintenance, can be used in the same manner in many facilities.

Use of Alternative Technology

Alternative technology has been addressed in many areas in the field of personal computers. As new equipment with significantly greater capability and many new software programs becomes available, teams are continually investigating and evaluating its applicability. Due to the rapid changes in costs and capabilities, comparisons are ongoing.

Voice mail is used extensively in the support functions. Communications have been vastly improved, and actual paper use has almost been eliminated. Bar codes are used in the support areas for routing of reports and documents.

Process teams in the support functions are continually researching and reviewing ideas for the application of alternative technologies. Inputs for ideas and actions derive from benchmarking visits of organizations outside the fastener industry, visits to trade shows, internal visits to other sectors, and combining business periodicals.

Information from Customers
CFI is focused on outside customers and has always maintained a good dialog with them. Although information transferred usually relates to products for today and in the future, many support processes are covered in customer discussions. Usually, they concern interfacing, such as billing or credit, and sometimes occur as a result of a visit from which an observation can lead to improvements.

Internal customers are also solicited for information, and actions are often taken as a result of their observations and suggestions.

Most of the sectors have utilized the PTP technique of having internal suppliers and customers meet at a regular time (such as Friday afternoons at 3:00 P.M.) to discuss mutual needs and services. These meetings allow better understanding between the parties and result in continually improved, more effective services.

All sectors are encouraged to take advantage of customer needs. The NSS recently learned of a better process to tabulate and maintain records of audits required by the Nuclear Regulatory Commission. The process utilized a portable device that transferred records by radio directly from the auditor to the records retention area. The device also produced a bar code strip that would be attached to the material.

This was faster and more accurate, with less overall cost, and was an application of new technology provided by an outside customer. In turn, this process was picked up by the CPS as a method of inventory counting by which counts from the end of the production line are fed into the data system

immediately. On receipt in the stockroom, a verification count would either accept the count or immediately alert the material handlers of possible misplaced material.

6.3 Management of Supplier and Partner Processes

6.3a(1) Process Design
CFI presently has 420 suppliers for both raw materials for products and materials integrated into salable products. Key materials are metals such as aluminum, carbon steel, stainless steel, monel, and brass. Chemicals for processing and cleaning are also considered to be key materials.

CFI has established a process called Pass Through Partnerships (PTP) to share lessons learned to improve quality, reduce cycle time, and pass on technology advances. This process establishes special relationships with suppliers by sharing benchmark information, training on process control concepts, and holding seminars in "lessons learned." When suppliers qualify with their processes attaining C_{pk}'s > 1.5 and pass other requirements to show the capabilities will be maintained, they become "certified" and their products are not subject to receiving inspection at any CFI facility.

There are five levels of suppliers: nonqualified, conditional, qualified, PTP, and certified. Continuing failure to meet appropriate requirements or to address inappropriate performance results in demotion of one or more levels.

Certification requirements include quality, delivery, and price. Certified Suppliers are connected with EDI, which provides them with product specifications and production requirements information as soon as CFI makes needs determinations. They receive special bar code strips to attach to products delivered. This simplifies the incoming process and results in the suppliers receiving payment earlier. The supplier certification program is shared with all sectors to minimize costs of developing suppliers.

CFI passes its process control philosophy on to suppliers. Suppliers are expected to have their processes measured and to have a C_{pk} of 1.5 or greater. This includes supplier support services.

CFI has a business strategy to be the technology leader in the introduction of revolutionary fasteners and has established a supplier base with similar goals. These knowledgeable suppliers have simplified the transfer of understanding of process control capability techniques.

6.3a(2) Meeting Requirements

Through the PTP and supplier certifications with process capability techniques in which many suppliers participate, incoming product quality is ensured. Many suppliers are part of large companies and have participated in similar programs with other customers.

Some suppliers are not certified, and alternative suppliers have not yet been developed to replace them, although an active program is in process. For suppliers not certified, product inspection is performed on all incoming materials. These inspections consist of samples for chemical analysis and physical properties. The measurements to be sampled are determined during the design process to maintain material capabilities that are utilized in the production process. Price and delivery are consistently monitored by the Purchasing group. The PTP program involves meetings with suppliers to concerned sectors at least quarterly.

All suppliers in the PTP program have the EDI link to receive real-time feedback on their performance, and most have electronic mail connectivity for regular communications with CFI. For suppliers not in the formal PTP program, information is mailed to them from the Purchasing organization once per quarter in the form of a printout from the ODS. This Supplier Rating System information is automatically compiled, and rejection rates are presented along with supplier receipt information.

If any lot rejection rate exceeds 250 ppm, the supplier is flagged with a Supplier Corrective Action Request (SCAR). A specific site visit is made to resolve the problem by determining the root cause and developing a Corrective Action Plan.

6.3a(3) Evaluation and Improvement

Improve Suppliers' Abilities

CFI utilizes several programs to improve suppliers' capabilities. CFI provides supplier training and recognition as incentives to improve. If the incentives and help are not enough, the supplier may well become one of those in the supplier base reduction plan.

A Cost of Doing Business (CODB) factor is used for all suppliers by calculating the costs to CFI due to suppliers' failure to meet requirements, such as the costs to return lots that fail to meet specifications. The CODB factor is used in subsequent procurements to give preference to high-performing suppliers.

Actions and Plans

The PTP program provides a two-way dialog with individual suppliers. This gives them the opportunity to point out situations for which the purchasing process can be improved.

Annually, a planning meeting is held with the top 40 volume suppliers to develop plans for improvements. In this planning meeting, action plans with targets are developed for both CFI and the supplier for the upcoming year. These action plans and targets are fed into the company's annual planning process.

Last year, CFI started a Preferred Customer Certification Program (PCCP). Our principal suppliers have helped develop a set of criteria for rating whether we are the customer of choice. These criteria include timeliness, quality, clarity of communication, and supplier satisfaction. Quarterly Survey, Incorporated, an independent contractor, sends all CFI suppliers a survey. Analysis is conducted on the survey, and ratings are established similar to the PTP program. Action plans are established by a multifunctional internal team to improve our procurement and supplier management process. Results of the survey and action plans are fed to all suppliers.

In 1996, one supplier that had not attained certification, Salter, Incorporated, explained in a memo that it was not provided a detailed set of reasons why its product, a special washer specification, had been modified for use in another sector. Further analysis proved that a second supplier of the same washer had agreed to the change and had been shipping to a tighter specification. The purchasing procedures were modified, Salter was able to make the changes, and the rejections stopped.

Minimize Costs of Inspection

The process control capability concept is directed toward reduced costs in receiving inspection. When suppliers have processes with a C_{pk} of 1.5 or greater, they also can cease final inspection. Thus, the thrust of capability studies is directed toward lower costs and reduced lead times.

The suppliers that have achieved certification send process performance data through the EDI system to CFI. When these data show that the supplier is attaining a C_{pk} of at least 1.5 and all inspections and audits continue to show the processes are under control, no audits or inspections are conducted. Further, if the supplier takes prompt actions for processes that are drifting out of control, inspections and audits are not resumed. Our PCCP survey

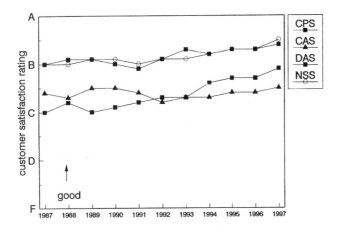

Figure 7.1-1 Composite customer satisfaction for product sectors.

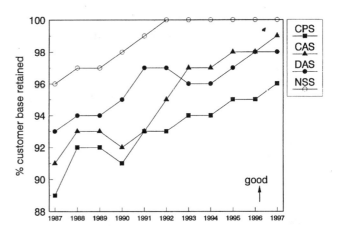

Figure 7.1-3 Customer retention.

results indicate that all suppliers find this proactive approach very helpful and meaningful.

7 BUSINESS RESULTS

7.1 Customer Satisfaction Results

7.1a Levels, Trends, and Comparisons

Customer Satisfaction
An overall chart for composite customer satisfaction by sector for a 10-year period is shown in Figure 7.1-1 (see Item 3.2).

Figure 7.1-2 shows CAS Composite Customer Satisfaction with comparisons to the best competitor, the goal, and the benchmark.

Another measure of customer satisfaction is retention. Figure 7.1-3 shows the improvement for each sector.

Figures 7.1-4 through 7.1-7 show 1996 measures for the five key requirements compared with 1997 goals, benchmarks, and the best competitor for each sector. CFI's five key business strategies address customer and stakeholder satisfaction:

1. To deliver products to customers on time and defect free.

2. To be recognized as the producer of the highest value fasteners (Figure 7.1-8). This figure shows the four sectors in the upper right quadrant, reflecting high satisfaction and high quality. Our customers define this as high value. The data come from aggregating many inputs explained in this application.

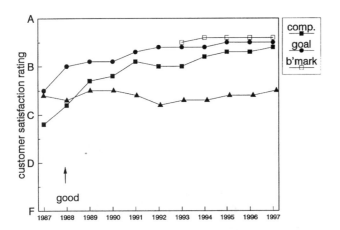

Figure 7.1-2 Commercial and Automotive Sector (CAS) composite customer satisfaction with comparisons.

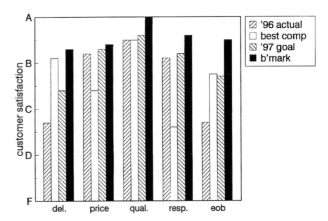

Figure 7.1-4 Consumer Products Sector (CPS) customer satisfaction with five key requirements.

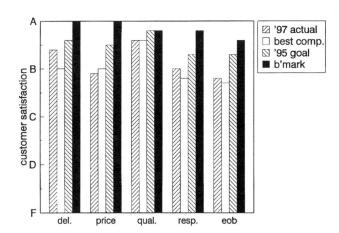

Figure 7.1-5 Commercial and Automotive Sector (CAS) customer satisfaction with five key requirements.

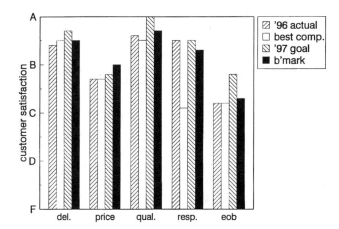

Figure 7.1-6 Defense and Aerospace Sector (DAS) customer satisfaction with five key requirements.

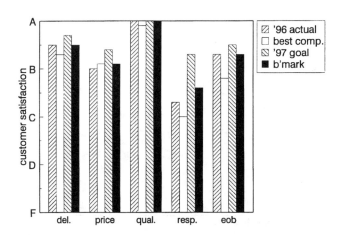

Figure 7.1-7 Nuclear and Specialty Sector (NSS) customer satisfaction with five key requirements.

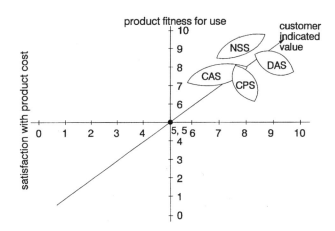

Figure 7.1-8 Customer satisfaction versus perceived value.

3. To be the technology leader in the introduction of revolutionary fastener products. Figure 7.1-9 shows the result of CFI's aggressive technology road map, which yields an increasing number of patents annually. The best competitor information comes from the IFI, which looks at a wide range of competitors. CFI is clearly ahead of the next closest competitor.

4. To protect the environment at all worldwide locations and set benchmark levels of compliance (Figure 7.5-17).

5. To be recognized as number one in employee satisfaction at all worldwide locations (Figure 7.3-3).

Customer Dissatisfaction
Each sector uses the same measure of customer dissatisfaction, customer complaints. Customer complaints include all customer concerns, whether

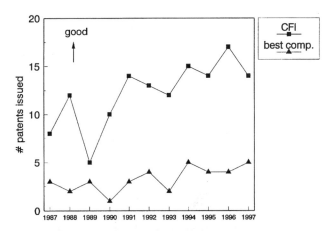

Figure 7.1-9 Technology leadership.

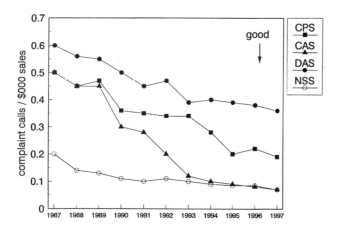

Figure 7.1-10 Customer complaint calls.

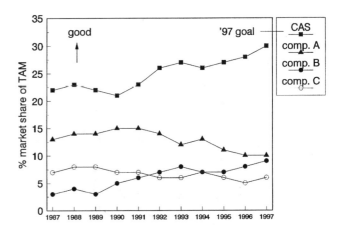

Figure 7.2-2 Commercial and Automotive Sector (CAS) gains and losses in market share versus competitors.

they are product or service related or concerned with the conditions of how CFI is conducting its business. Process, service, and business complaints are often related to time, with some product-related complaints delayed by weeks or months due to shipping, warehousing, or distribution lead time. Figure 7.1-10 shows a reduction in the last 10 years for all the sectors.

7.2 Financial and Market Results

7.2a Levels, Trends, and Comparisons

Market share is an end result of the total business activity. It reflects on all aspects of business, including price, quality, delivery, and customer relationships. Markets increase and decrease as the result of international financial changes, so market share is related to the individual business and total

available market (TAM). CFI has performed well in market share in all sectors. Each sector is compared to its three best competitors in Figures 7.2-1 through 7.2-4.

The best indication of success for any company is substantial profit results over continuing years. CFI has experienced an impressive increase in profit margins across all products except DAS. The DAS profit margin has been dropping due to the extreme pressures from both competitors and the government buyers. Since supply to the defense industry was a core business during the establishment of the company, CFI will continue to remain a dominant supplier to the country. Figure 7.2-5 shows that profit margins have increased directly as a result of the capability process techniques (see Figure 7.5-1) through the leverage of increased volume with increased productivity and lower costs.

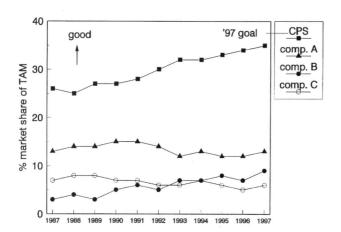

Figure 7.2-1 Consumer Products Sector (CPS) gains and losses in market share versus competitors.

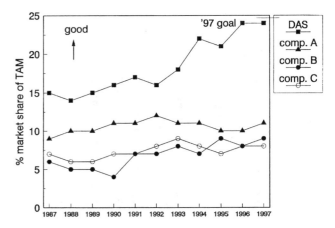

Figure 7.2-3 Defense and Aerospace Sector (DAS) gains and losses in market share versus competitors.

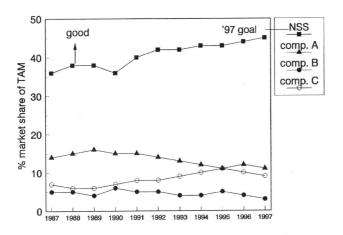

Figure 7.2-4 Nuclear and Specialty Sector (NSS) gains and losses in market share versus competitors.

7.3 Human Resource Results

7.3a Levels, Trends, and Comparisons

Many favorable accomplishments have resulted from efforts in Human Resources. One example of success in this function is shown in Figure 7.3-1. This figures demonstrates the reduction in lost days of work due to accidents. The number of cases corporatewide in the United States has been significantly reduced, from a high of 1.4 per employee per year in 1989 to under 0.7 per employee in 1996 and nearing the benchmark of 0.38. This reduction indicates the results of the company's efforts to emphasize safety through training, investment in equipment, and constantly remind employees about safety concerns.

Additional accomplishments in the Human Resources function are shown in Figures 7.3-2

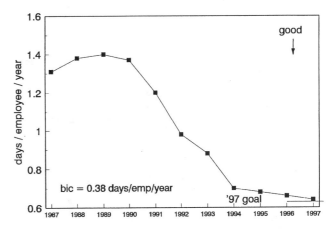

Figure 7.3-1 Lost work day cases.

through 7.3-9. Workers' compensation, although not yet attaining the benchmark, has been reduced every year but one for the last six years, as illustrated in Figure 7.3-2.

A composite picture of employee satisfaction and working relationships—indicating a good company to work for—is created using Employee Survey Results (Figure 7.3-3), Employee Turnover (Figure 7.3-4), and Employee Years of Service (Figure 7.3-5). These key indicators point to employees well satisfied with the way they are respected and compensated for their accomplishments. The salary-exempt longevity drop in Figure 7.3-5 indicates many long-term employees retiring (e.g., World War II and Korean War veterans).

The hours of training per employee are reflected in Figure 7.3-6. Recognition of individuals and teams is shown in Figure 7.3-7. Figure 7.3-8 demonstrates that activity and team growth have been substantial over the last five years. Figure 7.3-9 shows the

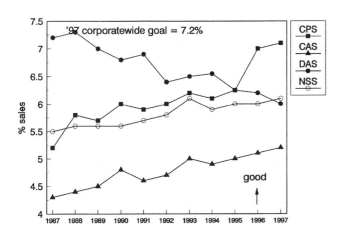

Figure 7.2-5 Profit margins for product sectors.

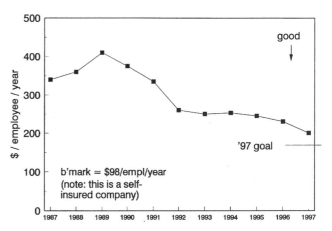

Figure 7.3-2 Workers' compensation.

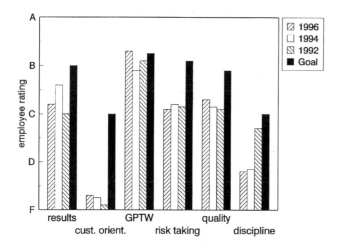

Figure 7.3-3 Employee survey results.

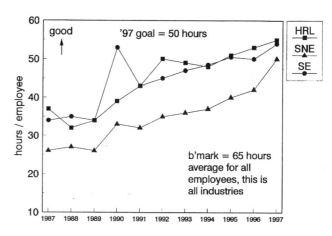

Figure 7.3-6 Hours of training per employee.

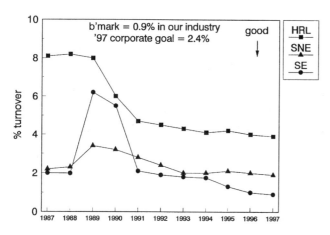

Figure 7.3-4 Employee turnover.

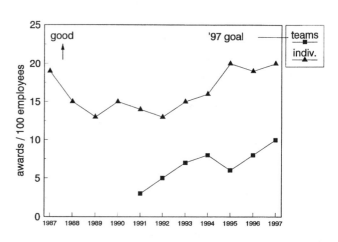

Figure 7.3-7 Team and individual awards.

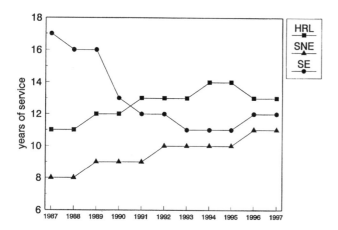

Figure 7.3-5 Employee years of service.

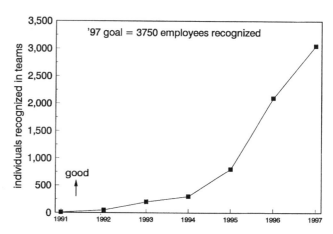

Figure 7.3-8 Recognition of individuals on teams.

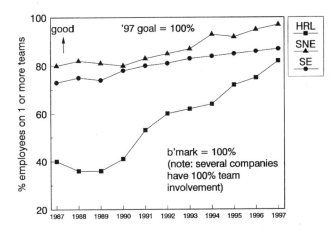

Figure 7.3-9   Employees engaged in teams.

growth rate of the percentage of employees who actively participate in teams.

Figure 7.3-10 shows growth in the rate of implementation of employee suggestions, with the 1997 goal increasing to at least 88%.

7.4   Supplier and Partner Results

7.4a   Levels, Trends, and Comparisons

Each sector maintains similar figures that are standardized to enable management to make comparison decisions among the sectors, so representative figures are shown.

There are 155 suppliers that deliver 80% of the supplies by dollar volume. The distribution and number of PTP suppliers are shown in Table 7.4-1 and Figure 7.4-1, respectively.

Table 7.4-1   Supplier Certification

Sector	Suppliers	Certified 1992	Certified 1996
CAS	83	60	80
CPS	33	15	30
DAS	28	20	27
NSS	11	4	11

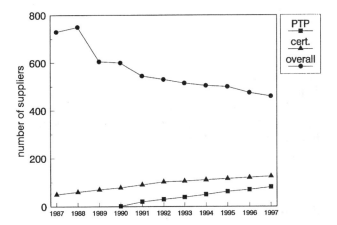

Figure 7.4-1   Supplier base transitions.

Delivery of parts is crucial when proprietary products are used by customers of CFI. The supplier's on-time delivery is shown in Figure 7.4-2. The results of the incoming material checks are shown in Figure 7.4-3.

Inspection results for noncertified suppliers' materials, sampled in the incoming area for physical

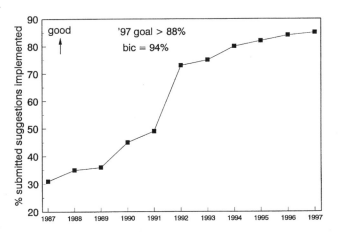

Figure 7.3-10   Suggestion implementation rate for Defense and Aerospace Sector (DAS).

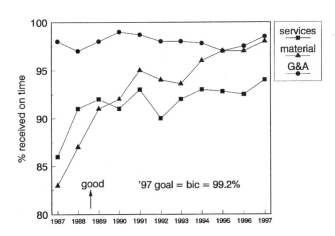

Figure 7.4-2   Supplier receiving history.

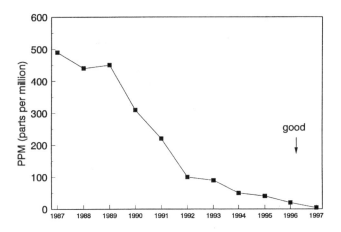

Figure 7.4-3   Certified supplier quality.

properties and chemical analysis, are shown in Figure 7.4-4. These results show great improvement over the 10-year period and are now at 0.04%, with the benchmark being 0.03%. The aim of CFI is to have all major suppliers certified and cease all incoming inspection.

Figure 7.4-5 demonstrates how suppliers have improved over the past 10 years as measured by the need to make requests for corrective action. This improvement is the result of many actions, including the establishment of the PTP program, certifications, and the reduction in the number of suppliers.

Figure 7.4-6 shows that the number of corrective action requests that have been made to suppliers are being closed in shorter and shorter cycle times, with a shift of the closure cycles being observed from 1987 to 1997 (projected). The program with suppliers has paid off with improved relationships, better

quality, lower cycle time, and improved customer relationships.

7.5   Company-Specific Results

7.5a   Levels, Trends, and Comparisons

Product/Service Quality
One CFI business strategy is to deliver six-sigma products on time. The quality of the product delivered is directly related to the C_{pk}'s of the processes. Figure 7.5-1 shows improvements over the last 10 years. CPS has the highest percentages of processes operating with high C_{pk} values as the company has more flexibility in setting limits.

Process yields vary for each type of product in each sector. To demonstrate the differences, a chart from

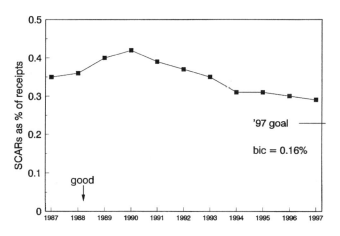

Figure 7.4-5   Supplier corrective action request (CAR).

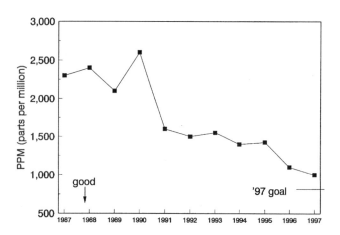

Figure 7.4-4   Noncertified supplier quality.

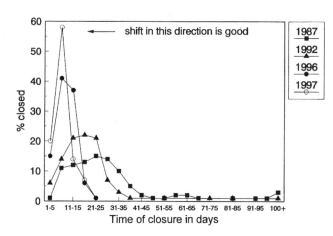

Figure 7.4-6   Velocity of corrective action request (CAR) closures.

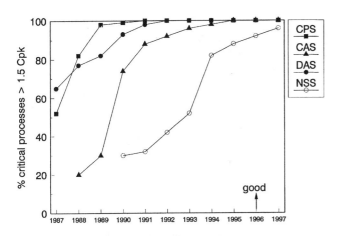

Figure 7.5-1 Percentage critical processes with $C_{pk} \geq$ 1.5.

the CPS is shown for four different products. Yields are related to the complexity of the part and the processes used (see Figure 7.5-2). Improved process capabilities have shown overall results in the yields. Figure 7.5-3 shows yields by sector.

DAS and NSS customers are continually attempting to get the most by pushing processes to their limits, making process capabilities smaller, and yields lower.

Problems with customers often relate more to mistakes in quantities or the wrong product being shipped than defective parts according to warranty returns. Figure 7.5-4 shows the reduction in warranty returns over the last 10 years for each sector. The highest warranty returns are in DAS, with just under 0.01% of sales, with CPS running under 0.005% of sales.

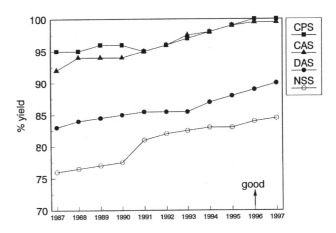

Figure 7.5-3 Sector operations yield.

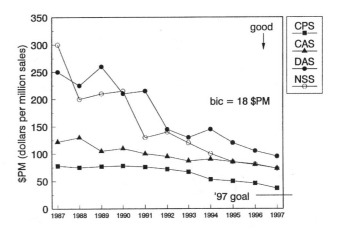

Figure 7.5-4 Sector warranty returns.

Significant to customers is the resolution of problems when they do occur. Figure 7.5-5 shows that, for 10 years, over 90% of the problems were resolved for all sectors except the Defense and Specialty Sector, with the Commercial and Specialty Sector having over 98% resolution.

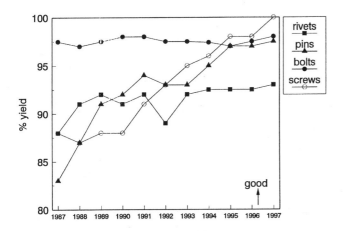

Figure 7.5-2 Process yield by product type.

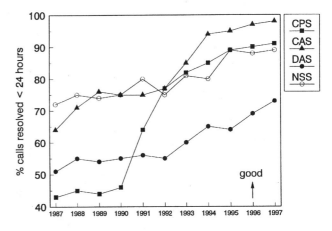

Figure 7.5-5 Problem calls resolved within 24 hours.

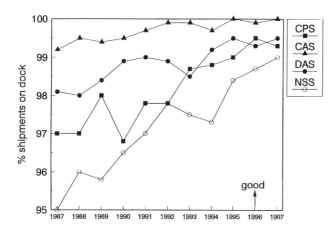

Figure 7.5-6 Sector on-dock performance.

The DAS still has a low resolution as a result of solving paperwork problems with defense contract administrators and the extensive checking that is required. Typically, warranty returns represent only about one-fourth of the problems, and the problem calls reflect about this same percentage.

On-time delivery, part of the first business strategy, is shown in Figure 7.5-6. For many years, CFI maintained that delivery was the date a product was shipped from the CFI facility. Customers explained that, from their standpoint, the date the material arrived at their dock is all that mattered. In 1992, CFI changed the measuring point, and the performance degraded until new processes were established to meet the customers' expectations.

On-dock performance for the Commercial and Automotive Sector is approximately 100%. NSS shipments are about 99%, often due to unreasonable dates requested by their customers and the promise

by CFI to try to make delivery in a very short time. Nuclear requirements are sometimes changed during production due to changes in government regulations.

Another important matter is delivery with very short lead times. Customers expect immediate delivery of an order, and the company has responded. Figure 7.5-7 shows significant improvement over the last 10 years. The exception is NSS, for which few speculative product actions can be taken prior to order receipt.

Operations
Figure 7.5-8 demonstrates productivity improvements over 10 years for product-related operations. Productivity has consistently improved in all sectors for the last 10 years. This is the result of team actions in all product areas and due primarily to the efforts in improving the process capabilities.

Figure 7.5-9 shows increases in productivity in nonproduct functions. This improvement in the support service areas has given CFI significant advantages in cost over the competition, which has not kept pace.

The recent improvement in CPS results is due to moving off-shore production work and the significant reduction in support personnel that has been customary in the United States. NSS has lagged as a result of regulation requirements that will not allow reductions even when process capability studies show that checking functions can be eliminated.

Figure 7.5-10 demonstrates the substantial improvement in overall quality for all the sectors in all actions. This figure is a compilation of quality figures throughout the company and is the information figure provided to top management for their assessment of

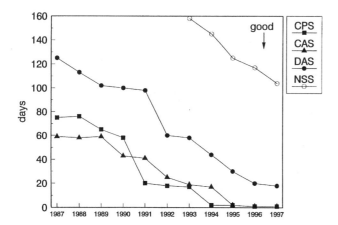

Figure 7.5-7 Lead time to order fulfillment.

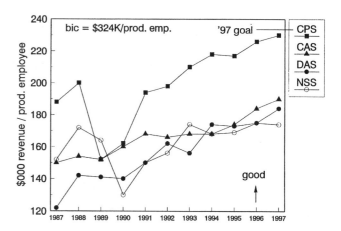

Figure 7.5-8 Product operational productivity.

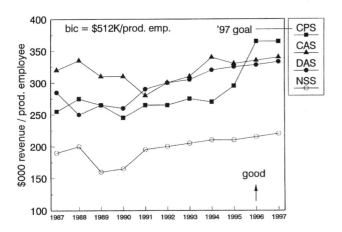

Figure 7.5-9 Nonproduct operational productivity.

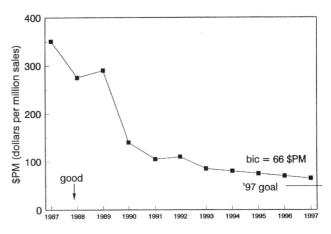

Figure 7.5-11 Consolidated Fastener, Incorporated, scrap material.

the total company. This figure demonstrates the power of the process capability approach.

The corporate quality index accounts for problems within the production facility, as well as customer complaints and problems. The index is structured so that 100 indicates organizational excellence with no problems being identified.

Another measure of operations is the scrap report. Figure 7.5-11 shows the significant reduction in scrap for the total company as a result of having all process steps operating with a C_p of at least 2.

Results of self-assessments are measured in corrective action requests (CARs) focused on internal operations. Figure 7.5-12 shows the trend decreasing while the number of internal self-assessments has been increasing. Today, CFI conducts 360% more self-assessments than it did in 1987.

Support Functions
The overall productivity data for the nonproduct functions are shown in Figure 7.5-9. Figures with more detailed results are shown for

- Engineering (Corporate R&D),
- Information Services (IS),
- Environmental (Corporate R&D),
- Human Relations (Human Resources), and
- Accounting (Administration).

Engineering—Figure 7.5-13 shows the reduction, which has been significantly reduced over the last 10 years, in product design cycle time for each sector. NSS creates product designs in a difficult area with ever-changing requirements due to the constant change in regulations. However, the improvement has been substantial.

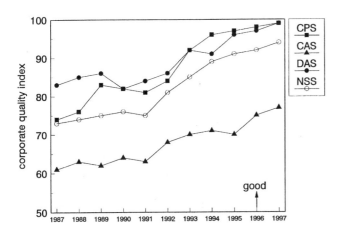

Figure 7.5-10 Sector operations quality.

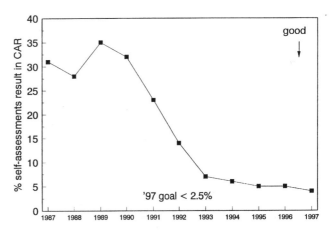

Figure 7.5-12 Self-assessment results.

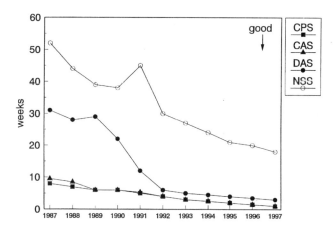

Figure 7.5-13   Sector product design cycle.

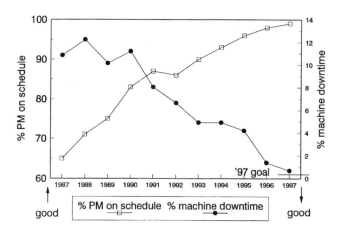

Figure 7.5-15   Preventive maintenance.

Another measure of the improvement in the engineering function has been the reduction in product setup cycle time. With the continual needs of customers for shortened time for deliveries and shorter production runs, engineering resources have been directed toward reducing the setup time for different products.

The single-minute die exchange (SMDE) program was initiated in 1991. This program moved the engineering organizations toward reducing the time for product setups and has resulted in significantly reduced cycle time (see Figure 7.5-14). This has allowed CFI to be more responsive to the customer and yet be more productive with less inventory for both cost and product obsolescence reasons.

A third example is preventive maintenance (PM), which has a significant effect on the overall

operations. When the maintenance is performed on time, the production equipment performs better. Figure 7.5-15 shows the results of improved maintenance over the last 10 years.

Information Systems—Figure 7.5-16 shows how the availability has increased and the response time has decreased at a time when the demands of the system have been expanding at a great rate.

Environmental—Another business strategy is to protect the environment at all worldwide locations, setting the benchmark for others to follow by complying to the tightest goals. Figure 7.5-17 shows the reduction in solid wastes over the last 10 years.

Liquid wastes have been reduced 97% over the last five years through the use of substitute materials such as water-soluble cleaning solutions. Vapor emissions were reduced 95% during this same period of time.

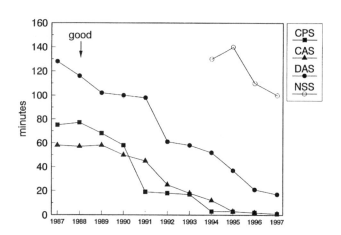

Figure 7.5-14   Product setup cycle time.

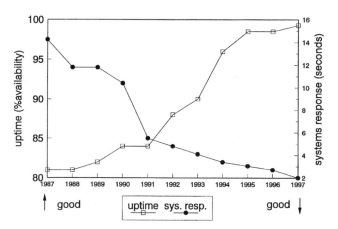

Figure 7.5-16   Information system availability.

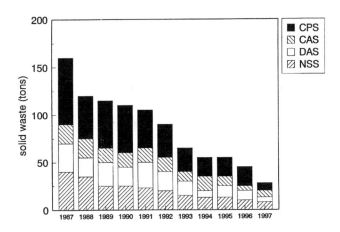

Figure 7.5-17   Reduction in solid waste.

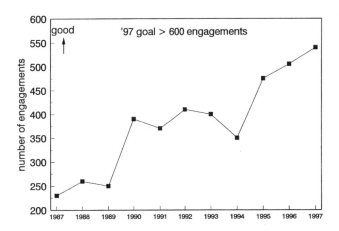

Figure 7.5-20   Corporate citizenship engagements.

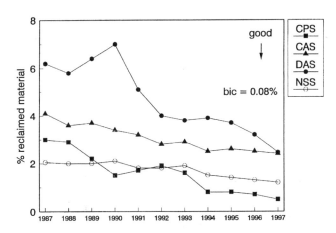

Figure 7.5-18   Percentage reclaimed material.

Other examples are the efforts to reduce the amount of material that requires recycling through more efficient use of material. This is shown in Figures 7.5-18 and 7.5-19.

Human Relations—Figure 7.5-20, Corporate citizenship engagements, shows the increase in outside contacts by employees to an average of about two engagements every working day.

Customer contact requirements are the same for all sectors; see Area 3.2a(1). Figures 7.5-21 through 7.5-25 show representative results for CAS. Figure 7.5-21 shows the peak is two rings and the majority is within three rings. The goal is to have all calls answered within two rings.

Figure 7.5-22 shows how CFI has shortened the cycle time to respond to customer problem calls from a

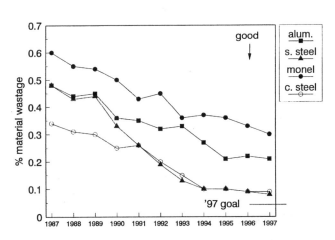

Figure 7.5-19   Wastage reduction.

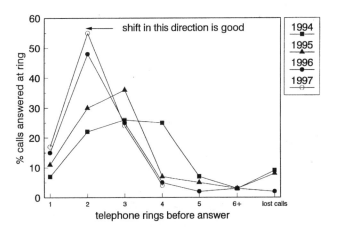

Figure 7.5-21   Response time to answer telephone calls, Commercial and Automotive Sector (CAS).

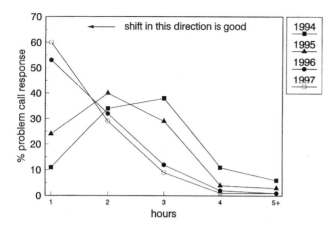

Figure 7.5-22 Time to respond to problem calls, Commercial and Automotive Sector (CAS).

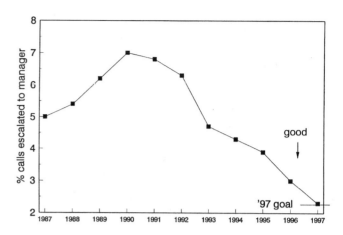

Figure 7.5-25 Problem escalation to manager, Colony Fastener, Incorporated.

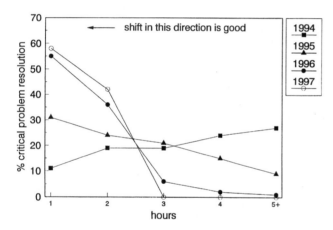

Figure 7.5-23 Time to resolve critical problems, Commercial and Automotive Sector (CAS).

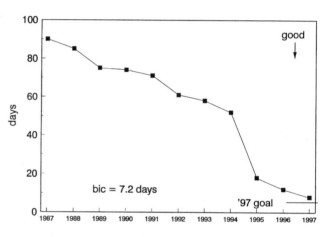

Figure 7.5-26 Time to pay invoices.

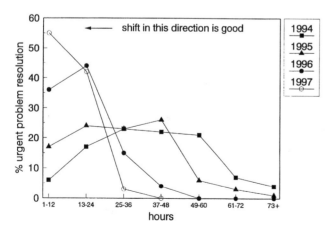

Figure 7.5-24 Time to resolve urgent problems, Commercial and Automotive Sector (CAS).

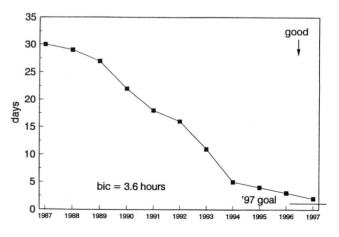

Figure 7.5-27 Days to close books.

peak of three hours in 1994 to projected 1997 results of about 90% answered within two hours.

The goal is to close all critical problems in two hours. Figure 7.2-23 shows CFI is projected to achieve 100% of its goal. A 93% attainment is shown for 1996.

CFI's commitment to customers is to close urgent problems in 24 hours or less. Figure 7.5-24 shows that in 1996, 79% were closed in 24 hours or less, and 1997 projections are 94% meeting the goal.

It is critical for customers to have the freedom to escalate their problems to appropriate managers if they have not been satisfied with the results offered by the customer contact personnel. CFI measures the effectiveness and empowerment of the customer contact personnel by the number of calls escalated to managers. CFI continues to improve (Figure 7.5-25).

Accounting—Two examples of the success of PITs in reducing cycle time for support services are from CAS (Figures 7.5-26 and 7.5-27).

1997 AWARD CRITERIA

1 Leadership (110 pts.)

The **Leadership** Category examines senior leaders' personal leadership and involvement in creating and sustaining values, company directions, performance expectations, customer focus, and a leadership system that promotes performance excellence. Also examined is how the values and expectations are integrated into the company's leadership system, including how the company continuously learns and improves, and addresses its societal responsibilities and community involvement.

1.1 Leadership System (80 pts.)

Approach – Deployment

> **Describe how senior leaders guide the company in setting directions and in developing and sustaining an effective leadership system.**
>
> In your response, address the following Area:
>
> **a. Leadership System**
> How the company's senior leaders provide effective leadership, taking into account the needs and expectations of all key stakeholders. Include:
>
> (1) how senior leaders set company directions and seek future opportunities for the company;
>
> (2) a description of the company's leadership system and how it incorporates clear values, company directions, high performance expectations, a strong customer focus, and continuous learning;
>
> (3) how senior leaders communicate and reinforce values, directions, expectations, customer focus, and their commitment to learning throughout the work force; and
>
> (4) how senior leaders review the company's overall performance, and use the review process to reinforce company directions and improve the leadership system.

Note:

Company performance reviews are addressed in Item 4.3. Responses to 1.1a(4) should therefore focus on the senior leaders' roles in the review of overall company performance, not on the details of the review.

1.2 Company Responsibility and Citizenship (30 pts.)

Approach – Deployment

> **Describe how the company addresses its responsibilities to the public and how the company practices good citizenship.**
>
> In your response, address the following Areas:
>
> **a. Societal Responsibilities**
> How the company addresses the current and potential impacts on society of its products, services, facilities, and operations. Include:
>
> (1) key practices, measures, and targets for regulatory, legal, and ethical requirements and for risks associated with managing company operations; and
>
> (2) how the company anticipates public concerns, assesses potential impacts on society, and addresses these issues in a proactive manner.
>
> **b. Community Involvement**
> How the company and its employees support and strengthen their key communities.

Notes:

N1. Public responsibilities in areas critical to the business also should be addressed in Strategy Development Process (Item 2.1) and in Process Management (Category 6). Key results, such as results of regulatory/legal compliance, environmental improvements or use of "green" technology, should be reported as Company-Specific Results (Item 7.5).

N2. Areas of community involvement and leadership appropriate for inclusion in 1.2b may include efforts by the company to strengthen local community services, education, the environment, and practices of trade or business associations.

N3. Health and safety of employees are not addressed in Item 1.2; they are addressed in Item 5.3.

2 Strategic Planning (80 pts.)

The *Strategic Planning* Category examines how the company sets strategic directions, and how it determines ke action plans. Also examined is how the plans are translated into an effective performance management system.

2.1 Strategy Development Process (40 pts.)

Approach – Deployment

Describe how the company sets strategic directions to better define and strengthen its competitive position. Describe also how the strategy development process leads to an action plan for deployin and aligning key plan and performance requirements.

In your response, address the following Areas:

a. Strategy Development

How the company develops strategy, taking into account the five factors listed below. Provide a brief description or diagram of the strategy development process and an outline of forecasts, models, etc., used to help select strategy.

(1) target customers; market requirements, including price; customer and market expectations; and new opportunities;

(2) the competitive environment;

(3) risks: financial, market, technological, and societal;

(4) company capabilities — human resource, technology, research and development, and business processes — to seek new opportunities and/or to prepare for key new requirements; and

(5) supplier and/or partner capabilities.

b. Strategy Deployment

How strategy is translated into action plans, including a clear basis for communicating and aligning critical requirements, and tracking performance relative to plans.

Notes:

N1. The strategy development process refers to the company's approach to a future-oriented basis for major business decisions, resource allocations, and companywide management. The strategy development process should include revenue growth as well as cost reduction thrusts.

N2. Item 2.1 addresses overall company directions and strategy. Although this might include changes in services, products, and/or product lines, the Item doe not address product and service design. Product and service design is addressed in Item 6.1.

2.2 Company Strategy *(40 pts.)*

Summarize the company's strategy and action plans and how they are deployed. Include key performance requirements and measures, and outline overall human resource plans. Estimate how the company's performance projects into the future relative to competitors and/or key benchmarks.

In your response, address the following Areas:

a. Strategy and Action Plans

Provide a summary of the action plans derived from the company's strategy and how these plans are deployed. Include performance requirements, key performance measures and/or indicators, and how plans, resources, and measures are deployed to ensure alignment of goals and actions. Note any important differences between short- and longer-term plans.

b. Human Resource Plans

Provide a brief summary of key human resource plans derived from overall strategy. Include the following elements:

(1) changes in work design and/or organization to improve knowledge creation/sharing, flexibility, innovation, and rapid response;

(2) employee development, education, and training;

(3) changes in compensation, recognition, and benefits; and

(4) recruitment, including critical skill categories and expected or planned changes in demographics of the work force.

c. Performance Projection

Provide a two-to-five year projection of key performance measures and/or indicators from the company's action plans. Include appropriate comparisons with competitors and/or key benchmarks. Briefly explain the comparisons, including any estimates or assumptions made in projecting competitor performance and/or benchmark data.

3 Customer and Market Focus (80 pts.)

The *Customer and Market Focus* Category examines how the company determines requirements and expectations of customers and markets. Also examined is how the company enhances relationships with customers and determines their satisfaction.

3.1 Customer and Market Knowledge (40 pts.)

Approach – Deployment

Describe how the company determines longer-term requirements, expectations, and preferences o target and/or potential customers and markets, to understand and anticipate needs and to develop business opportunities.

In your response, address the following Area:

a. Customer and Market Knowledge

Provide a brief outline of how the company learns from its current and potential customers and markets to support the company's overall business needs and opportunities. Include:

(1) how customer groups and/or market segments are determined or selected, including the consideration of customers of competitors and other potential customers and markets. Describe how the approaches to listening and learning vary for different customer groups;

(2) how key product and service features and their relative importance/value to customers are determined and/or projected. Describe how key information from current customers and markets, including customer retention and complaint information, is used in this determination; and

(3) how the company's approach to listening to and learning from customers and markets is evaluated, improved, and kept current with changing business needs.

Notes:

N1. The company's products and services might be sold to end users via other businesses such as retail stores or dealers. Thus, "customer groups" should take into account the requirements and expectations of both the end users and these other businesses.

N2. Product and service features [3.1a(2)] refer to all important characteristics and to the performance of products and services. These features affect customers

throughout their overall purchase and ownership experiences. The focus should be primarily on feature that bear upon customer preference and repurchase loyalty — for example, those features that differentiate products and services from competing offerings. This might include price and value.

N3. Information about customers and markets is requested as key input to strategic planning (Item 2.

3.2 Customer Satisfaction and Relationship Enhancement (40 pts.)

Approach – Deployment

Describe how the company determines and enhances the satisfaction of its customers to strengthen relationships, to improve current offerings, and to support customer- and market-related planning.

In your response, address the following Areas:

a. Accessibility and Complaint Management

How the company provides access and information to enable customers to seek assistance, to conduct business, and to voice complaints. Include:

(1) how the company determines customer contact requirements, deploys the requirements to all employees who are involved in meeting the requirements, and evaluates and improves customer contact performance; and

(2) a description of the company's complaint management process. In this description, explain how the company ensures that complaints are resolved effectively and promptly, and that complaints received by all company units are aggregated and analyzed for use throughout the company.

b. Customer Satisfaction Determination

How the company determines customer satisfaction. Include:

(1) how the company follows up with customers on products, services, and recent transactions to receive prompt and actionable feedback;

(2) a brief description of other customer satisfaction determination processes and measurements used. Describe how the measurements capture actionable information that reflects customers' future business with the company and/or positive referral. Indicate significant differences, if any, in methods and/or measurement scales for different customer groups or segments; and

(3) how the company obtains objective and reliable information on customer satisfaction relative to its competitors.

Notes:

N1. Customer satisfaction measurement might include both a numerical rating scale and descriptors for each unit in the scale. Effective (actionable) customer satisfaction measurement provides reliable information about customer ratings of specific product and service features and the relationship between these ratings and the customer's likely future actions — repurchase and/or positive referral. Product and service features might include overall value and price.

N2. The company's products and services might be sold to end users via other businesses such as retail stores or dealers. Thus, "customer groups or segments" should take into account these other businesses as well as the end users.

N3. Information on trends and levels in measures and/or indicators of complaint handling effectiveness such as complaint response time, effective resolution, and percent of complaints resolved on first contact should be reported in Item 7.5.

4 Information and Analysis (80 pts.)

The *Information and Analysis* Category examines the management and effectiveness of the use of data and information to support key company processes and the company's performance management system.

4.1 Selection and Use of Information and Data (25 pts.)

Approach – Deployment

Describe the company's selection, management, and use of information and data needed to support key company processes and improve company performance.

In your response, address the following Area:

a. Selection and Use of Information and Data
Describe:

(1) the main types of information and data, financial and non-financial, and how each type relates to key company processes and goals. Briefly explain how the information and data are integrated into measurements that can be used to track and improve the company's performance.

(2) how the information and data are deployed to users to ensure alignment with key company goals;

(3) how key user requirements, including rapid access and reliability, are met; and

(4) how information and data, their deployment, and effectiveness of use are evaluated, improved, and kept current with changing business needs.

Notes:

N1. "Users" [4.1a(2,3)] refers to company work units and to those outside the company who have access — customers, suppliers, and business partners, as appropriate.

N2. Deployment of information and data might be via electronic or other means. Reliability [4.1a(3)] includes software and delivery systems.

4.2 Selection and Use of Comparative Information and Data (15 pts.)

Approach – Deployment

Describe the company's selection, management, and use of comparative information and data to improve the company's overall performance and competitive position.

In your response, address the following Area:

a. Selection and Use of Comparative Information and Data
Describe:

(1) how needs and priorities for comparative information and data are determined;

(2) the company's criteria for seeking sources of appropriate comparative information and data — from within and outside the company's industry and markets;

(3) how comparative information and data are used to set stretch targets and/or to encourage performance breakthroughs; and

(4) how comparative information and data, their deployment, and effectiveness of use are evaluated, improved, and kept current with changing business needs.

Note:

Comparative information and data include benchmarking and competitive comparisons. Benchmarking refers to processes and results that represent best practices and performance for similar activities, inside or outside the company's industry. Competitive comparisons refer to performance relative to direct competitors in the company's markets.

4.3 Analysis and Review of Company Performance *(40 pts.)*

Approach – Deployment

Describe how the company analyzes and reviews overall performance to assess progress relative to plans and to identify key areas for improvement.

In your response, address the following Areas:

a. Analysis of Data

How performance data from all parts of the company are integrated and analyzed to assess overall company performance in key areas. Describe the principal financial and non-financial measures integrated and analyzed to determine:

(1) customer-related performance;

(2) operational performance, including product and service performance;

(3) competitive performance; and

(4) financial and market-related performance.

b. Review of Company Performance

How company performance and capabilities are reviewed to assess progress relative to goals, plans, and changing business needs. Describe how review findings are translated into improvement priorities and deployed throughout the company and, as appropriate, to the company's suppliers and/or business partners.

Notes:

N1. Analysis includes trends, projections, comparisons, and cause-effect correlations intended to support the setting of priorities for resource use. Accordingly, analysis draws upon all types of data: operational, customer-related, financial, and economic.

N2. Performance results should be reported in Items 7.1, 7.2, 7.3, 7.4, and 7.5.

5 Human Resource Development and Management (100 pts.)

The *Human Resource Development and Management* Category examines how the work force is enabled to develop and utilize its full potential, aligned with the company's objectives. Also examined are the company's efforts to build and maintain an environment conducive to performance excellence, full participation, and personal and organizational growth.

5.1 Work Systems (40 pts.)

Approach – Deployment

> **Describe how the company's work and job design and its compensation and recognition approaches enable and encourage all employees to contribute effectively to achieving the company's performance and learning objectives.**
>
> In your response, address the following Areas:
>
> **a. Work and Job Design**
> How work and jobs, including those of managers at all levels in the company, are designed, organized, and managed to ensure:
>
> (1) opportunities for individual initiative and self-directed responsibility in designing, managing, and improving company work processes;
>
> (2) flexibility, cooperation, rapid response, and learning in addressing current and changing customer and operational requirements; and
>
> (3) effective communications, and knowledge and skill sharing across work functions, units, and locations.
>
> **b. Compensation and Recognition**
> How the company's compensation and recognition approaches for individuals and groups, including managers at all levels in the company, reinforce the overall work systems, performance, and learning objectives.

Notes:

N1. Work design refers to how employees are organized and/or organize themselves in formal and informal, temporary, or longer-term units. This includes work teams, problem-solving teams, functional units, cross-functional teams, and departments — self-managed or managed by supervisors.

Job design refers to responsibilities, authorities, and tasks assigned to individuals.

N2. Compensation and recognition refer to all aspects of pay and reward, including promotions and bonuses. This includes monetary and non-monetary, formal and informal, and individual and group compensation and recognition.

5.2 Employee Education, Training, and Development *(30 pts.)*

Approach – Deployment

> **Describe how the company's education and training address key company plans and needs, including building knowledge and capabilities, and contributing to improved employee performance and development.**
>
> In your response, address the following Area:
>
> **a. Employee Education, Training, and Development**
> Describe:
>
> (1) how education and training address the company's key performance plans and needs, including longer-term employee development objectives;
>
> (2) how education and training are designed to support the company's approach to work and jobs. Include how the company seeks input from employees and their managers in education and training design;
>
> (3) how education and training, including orientation of new employees, are delivered;
>
> (4) how knowledge and skills are reinforced on the job; and
>
> (5) how education and training are evaluated and improved, taking into account company performance, employee development objectives, and costs of education and training.

Notes:

N1. Education and training address the knowledge and skills employees need to meet their overall work and development objectives.

N2. Education and training delivery [5.2a(3)] might occur inside or outside the company and involve on-the-job, classroom, computer-based, or other types of delivery.

5.3 Employee Well-Being and Satisfaction *(30 pts.)*

Approach – Deployment

> **Describe how the company maintains a work environment and work climate that support the well-being, satisfaction, and motivation of employees.**
>
> In your response, address the following Areas:
>
> ### a. Work Environment
> How the company maintains a safe and healthful work environment. Include how employee well-being factors such as health, safety, and ergonomics are included in improvement activities. Briefly describe key measures and targets for each important factor. Note significant differences, if any, based upon different health and safety factors in the work environments of employee groups or work units.
>
> ### b. Employee Support Services
> How the company supports the well-being, satisfaction, and motivation of employees via services, facilities, activities, and opportunities.
>
> ### c. Employee Satisfaction
> How the company determines employee well-being, satisfaction, and motivation. Include:
>
> (1) a brief description of formal and informal methods used. Outline how the company determines the key factors that affect employee well-being, satisfaction, and motivation and assesses its work climate. Note important differences in methods, factors, or measures for different categories or types of employees, as appropriate; and
>
> (2) how the company relates employee well-being, satisfaction, and motivation results to key business results and/or objectives to identify improvement activities.

Notes:

N1. Services, facilities, activities, and opportunities (5.3b) might include: counseling; career development and employability services; recreational or cultural activities; non-work-related education; day care; special leave for family responsibilities and/or for community service; safety off the job; flexible work hours; out-placement; and retiree benefits, including extended health care.

N2. Specific factors that might affect satisfaction, well-being, and motivation include: effective employee problem or grievance resolution; safety; employee views of management; employee development and career opportunities; employee preparation for changes in

technology or work organization; work environment; workload; cooperation and teamwork; recognition; benefits; communications; job security; compensation; equality of opportunity; and capability to provide required services to customers.

N3. Measures and/or indicators of well-being, satisfaction, and motivation (5.3c) might include safety, absenteeism, turnover, turnover rate for customer-contact employees, grievances, strikes, and worker compensation, as well as results of surveys. Results relative to such measures and/or indicators should be reported in Item 7.3.

Process Management (100 pts.)

The *Process Management* Category examines the key aspects of process management, including customer-focused design, product and service delivery processes, support processes, and supplier and partnering processes involving all work units. The Category examines how key processes are designed, effectively managed, and improved to achieve better performance.

6.1 Management of Product and Service Processes (60 pts.)

Approach – Deployment

> **Describe how new, significantly modified, and customized products and services are designed. Describe how production/delivery processes are designed, implemented, and improved.**
>
> In your response, address the following Areas:
>
> **a. Design Processes**
>
> How products, services, and production/delivery processes are designed. Include:
>
> (1) how changing customer requirements and technology are incorporated into product and service designs;
>
> (2) how production/delivery processes are designed to meet quality and operational performance requirements; and
>
> (3) how design and production/delivery processes are coordinated to ensure trouble-free introduction and delivery of products and services.
>
> **b. Production/Delivery Processes**
>
> How the company's key product and service production/delivery processes are managed and improved. Include:
>
> (1) a description of the key processes and their principal requirements;
>
> (2) how the processes are managed to maintain process integrity and to ensure products and services will meet operational and customer requirements. Include a description of key in-process measurements and customer interactions, as appropriate; and
>
> (3) how product and service processes are evaluated and improved to achieve better performance, including improvements to products and services, and the transfer of learning to other company units and projects.

Notes:

N1. The exact relationship of design processes to production/delivery processes and the relative importance of design processes depend on a company's specific business. For example, a developer of customized products or services would address this Item differently than an innovation-intensive manufacturer of high volume, high technology products. Other approaches would be appropriate for a small manufacturer that receives design information from its customers or for a service company that develops new services where delivery processes change depending on an ongoing dialog with the customer.

N2. Responses to 6.1a(1) should include how customer review of designs is accomplished, if appropriate.

N3. Responses to 6.1a(3) should include key supplier participation, as appropriate.

N4. Process evaluation and improvement [6.1b(3)] could include process analysis, research and development results, benchmarking, use of alternative technology, and information from internal and external customers.

N5. Results of improvements in product and service design and delivery processes, product and service quality results, and results of improvements in products and services should be reported in Item 7.5.

N6. Significant changes in products, services, and production/delivery processes will often result from strategic directions discussed in Item 2.2.

6.2 Management of Support Processes *(20 pts.)*

`Approach – Deployment`

Describe how the company's key support processes are designed, managed, and improved.

In your response, address the following Area:

a. Management of Support Processes

How key support processes are designed, managed, and improved so that current and future requirements are met. Include:

(1) how key requirements are determined or set, incorporating input from internal and external customers;

(2) how key support processes are designed to meet overall performance requirements;

(3) a description of the key support processes and their principal requirements;

(4) how the processes are managed to maintain process performance and to ensure results will meet operational and customer requirements. Include a description of key in-process measurements and customer interactions, as appropriate; and

(5) how the processes are evaluated and improved to achieve better performance, including cycle time.

Notes:

N1. The purpose of Item 6.2 is to permit companies to highlight separately the processes that support the product and service design, production, and delivery processes addressed in Item 6.1. The support processes included in Item 6.2 depend on the factors relevant to the company's business. Thus, this selection should be made by the company. Together, Items 6.1, 6.2, and 6.3 should cover all key operations, processes, and activities of all work units.

N2. Process evaluation and improvement [6.2a(5)] co include process analysis and research, benchmarking use of alternative technology, and information from internal and external customers. Information from external customers could include information describe in Items 3.2 and 4.3.

N3. Results of improvements in support processes ar performance of key support processes should be reported in Item 7.5.

6.3 Management of Supplier and Partnering Processes *(20 pts.)*

`Approach – Deployment`

Describe how the company's supplier and partnering processes, relationships, and performance are managed and improved.

In your response, address the following Area:

a. Management of Supplier and Partnering Processes

Describe:

(1) how supplier and partnering processes are designed to meet overall performance requirements, including how preferred suppliers and partners are selected, as appropriate. Include a brief summary of the principal performance requirements for key suppliers and partners;

(2) how the company ensures that these requirements are met. Include a description of key measures, expected performance levels, and how performance information is fed back to suppliers and partners; and

(3) how the company evaluates and improves its management of supplier and partnering processes to achieve better performance. Discuss current actions and plans to improve suppliers' and partners' abilities to contribute to achieving your company's performance goals. Include actions to minimize costs associated with inspection, test, or other performance audits; and actions to enhance supplier and partner knowledge of your company's needs and their ability to respond to those needs.

Note:

Results of improvements in supplier and partnering processes and supplier/partner performance results should be reported in Item 7.4.

Business Results (450 pts.)

The *Business Results* Category examines the company's performance and improvement in key business areas — customer satisfaction, financial and marketplace performance, human resource, supplier and partner performance, and operational performance. Also examined are performance levels relative to competitors.

7.1 Customer Satisfaction Results (130 pts.)

Results

Summarize the company's customer satisfaction and dissatisfaction results.

In your response, address the following Area:

a. Customer Satisfaction Results

Summarize current levels and trends in key measures and/or indicators of customer satisfaction and dissatisfaction, including satisfaction relative to competitors.

Notes:

N1. Customer satisfaction results reported in this Item derive from determination methods described in Item 3.2.

N2. Measures and/or indicators of customer satisfaction and satisfaction relative to competitors may include information on customer-perceived value.

N3. Measures and/or indicators of satisfaction relative to competitors might include objective information and data from customers and independent organizations. Comparative performance of products and services should be addressed in Item 7.5.

7.2 Financial and Market Results (130 pts.)

Results

Summarize the company's key financial and marketplace performance results.

In your response, address the following Area:

a. Financial and Market Results

Provide results of:

(1) financial performance, including aggregate measures of financial return and/or economic value, as appropriate; and

(2) marketplace performance, including market share, business growth, and new markets entered, as appropriate.

For all quantitative measures and/or indicators of performance, provide current levels and trends. Include appropriate comparative data.

Note:

Aggregate measures such as return on investment (ROI), margin rates, operating profit rates, and other profitability, liquidity, and financial activity measures are appropriate for responding to 7.2a(1).

7.3 Human Resource Results *(35 pts.)*

Summarize the company's human resource results, including employee well-being, satisfaction, development, and work system performance.

In your response, address the following Area:

a. Human Resource Results
Summarize current levels and trends in key measures and/or indicators of employee well-being, satisfaction, development, work system improvement, and effectiveness. Address all categories and types of employees, as appropriate. Include appropriate comparative data.

Notes:

N1. The results reported in this Item should address results from activities described in Category 5. The results should be responsive to key process needs described in Category 6, and the company and human resource strategy described in Item 2.2.

N2. Appropriate indicators of employee satisfaction, well-being, development, and effectiveness include safety, absenteeism, turnover, turnover rate for

customer-contact employees, grievances, strikes, worker compensation, innovation and suggestion rates courses completed, and cross-training, as well as results of employee surveys.

N3. Appropriate measures and/or indicators of work system improvements and effectiveness might includ' job and job classification simplification, job rotation, wc layout, work locations, and changing supervisory rati(

7.4 Supplier and Partner Results *(25 pts.)*

Summarize results of the company's supplier and partner performance.

In your response, address the following Area:

a. Supplier and Partner Results
Summarize current levels and trends in key measures and/or indicators of supplier and partner performance. Include company cost and/or performance improvements attributed to supplier and partner performance, as appropriate. Include appropriate comparative data.

Note:

The results reported in this Item should relate directly to processes and requirements described in Item 6.3.

7.5 Company-Specific Results *(130 pts.)*

> **Summarize key company operational performance results that significantly contribute to key company goals — customer satisfaction, operational effectiveness, and financial/marketplace performance.**
>
> In your response, address the following Area:
>
> **a. Company-Specific Results**
> Summarize key company-specific results derived from: product and service quality and performance; key process performance; productivity, cycle time, and other effectiveness and efficiency measures; regulatory/legal compliance; and other results supporting the company's strategy, such as new product/ service introductions. For all quantitative measures and/or indicators of performance, provide current levels and trends. Include appropriate comparative data.

Notes:

N1. Results reported in Item 7.5 should include results not reported in Items 7.1, 7.2, 7.3, and 7.4, and that address key company requirements and progress toward key company goals as presented in the Business Overview, Items 1.1, 2.2, 6.1, and 6.2.

N2. Results reported in Item 7.5 should provide key information for analysis and review of company

performance (Item 4.3) and should provide the operational basis for company financial and market results (Item 7.2) and customer satisfaction (Item 7.1).

N3. Regulatory/legal compliance results reported in Item 7.5 should address requirements described in Item 1.2.

Quality Resources offers several titles that can help you with the assessment process...

Keeping Score: Using the Right Metrics to Drive World-Class Performance
Mark Graham Brown
224 pp., 1996, hardcover, Item No. 763128

Baldrige Award Winning Quality (Seventh Edition)
Mark Graham Brown
276 pp., 1997, paperback, Item No. 763306

The Pocket Guide to the Baldrige Award Criteria (Fourth Edition)
Mark Graham Brown
66 pp., 1997, paperback, Item No. 763314

The Small Business Pocket Guide to the Baldrige Award Criteria
Mark Graham Brown
60 pp., 1997, paperback, Item No. 763292

The Basics of Performance Measurement
Jerry L. Harbour, Ph.D.
76 pp., 1997, paperback, Item No. 76328

The Basics of Process Mapping
Robert Damelio
77 pp., 1996, paperback, Item No. 763160

For additional information on any of the above titles, or to request a catalog, call 800-247-8519.